First Steps in SAP® S/4HANA Finance

2nd, revised edition

Janet Salmon

Thank you for purchasing this book from Espresso Tutorials!

Like a cup of espresso coffee, Espresso Tutorials SAP books are concise and effective. We know that your time is valuable and we deliver information in a succinct and straightforward manner. It only takes our readers a short amount of time to consume SAP concepts. Our books are well recognized in the industry for leveraging tutorial-style instruction and videos to show you step by step how to successfully work with SAP.

Check out our YouTube channel to watch our videos at
https://www.youtube.com/user/EspressoTutorials.

If you are interested in SAP Finance and Controlling, please join us at http://www.fico-forum.com/forum2/ to get your SAP questions answered and contribute to discussions.

Related titles from Espresso Tutorials:

- Oona Flanagan:
  A Practical Guide to SAP® S/4HANA Financial Accounting
  http://5320.espresso-tutorials.com

- Oona Flanagan:
  Delta from SAP ERP Financials to SAP® S/4HANA Finance
  http://5321.espresso-tutorials.com

- Kees van Westerop:
  New Fixed Asset Accounting in SAP® S/4HANA
  http://5409.espresso-tutorials.com

- Ann Cacciottolli: **First Steps in SAP® Financial Accounting (FI)**
  http://5095.espresso-tutorials.com

- Mary Loughran, Praveen Gupta:
  Bank Communication Management in SAP® S/4HANA
  http://5469.espresso-tutorials.com

- Robin Schneider: **Practical Guide to SAP® Business Partner Functions and Integration with SAP S/4HANA**
  http://5494.espresso-tutorials.com

- Oona Flanagan:
  A Practical Guide to Accounts Payable in SAP® S/4HANA Fiori
  http://5543.espresso-tutorials.com

- Oona Flanagan:
  Introduction to New Asset Accounting in SAP® S/4HANA (FI-AA)
  http://5567.espresso-tutorials.com

The SAP eBook Library: Team and Company Access

Did you know that you can provide your team with effective SAP training with access to the SAP eBook Library and reduce travel and training costs? You can!

Curious about how we stack up against the competition?

	Espresso Tutorials	Other Offerings
Price per Year	$159 annually	$699 annually
SAP eBooks	✓	✓
SAP video tutorials	✓	✗
Mobile app	✓	✓
Immediate access to new titles	✓	✓
Self service to maintain users (for companies)	✓	✗

Pricing available for teams of 5+. A team of 10 can access the library for one year for $850 (pre-tax). That's a 42% discount. The larger your team, the more you save.

Try a free 7-day, no obligation trial:
http://free.espresso-tutorials.com

Get a quote for your team today:
http://company.espresso-tutorials.com

Janet Salmon
First Steps in SAP® S/4HANA Finance—2nd, revised edition

ISBN:	978-3-96012-115-2
Editor:	Karen Schoch
Cover Design:	Philip Esch
Cover Photo:	fotolia #16757910 © Stefan Richter
Interior Book Design:	Johann-Christian Hanke

All rights reserved.

2nd Edition 2020, Gleichen

© 2020 by Espresso Tutorials GmbH

URL: *www.espresso-tutorials.com*

All rights reserved. Neither this publication nor any part of it may be copied or reproduced in any form or by any means or translated into another language without the prior consent of Espresso Tutorials GmbH, Bahnhofstr. 2, 37130 Gleichen, Germany.

Espresso Tutorials makes no warranties or representations with respect to the content hereof and expressly disclaims any implied warranties of merchantability or fitness for any particular purpose. Espresso Tutorials assumes no responsibility for any errors that may appear in this publication.

Feedback
We greatly appreciate any feedback you may have concerning this book. Please send your feedback via email to: *info@espresso-tutorials.com*.

Table of Contents

Introduction		7
1	**SAP S/4HANA Finance—the next big thing**	**9**
1.1	A little history	9
1.2	SAP HANA	12
1.3	Changes to the Finance applications	16
1.4	SAP Fiori	20
1.5	A simplified architecture for Finance	23
2	**Accounting and Controlling**	**27**
2.1	Introducing the universal journal	27
2.2	General Ledger Accounting	39
2.3	Asset Accounting	51
2.4	Cost Center Accounting, Order Accounting, and Project Accounting	55
2.5	Margin Analysis	63
2.6	Material Ledger and Actual Costing	78
3	**Planning and S/4HANA Finance**	**87**
3.1	The case for a single planning model	87
3.2	SAP Analytics Cloud for planning	94
3.3	Using financial plan data in SAP S/4HANA	107
4	**Migrating to SAP S/4HANA Finance**	**115**
4.1	Documenting a migration	115
4.2	Preparation	118
4.3	Installation	123
4.4	Customizing	124
4.5	Migration steps	130
4.6	Activities after migration	135
5	**Deploying Central Finance**	**137**
5.1	Replication approach for documents	137

	5.2	System landscape	140
	5.3	Group reporting	155
6	**SAP Fiori**	**163**
	6.1	Roles and business catalogs	164
	6.2	Fiori apps for My Spend	167
	6.3	SAP Smart Business apps	169
	6.4	Fiori apps for professional users	171
	6.5	Hierarchies in Finance	177
	6.6	Extensibility in SAP Fiori	181
	6.7	Semantic tags in Accounting	185
	6.8	Digitizing the finance function	187
7	**Outlook**	**191**
	7.1	On-premise and cloud editions	191
	7.2	SAP S/4HANA professional services cloud	192
	7.3	SAP S/4HANA Cloud for other industries	193
	7.4	SAP S/4HANA as the digital core	194
A	**The Author**	**198**
B	**Index**	**199**
C	**Disclaimer**	**203**

Introduction

If you work in finance, you might think that discussions about databases are best left to your colleagues in IT. In this book, however, we show you how a new database technology changes the way your financial data is stored and thus allows SAP to completely re-architect its solution. We explain how the High-Performance Analytic Appliance (HANA) differs from a conventional database. We explain concepts such as the universal journal, which combines data from multiple application components, and Central Finance, which enables you to merge accounting documents from multiple source systems. We discuss how the various applications are being rebuilt to take advantage of the new database, explaining what changes, but also what stays the same, so that you have the skills to help your organization improve the efficiency of its finance function.

We have added a few icons to highlight important information. These include:

Tips

 Tips highlight information that provides more details about the subject being described and/or additional background information.

Attention

 Attention notices highlight information that you should be aware of when you go through the examples in this book on your own.

Finally, a note concerning the copyright: all screenshots printed in this book are the copyright of SAP SE. All rights are reserved by SAP SE. Copyright pertains to all SAP images in this publication. For the sake of simplicity, we do not mention this specifically underneath every screenshot.

1 SAP S/4HANA Finance—the next big thing

SAP S/4HANA Finance is being marketed as the next big thing in terms of software architecture. In this chapter, we look briefly at how the technology has evolved from the mainframes of the 1980s, to the client/server architecture of the 1990s, to web services in the Internet era, and finally, to the revolution of in-memory computing that we are experiencing today. We explain what is special about SAP HANA and why it enables SAP to firstly re-architect its financial applications to store data, thus making this data easier to consume in reporting, and secondly, to present this data more intuitively to provide instant insight into the state of the business. Finally, we introduce the three pillars of SAP S/4HANA Finance.

1.1 A little history

As a product name, SAP S/4HANA Finance gives an indication of SAP's aspirations for its latest product. The company was founded back in 1972 and its first products, R/1 and R/2, were ERP systems designed for the *mainframes* that most large companies ran in the 1970s and 1980s. The "R" in the product names stood for *real time*, the idea being that financial transactions could be captured in real time using online terminals rather than relying on batch processes to update the journals periodically. Back in the early 1990s, SAP trainers and consultants would patiently explain to customers what it meant to capture materials movements as they happened, along with the related journal entries, rather than waiting for a batch process to load the data to the finance system nightly or at period close.

In the summer of 1992, SAP introduced a new product, SAP R/3, designed to maintain the concept of real time but to work with the then revolutionary *client/server architecture*. The UNIX servers were significantly cheaper than the mainframe equivalent and it was possible to link multiple servers whenever more processing power was required. The client/server architecture comprised three layers: the database layer, the application layer, and the presentation layer. Without going into too much detail, this architecture meant that the customer could choose the *database* they preferred (and there was a regular flow of announcements as new databases were certified); the *application layer* contained the code for the various software modules (Materials Management, Production Planning, Financial Accounting, Controlling, and so on), and the *presentation layer* provided a graphical user interface. Let's not forget that in the days before smartphones and consumer websites, the graphical user interface delivered with SAP R/3 was more attractive and easier to use than the mainframe interfaces that most accounting clerks were using at the time.

This three-tier architecture is still the heart of many SAP applications today. When the R/3 product was renamed SAP ERP in 2004, the key technology change was the underlying SAP NetWeaver stack which enabled the use of *web services*. This meant that the ERP system could communicate with other applications such as Customer Relationship Management and Supplier Relationship Management using standard protocols. It also enabled significant changes to the user interface because new web applications could be built and delivered in the Enterprise Portal, such as those in Manager Self-Service or Employee Self-Service. The ERP world focused ever more strongly on transactional processing, capturing the sales orders, invoices, purchase orders, and goods movements at the heart of a company's operations.

Sometime in the late 1990s, many companies also started to work with dedicated *management information systems*—data warehouses and data marts that were designed to make the vast quantities of data being captured in the company's various operations easy to query and report on. SAP's Business Information Warehouse (BW) offered online analytical processing (OLAP), as did many other products on the market. The result was that each night, huge quantities of data would be loaded from SAP ERP, SAP CRM, and other systems into the data warehouse and transformed for reporting purposes.

At its simplest, this meant putting the data associated with an invoice or an order into a *star schema* to enable *multidimensional reporting* on the customers served and the products sold in the relevant regions. In many cases, it also involved significant *data cleansing* to solve underlying master data issues as well as transformation into a group chart of accounts, a group profit center structure, and so on. Multi-national companies needed a data warehouse to handle the volumes of data generated in their operations, but the nightly load was at odds with the "R" in real time. These organizations were paying a high price for the flexibility of their management information systems in terms of the timeliness of their data.

More to the point, if you were to ask most financial analysts how they actually worked in those days, the answer would be neither in SAP ERP nor in a data warehouse directly, but in a *spreadsheet*. This was the era of Microsoft Excel, with the operations of vast companies being run from "spreadmarts".

In 2011, Hasso Plattner, one of the founders of SAP, published his book, "In-Memory Data Management" (Springer-Verlag, Berlin Heidelberg). This book described the architecture of SAP HANA and envisioned a management meeting of the future: instead of the participants arriving with a set of laboriously compiled briefing books—which tried to anticipate every question that might be asked and by their very nature, were out of date by the time the managers entered the meeting room—the managers would have instant access to real-time business information and could spend the meeting simulating the effect of various assumptions on their bottom line before agreeing on the actions to follow. Essentially, SAP S/4HANA Finance is the realization of the vision illustrated in Figure 1.1. SAP CFO Luka Mucic really does use the SAP Digital Boardroom to guide his fellow executives through the key KPIs for the organization and discuss scenarios for the future.

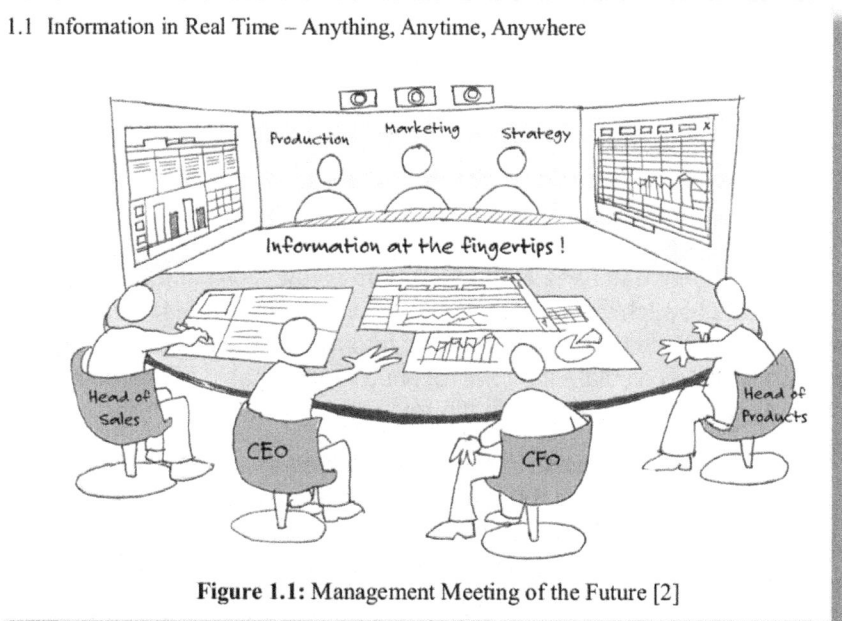

Figure 1.1: Management Meeting of the Future [2]

Figure 1.1. Hasso Plattner's vision of a management meeting of the future

Of course, this vision does not apply only to the time the board members are in the meeting room; they need the same information in real time on every device they use. We will look at how SAP Fiori is helping them to access this information while they are on the move. And this real-time information is required not only by the board members but also by every manager in the organization, with the approach being extended to professional users from accountants to warehouse clerks.

As this vision becomes reality, we are seeing the re-architected system becoming the *digital core* and organizations connecting cloud services to this digital core using HANA Cloud Integration. But first, let us focus on how SAP HANA enables SAP to re-architect the Financial Accounting, Asset Accounting, Controlling, and Inventory Accounting applications to be ready for the digital age.

1.2 SAP HANA

SAP HANA evolved from Hasso Plattner's work with his students at the Hasso Plattner Institute (*http://hpi.de/en.html*) in Potsdam, Germany. From a technical point of view, the radical changes are that all data is kept in main memory rather than on a hard disk and that massive parallel processing is possible. Both of these changes significantly accelerate data processing.

1.2.1 From row stores to column stores

For a financial analyst, the key difference between an SAP HANA database and a traditional database is the shift from a *row store* to a *column store*. Because this switch is critical to understanding how SAP S/4HANA Finance works, let us spend a moment thinking through a simple example. Imagine that we want to calculate the total revenue for Germany in a particular period by aggregating the figures in the relevant invoices:

- ▶ In a row store, each invoice line is stored as a row in the database. This row contains the amount in the invoice together with the data used to select the relevant invoices for reporting, such as the accounting period, the fiscal year, the company code, and the account. To determine the rows containing the German company code, the system has to read **every line** in the database and then aggregate the amounts for the relevant lines. Because there are typically millions of invoice lines on the database, if aggregating revenue by company code is a common query, there will probably be an *index*—an additional table to support selection by company code.

In some cases, the query may still be too slow and the chances are that the developer will have added a totals table to pre-aggregate the data by accounting period and fiscal year.

▶ In a column store, the data is organized in columns. If you are querying the document number, then the number of lines to be queried will be the same in both the column store and the row store. However, if you are selecting the revenue lines by company code, then the **column** for the company code will only contain one entry per company code and even a major multi-national organization probably will not have more than a few hundred company codes in that column. Instead of querying millions of lines, the system can select the German company from a couple of hundred lines. The result is available in seconds with no need to create an additional index table. The period selection works in the same way, aggregating the relevant figures for the selected periods on the fly with no need to create an additional totals table.

Now imagine that the data record includes not only the period, the year, the company code, and the account, but all sixty characteristics that can currently be included in an operating concern for Profitability Analysis (CO-PA). A typical operating concern contains reporting characteristics such as product, product group, customer, customer group, region, sales office, and so on. Multidimensional reporting in Profitability Analysis was already available in R/2; what is new is that you can now change a single setting in your existing profitability drill-down reports (READ UPON EACH NAVIGATION STEP) to ensure that instead of reading *pre-aggregated* data, the system executes a new *select statement* each time you navigate to a new view of the report data. This means that when you have finished looking at the revenue for Germany and decide to look at the revenue for France, this triggers a new select statement on the invoice data in real time. If you drill down from there to the sales office in Paris, this triggers another select statement. If you then pull in the product categories that are selling well in the Paris office, the system begins another select statement. These fast select statements are what make Hasso Plattner's vison for the future possible today. This is technically what happens as Luka Mucic navigates through the SAP Digital Boardroom. However, if you choose to continue to use the drill-down reports (transaction KE30) that have been available since the 1990s, you do not need to retrain your entire user community and can move ahead with the new technology at your own speed. This stability is key to the idea of offering *innovation without disruption*. You can continue to use all the CO-PA reports your organization has built up over the years and simply change one parameter to benefit from the new architecture.

What changes is that you no longer need to maintain summarization levels in Profitability Analysis. Assessment cycles that previously relied on pre-aggregated data to determine the drivers for the allocation can aggregate such data on the fly. You no longer need to load profitability data to a data warehouse; instead, you can work with a virtual data model to achieve multidimensional data analysis without a data warehouse, or build data marts to prepare this data for the briefing books.

1.2.2 From updates to inserts

Another key element to understand about SAP HANA is that it is much faster to *insert* a single record than to *update* (or change) a totals table (or several totals tables). If a single business transaction, such as an invoice or a goods movement, can be captured as one document in Financials, the system simply needs to issue a document number and record the relevant information in the document. This is what we mean by an insert.

Every time an update is required to store totals by period and cost center, profit center, and so on, the system has to **lock** that record to perform the update, which can significantly slow down period-end processes, such as huge allocations or top-down distributions. Each application in Financials has its own line item and totals table, so one simple invoice could trigger updates to the totals in Asset Accounting, Cost Center Accounting, Profit Center Accounting, and Accounts Payable.

This situation becomes even more critical when we are posting goods movements, where the same material may be required in multiple production orders or where the same material is going from a retail distribution center to several stores on different trucks. In an extreme case, these locks on the various tables can stop a production line if several production orders try to record their usage of a common part or the trucks at a retail center because the goods issues for each store lock each other out. If you can get rid of the locks, you can record more goods movements on the same system and the whole dynamics of your system sizing changes dramatically. This is essentially what is happening as SAP re-architects its solution for SAP HANA.

1.2.3 The move to SAP HANA

Although the last two sections sound radical, it is important to understand that you can make the move to SAP HANA in a series of small steps:

- You may already have heard of the *CO-PA accelerator* or the *side-car approach* introduced in 2011. This just meant that the transactional data for Profitability Analysis (table CE1 for costing-based Profitability Analysis or table COEP for account-based Profitability Analysis) was moved to a separate SAP HANA database and updated in near real time whenever a new invoice or cost posting was added to the ERP database (the *primary database* in this context). Drill-down reporting for Profitability Analysis was then redirected to read from the SAP HANA database (the *secondary database*) rather than the ERP database. Similar accelerators are available for General Ledger Accounting (new and classic), Special Ledger, Profit Center Accounting, Cost Center Accounting, Order and Project Accounting, Asset Accounting, Investment Management, and the Material Ledger. The charm of this approach was that it posed no risk. If the SAP HANA database was unavailable for any reason, then the report would simply select from the main database. The response might be slower, but the report would still return a result.

- *SAP Business Suite powered by HANA* was introduced in 2012 and goes one stage further, replacing the standard database with an SAP HANA database. At first glance, not much has changed. You still find the familiar menus for Financial Accounting, Controlling, Materials Management, Production Planning, and so on, but you benefit from all the accelerations due to the faster select statements detailed above. You also find a handful of new transactions in the menu, such as:
  - KSB1N for faster cost center line item reporting,
  - KOB1N for faster order line item reporting,
  - CJ13N for faster project line item reporting, and
  - drill-down reporting for the material ledger using transaction KKML0.

To find out more about these approaches, refer to my previous, co-authored book "SAP HANA for ERP Financials"[1].

---

[1] "SAP HANA for ERP Financials"—by Ulrich Schlüter and Janet Salmon (Espresso Tutorials 2011).

1.3 Changes to the Finance applications

SAP S/4HANA Finance is more than just a database change. Over recent years, SAP has been rewriting its financial applications because the programming paradigms that prevailed back in the 1990s no longer apply and the software architecture can be simplified. To help you understand what is happening, we will look at some examples of the major changes under way.

1.3.1 Index and totals tables

Index tables were originally used to improve selection, as we saw when we looked at the selection of revenues by company code. By comparison, *totals tables* pre-aggregate the financial data into period blocks to make it easy to select the total cost center costs for the relevant fiscal period, either for reporting or for use in a process such as allocations or settlement.

- As a first step, let us take a look at the index tables in Financial Accounting. In the past, when you selected a list of open items for a supplier, the application used index table BSIK to find the relevant items. To select those supplier items that had been cleared, the application used index table BSAK. For a list of open items for a customer, it was index table BSID, and for those customer items that had been cleared, index table BSAD. There were index tables BSIS and BSAS for G/L accounts (or index tables FAGLBSIS and FAGLBSAS for new G/L) and index table BSIM for materials. With SAP HANA, these index tables have become superfluous because the selection can work directly on the primary tables for the open items or the accounts. That is already seven fewer tables that require synchronization when building an application, and seven fewer tables occupying space on the database.

- When we looked at navigation within a profitability report, we said that we were selecting with each navigation step rather than reading from pre-aggregated data. Almost all standard reports read from such pre-aggregated tables or totals tables. Customer data is updated to KNC1 and KNC3, supplier data to LFC1 and LFC3, data in Classic General Ledger Accounting to GLT1 and GLT3, data in new General Ledger Accounting to FAGLFLEXT, and in Controlling, to COSP and COSS. In the past, the challenge here was two-fold: on the one hand, you had aggregated data that had to be kept synchronized with the supporting line item data. The result of aggregating the general ledger line items by company code and business area should always be the **same** as the total stored in the totals table for the period of aggregation. As we discussed in Section 1.2.2, you might have experienced **locking** problems when trying to perform huge data loads or large allocations at period close. To write a new line item, the system simply issues a new document number and creates a record, but to update the totals table, the system has to lock the totals table for cost center XYZ in the relevant period and then release it again once the new line item has been included in the totals for the period. If you have a lot of data records trying to update a small number of totals tables because you only have a small number of profit centers, this can cause significant problems.

- This locking of the aggregate tables was particularly problematic in Inventory Management, where there are many tables storing inventory values by plant, storage location, and so on and for the various stock types. The impact of changing this data structure can be significant, sometimes making postings faster by a factor of up to ten.

If SAP were to rebuild its applications from scratch, then the fact that the index tables and the totals tables are no longer needed would be of minor academic interest. In practice, however, hundreds of programs read from these totals tables and not all of them were built by SAP. In Controlling, around 180 standard programs read from tables COSP and COSS in the course of the period close. This is because it was easier to select the cost center data to be allocated during the period-end close from a table that has already pre-aggregated this data rather than aggregating on the fly.

The technical trick to enable a smooth changeover is to provide *compatibility views* for all the tables that have been removed. Figure 1.2 shows the compatibility view for the general ledger totals (the former table GLT0). This has exactly the same structure as the old totals table and ensures that any program—either an SAP program or a program from a partner or customer—that previously read from this table works as before, but aggregates the data on the fly from the underlying line item table rather than reading the totals table. SAP is gradually rewriting the programs for allocations, settlement, and so on to read directly from the line items. However, this simple technical trick means that you can make the move to SAP HANA at your own pace. Note also table GLT0_BCK in Figure 1.2; this is used during migration as a back-up to store the contents of the original totals tables to make sure that no data is missing in the line item table. New journal entries created after migration is complete will not be added to this table, and are only accessed via the view.

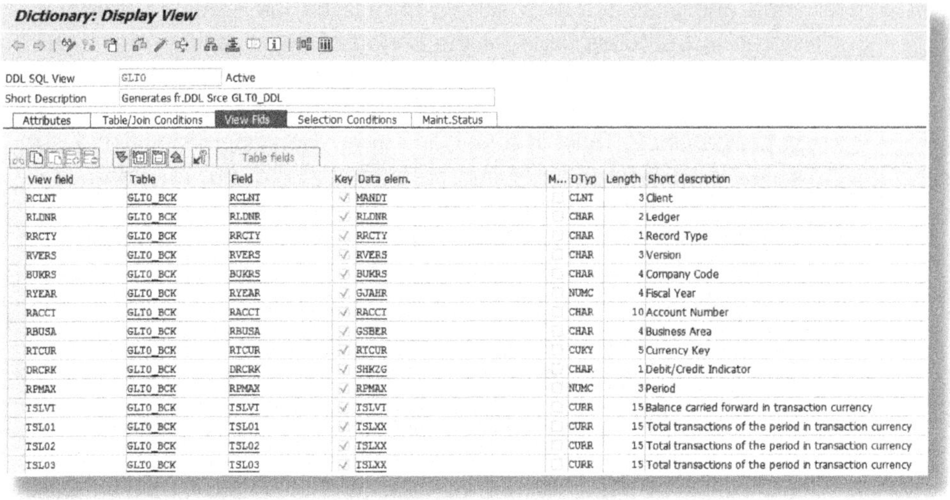
Dictionary: Display View

DDL SQL View GLT0 Active

Short Description Generates fr.DDL Srce GLT0_DDL

Attributes | Table/Join Conditions | View Flds | Selection Conditions | Maint.Status

Table fields

View field	Table	Field	Key	Data elem.	M...	DTyp	Length	Short description
RCLNT	GLT0_BCK	RCLNT	✓	MANDT		CLNT	3	Client
RLDNR	GLT0_BCK	RLDNR	✓	RLDNR		CHAR	2	Ledger
RRCTY	GLT0_BCK	RRCTY	✓	RRCTY		CHAR	1	Record Type
RVERS	GLT0_BCK	RVERS	✓	RVERS		CHAR	3	Version
BUKRS	GLT0_BCK	BUKRS	✓	BUKRS		CHAR	4	Company Code
RYEAR	GLT0_BCK	RYEAR	✓	GJAHR		NUMC	4	Fiscal Year
RACCT	GLT0_BCK	RACCT	✓	RACCT		CHAR	10	Account Number
RBUSA	GLT0_BCK	RBUSA	✓	GSBER		CHAR	4	Business Area
RTCUR	GLT0_BCK	RTCUR	✓	RTCUR		CUKY	5	Currency Key
DRCRK	GLT0_BCK	DRCRK	✓	SHKZG		CHAR	1	Debit/Credit Indicator
RPMAX	GLT0_BCK	RPMAX	✓	RPMAX		NUMC	3	Period
TSLVT	GLT0_BCK	TSLVT	✓	TSLVT		CURR	15	Balance carried forward in transaction currency
TSL01	GLT0_BCK	TSL01	✓	TSLXX		CURR	15	Total transactions of the period in transaction currency
TSL02	GLT0_BCK	TSL02	✓	TSLXX		CURR	15	Total transactions of the period in transaction currency
TSL03	GLT0_BCK	TSL03	✓	TSLXX		CURR	15	Total transactions of the period in transaction currency

Figure 1.2: Compatibility view for table GLT0

The one table without an equivalent view in Accounting and Controlling is the old reconciliation ledger (COFIT table). You no longer need the reconciliation ledger to keep your postings in synch. However, this absence means that you should not use the reports offered in the Cost Element Accounting menu after migration. Instead, you should use the newer SAP Fiori options that we will discuss in Chapter 7.

1.3.2 Universal journal

The *universal journal* is probably the most fundamental change with SAP S/4HANA Finance; it alters the way the transactional data is stored. Instead of using separate tables for General Ledger Accounting, Asset Accounting, Controlling, Inventory Accounting and Profitability Analysis, the transactional data for these applications is stored in the universal journal, which, from a technical perspective, is a single table—ACDOCA. This means that there is no longer any need to reconcile the data in the separate applications and it is easy to build reports that cross the old component boundaries because all the reporting dimensions are contained in a single data string. To understand what this means, let us think through a simple business example. Previously, when an asset was acquired, the value of the asset was stored in Asset Accounting, and the vendor and payment details were stored in Accounts Payable. In addition, if the asset was assigned to a cost center so that the asset costs could be depreciated later, then the asset acquisition was also recorded in Cost Center Accounting.

The operational part of these applications remains largely unchanged—there is a purchase order for the asset with an account assignment to the cost center. The asset is delivered, and the supplier sends their invoice which you pay, having performed a three-way match. What changes is that a **single table** provides details of the asset, the vendor, the G/L account, and the assigned cost center, meaning that you can report on that business transaction in ways that were not possible before. Essentially, you can see relationships that were inherent in the business process (the asset, the vendor, the cost center) but were lost in the past because the business transaction was chopped up for storage in the Asset Accounting, Accounts Payable, and Cost Center Accounting modules.

Figure 1.3 shows the key fields in the new line item table for the universal journal. We will return to this table to look at the various reporting dimensions for Accounting and Controlling in Chapter 2. For now, note that the table contains more than 370 fields (this varies depending on the industry solutions active, the use of coding block extensions, and the number of columns generated for the fields in Profitability Analysis) and that the posting item now allows **six digits**, whereas previously, you could only post 999 items in a single document. Other fields, such as COMPANY CODE, FISCAL YEAR, and RECORD TYPE will look completely familiar. One myth is that the ACDOCA table is the only table in SAP S/4HANA Finance. This is not true—the BSEG table still exists and captures all FI line items, including open and cleared payment line items and line items arriving from Materials Management, Payroll, and so on. What has changed is that you can now radically summarize the BSEG line items (remove material line items from an invoice, cost center line items from a payroll posting, etc.) but pass the detail on to the ACDOCA table. This means, for example, that the huge POS (point-of-sales) documents that are created in an IS-Retail system can be summarized for update in the BSEG table but can include the quantities and values per store and article in the ACDOCA table; or that backflush updates with huge bills of materials in an engineering system can be summarized to remove the material components in the BSEG table but can include the quantities and values for each component in the ACDOCA table.

Field	Key	Initi...	Data element	Data Type	Length	Decim...	Coordinate	Short Description
RCLNT	✓	✓	MANDT	CLNT	3	0	0	Client
RLDNR	✓	✓	FINS_LEDGER	CHAR	2	0	0	Ledger in General Ledger Accounting
RBUKRS	✓	✓	BUKRS	CHAR	4	0	0	Company Code
GJAHR	✓	✓	GJAHR	NUMC	4	0	0	Fiscal Year
BELNR	✓	✓	BELNR_D	CHAR	10	0	0	Accounting Document Number
DOCLN	✓	✓	DOCLN6	CHAR	6	0	0	Six-Character Posting Item for Ledger
RYEAR			GJAHR_POS	NUMC	4	0	0	General Ledger Fiscal Year
DOCNR_LD			FINS_DOCNR_LD	CHAR	10	0	0	Ledger specific Accounting Document Number
RRCTY		✓	RRCTY	CHAR	1	0	0	Record Type

Figure 1.3: Universal Journal Entry Line Items table

1.4 SAP Fiori

These architectural changes might be interesting to the system administrator, but if we return to Hasso Plattner's vision of the management meeting of the future, it becomes clear that the user interface plays just as important a role as the data structures that support the reporting tasks. With the briefing book consigned to history, new user interfaces have to be intuitive enough for everyone from the CFO to a line manager to use and to make it easy for an accounts payable clerk to work efficiently with only minimal training.

To get a sense of what has changed, we will show how Accounts Receivable will look going forward. Figure 1.4 shows a sample starting page for an ACCOUNTS RECEIVABLE MANAGER. We accessed the tiles via a URL that can be called from a desktop, a tablet device, or a smartphone. This URL shows only those applications assigned to the user's role (no searching in a menu for the relevant transactions) and the figures shown in the tiles are color-coded to make it immediately clear what is positive and negative. From there, the manager can intuitively drill down to the details, with no training in how to set up report variants. We are worlds away from the classic SAP GUI transactions for customer line item analysis and, in this example, we can immediately see that there is cause for concern in that the overdue receivables are way too high and there are a worrying number of outstanding promises to pay, while the other key performance indicators are currently green.

Figure 1.4: SAP Fiori launchpad for Accounts Receivable Manager

To find out more about overdue receivables, click on the OVERDUE RECEIVABLES tile in Figure 1.4. Figure 1.5 shows details of the overdue receivables grouped by due date. Each column represents the sum of the open items for each band of due dates. To understand exactly where the problems lie, you can select from a drop-down list: BY DUE PERIOD, BY ACCOUNTING CLERK, BY COMPANY CODE, BY CUSTOMER, BY CUSTOMER COUNTRY, and BY CUSTOMER REGION. Technically, each of these analysis options provides a *view* that accesses data from the underlying tables and extends it to include master data texts, hierarchy information, and so on.

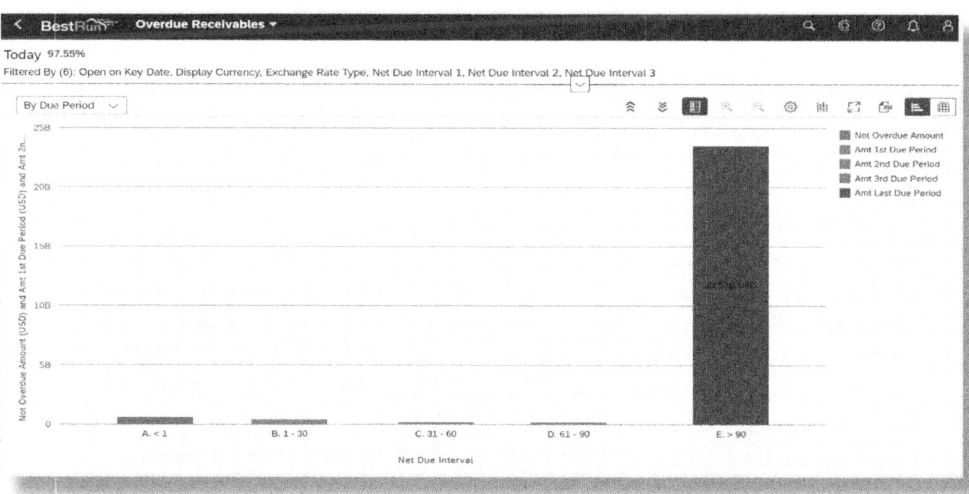

Figure 1.5: Overdue Receivables app, view by Due Period

From this view, we can drill down to see the receivables by customer, as shown in Figure 1.6. From there, we can access further views showing the receivables by company code or accounting clerk using the drop-down box in the upper left of the screen.

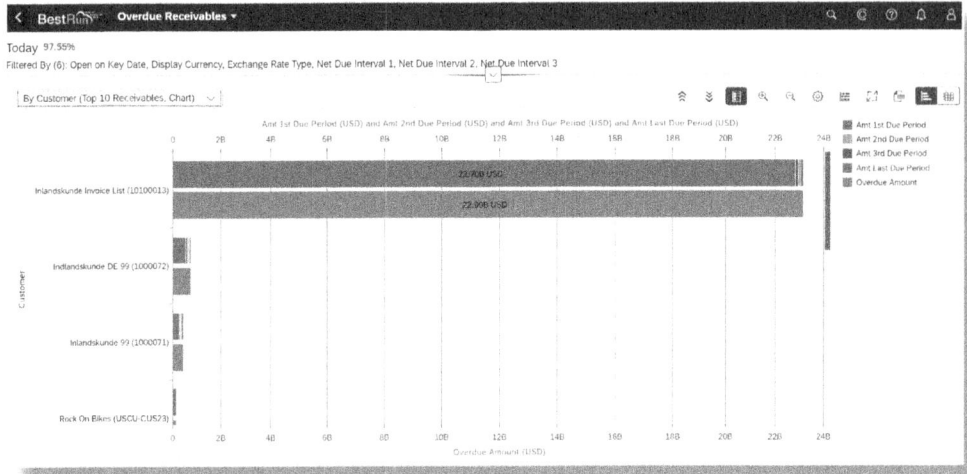

Figure 1.6: Overdue Receivables app, view by Customer

Clearly, we are scratching the surface of accounts receivables management here, but these views already give an idea of how easy the system is to use. What we cannot show in a book format is that these applications read the data in real time. There is no data mart or data warehouse behind the amounts shown in Figure 1.5 and Figure 1.6. If a new open item is created for one of these customers, it is instantly visible to the Accounts Receivable Manager without any interim steps, providing instant insight in a user interface that makes sense to any accountant.

Another example of how SAP is redesigning its applications from a business perspective is the display of journal entries as T-accounts, as shown in Figure 1.7. This format is universally used by accountants to record business transactions—with debits on the left, credits on the right, and the name of the account across the top of the "T". This example is the simplest set of T-accounts imaginable, with revenue being offset against receivables. Where a journal entry updates several accounts, color coding is used to show how the selected journal entries have impacted the various accounts.

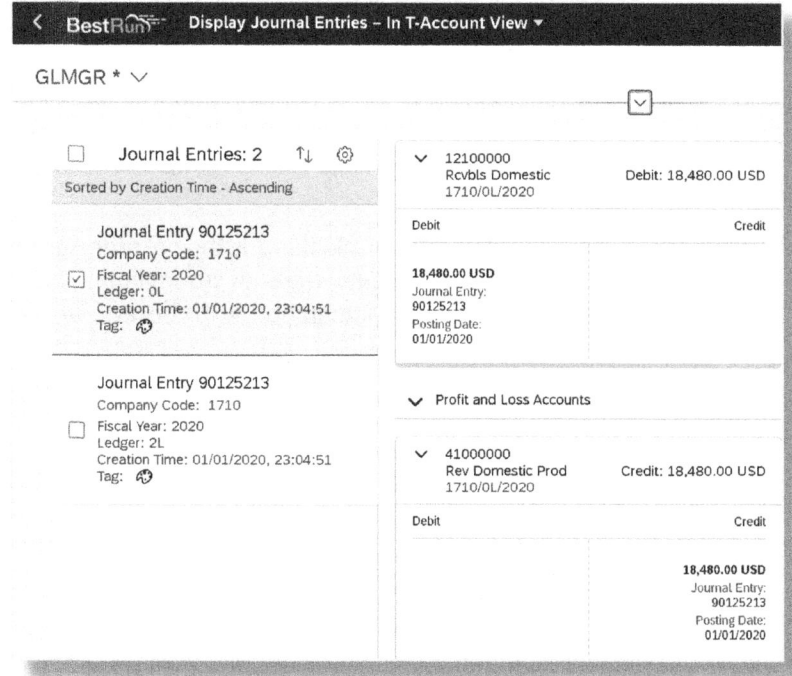

Figure 1.7: Display Journal Entries—T-Account View app

We will come back to how to work with these roles and business catalogs when we look at SAP Fiori in more detail in Chapter 5.

1.5 A simplified architecture for Finance

Figure 1.8 illustrates how the universal journal acts as the central table where all the reporting dimensions from the various financial applications are captured. On the left, we can see how the organizational and market-related dimensions are captured in a single table. SAP S/4HANA Finance includes three sister tables. We previously saw the line item table that captures all financial transactions in Figure 1.3, but there is also a planning table that enables organizations to create plan data for each of the reporting dimensions, and a group reporting table that displays the information captured for, and processed, during consolidation. In the chapters that follow we will look at each of these areas in turn:

- In Chapter 2, we will examine SAP Accounting, and the impact of the architectural changes on General Ledger Accounting, Controlling, Margin Analysis, Asset Accounting, and Inventory Accounting will be explained.
- In Chapter 3, we will explore how planning is being redesigned to include the learnings from the data warehouse environment of recent years and look at the tight integration with the accounting system.
- In Chapter 4, we will look at how to migrate to the new structures for Accounting and Controlling.
- In Chapter 5, we will examine how group reporting has been redesigned to work with data sourced directly from accounting without transformation and how to collect data from multiple source systems using Central Finance.
- In Chapter 6, we will take a detailed look at SAP Fiori, particularly its impact on financial reporting.

How does the Universal Journal manage to be the single-source-of-truth for your entire company?

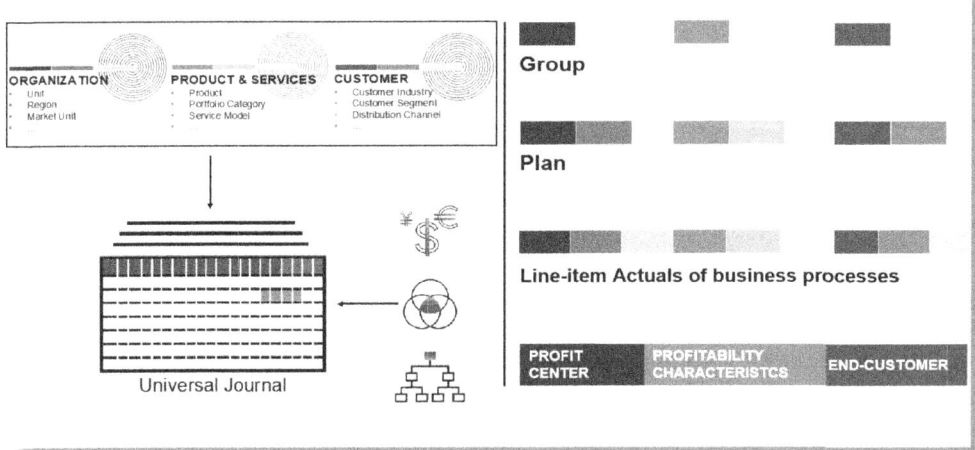

Figure 1.8: The universal journal in SAP S/4HANA Finance

At this stage, it makes sense to run through the software evolution:

- ► SAP Business Suite powered by HANA was introduced in 2012 and uses an SAP HANA database instead of a standard database. There are some optimizations to make use of the SAP HANA database.

- ► SAP Simple Finance Add-On for SAP Business Suite powered by HANA was introduced in 2014 and simplifies the data structure in Financials by removing the index tables and totals tables for many of the key finance tables. You can access the documentation via this link: *http://help.sap.com/sfin100*.

- ► SAP S/4HANA Finance was introduced in March 2015 and brings together the transactional tables for General Ledger Accounting, Asset Accounting, Controlling, and the Material Ledger into a single table, the universal journal. You can access the documentation via this link: *http://help.sap.com/sfin200*.

- ► SAP S/4HANA was introduced in November 2015 and includes new tables for inventory valuation. You can access the documentation via this link: *https://help.sap.com/s4hana*. It offers both on-premise and cloud editions. On-premise editions are released once a year and cloud editions once a quarter.

- ► The new tables for planning and for group reporting were introduced in November 2016. Actual Costing was also significantly rewritten in this edition.

In this context, it also makes sense to explain the naming conventions. Releases (editions) are given numbers based on calendar year and month; i.e., version "1503" means that it was released in 2015 (15), in March (3rd month of the calendar year—03). There are two versions of SAP S/4HANA Finance:

- ► SAP S/4HANA Finance 1503, introduced in March 2015 as SAP Simple Finance and requiring SAP ERP 6.0 EHP 7

- ► SAP S/4HANA Finance 1605, introduced in May 2016 and requiring SAP ERP 6.0 EHP 8

What is important here is the word **Finance**. With these software versions you have access to the universal journal, new Cash Management, and the connectors for Central Finance, but the logistics modules (Production Planning, Plant Maintenance, Sales and Distribution) and the industry solutions do not change. Customers are now advised to move directly to SAP S/4HANA rather than via SAP S/4HANA Finance.

There are multiple versions of SAP S/4HANA on the market:

- SAP S/4HANA 1511, introduced in November 2015
- SAP S/4HANA 1610, introduced in October 2016
- SAP S/4HANA 1709, introduced in September 2017
- SAP S/4HANA 1809, introduced in September 2018
- SAP S/4HANA 1909, introduced in September 2019

Here, in addition to the universal journal, new Cash Management, and the connectors for Central Finance, you will find changes in the logistics modules. From a finance perspective, the major changes with SAP S/4HANA are:

- The replacement of the customer and vendor transactions by the *business partner*
- The extension of the material number (now 40 characters)
- The introduction of the new inventory management table MATDOC
- Transaction-based material ledger becomes compulsory for inventory valuation

With SAP S/4HANA 1610, there is an additional change for customers using Actual Costing, with the introduction of two new tables: MLDOC, to record the material movements and price changes to be included in actual costing, and MLDOCCCS, to record the associated cost component split. The steps of the costing run have been completely reworked to benefit from the new architecture.

We will come back to these changes in subsequent chapters, but it is worth having a clear understanding of the relevant differences before you start to look at the details of the universal journal.

2 Accounting and Controlling

The German-speaking world has long since separated the Accounting modules from the Controlling modules and the move to bring the two applications into a single journal entry is one of the most significant changes with SAP S/4HANA Finance. The goal of this move is to provide internal and external reporting from the same data source. If you have struggled in the past to make sense of the SAP approach, the idea of having accounts, cost centers, profit centers, and so on in a single posting string, the universal journal, will make immediate sense.

2.1 Introducing the universal journal

The universal journal (ACDOCA table) significantly changes the way transactional data is stored for financial reporting. It offers huge benefits in terms of the ability to harmonize internal and external reporting requirements by having both read from the same document store where the account is the unifying element for all forms of financial reporting. You will still need to understand the different applications to the extent that you need to perform different business transactions in each application. This means that you still have to create general journal entries in General Ledger Accounting, acquire and retire assets in Asset Accounting, run allocations and settlement in Controlling, capitalize research and development costs in Investment Management, and so on, but in reporting, you read from one source, regardless of whether you want to supply data to your consolidation system, report to the tax authorities, or make internal management decisions.

Figure 2.1 illustrates the way the universal journal combines reporting dimensions from the separate applications (General Ledger Accounting, Profitability Analysis, Controlling, Asset Accounting, and Material Ledger) to provide a unified data structure for reporting that includes all relevant dimensions.

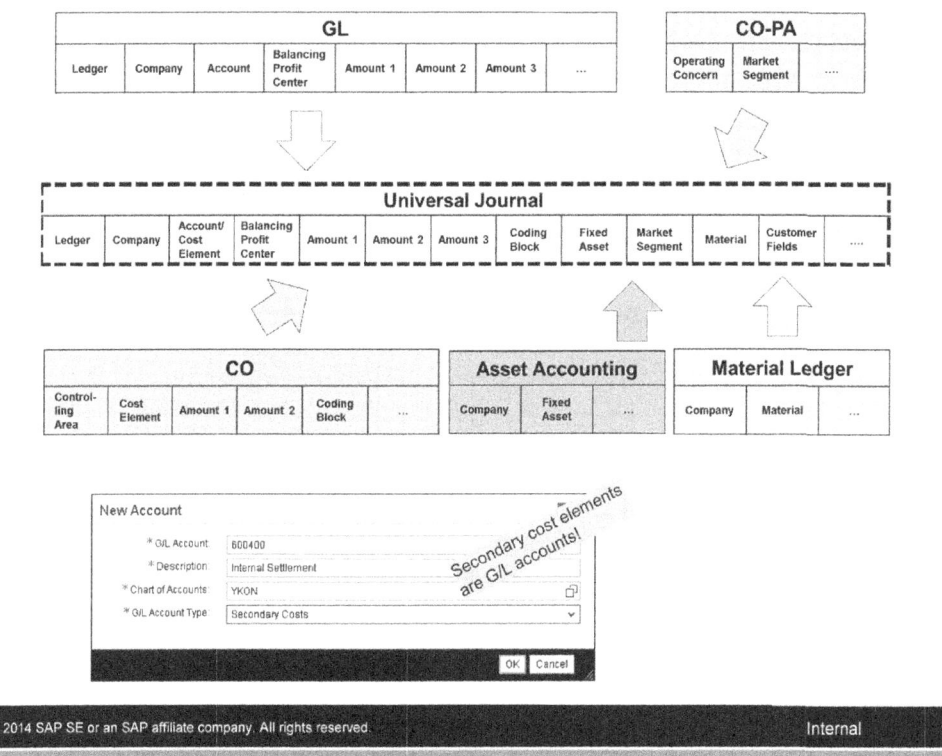

Figure 2.1: Combining reporting dimensions in the universal journal

We previously saw the key fields of the universal journal in Figure 1.3. If we now look at the details of the new line item table in Figure 2.2, we see how the existing fields for General Ledger Accounting, Asset Accounting, the Material Ledger, and Controlling are combined in the universal journal using a series of include structures, bringing data from the many different business transactions to deliver a single source of truth for financial reporting in SAP S/4HANA.

The massive simplification inherent in this structure is that instead of having a separate set of revenue lines in Profitability Analysis, Profit Center Accounting, and Financial Accounting, each offering a different amount of detail about the same business transaction, you can report from a single *source document* in the ACDOCA table. For internal reporting, for example, you might select revenue lines for a particular product or customer (information captured as characteristics that you can choose when you generate your operating concern in Profitability Analysis) and for external reporting, you select the same revenue lines based on the profit center or company code in the document.

Field	Key	Initi...	Data element	Data Type	Length	Decim...	Coordinate	Short Description
.INCLUDE			ACDOC_SI_VALUE_DAT	STRU	0	0	0	Universal Journal Entry: Value Fields
.INCLUDE		✓	ACDOC_SI_FIX	STRU	0	0	0	Universal Journal Entry: Mandatory fields for G/L
.INCLUDE		✓	ACDOC_SI_GEN	STRU	0	0	0	Universal Journal Entry: Fields for several subledgers
.INCLUDE		✓	ACDOC_SI_FI	STRU	0	0	0	Universal Journal Entry: Fields for FI subledgers
.INCLUDE		✓	ACDOC_SI_FAA	STRU	0	0	0	Universal Journal Entry: Fields for Asset Accounting
.INCLUDE		✓	ACDOC_SI_ML	STRU	0	0	0	Universal Journal Entry: Fields for Material Ledger
.INCLUDE		✓	ACDOC_SI_CFIN	STRU	0	0	0	Universal Journal Entry: Fields for Central Finance
.INCLUDE		✓	ACDOC_SI_CO	STRU	0	0	0	Universal Journal Entry: CO fields
.INCLUDE		✓	ACDOC_SI_LOG	STRU	0	0	0	Universal Journal Entry: Fields for Logistics

Figure 2.2: Merging the SAP ERP applications in the universal journal

When we talk about a *single source of truth*, what we mean is that instead of looking at datasets in multiple applications, we are looking at different aggregations of the same dataset by selecting fields from the various include structures shown in Figure 2.2. As we discussed in Section 1.2.1, the idea of the column store is significant. We may have hundreds of company codes, thousands of profit centers, and tens of thousands of customers, but these can be queried much more efficiently than in the past when each application built its own data store to record information about these entities.

In this context, it is also worth understanding how the different applications used to aggregate their data in the past. Even though many of the relevant fields were included in the BSEG table, organizations would configure their Financial Accounting applications to remove the individual cost centers from a large payroll document using *summarization*, or to remove the individual materials from a large invoice and only keep the cost center detail in Cost Center Accounting and the material detail in Profitability Analysis. This different granularity provided its own challenges when reconciling the various applications as key information was lost in the aggregation.

Before we look at what is new, let us remind ourselves of the high-level differences between the datasets in the various applications. However, if you are new to SAP S/4HANA Finance, you can skip straight to the next section because you do not have to worry about the historical differences between the various applications. All the Financials applications aggregate by period and fiscal year, but the other reporting dimensions are different in each application, making reconciliation tricky and meaning that management meetings are often spent discussing whose version of the truth is correct rather than what to do about the business situation the figures are showing.

2.1.1 Structure of General Ledger Accounting

Depending on which version of the SAP software you are using, you can approach a move to SAP S/4 HANA with two different options for General Ledger Accounting:

- *Classic General Ledger Accounting*—available from SAP R/3 onwards, stores data by account, company code, and business area, as we saw when we looked at table GLT0 in Figure 1.2. If you need reporting dimensions other than company code and business area, you can activate additional applications for Profit Center Accounting and Consolidation Preparation or build your own special ledger applications for Cost of Goods Sold Reporting, Segment Reporting, and so on. The separate ledgers for Profit Center Accounting, Consolidation Preparation, and so on, are no longer required since the information is in the universal journal, but these ledgers are still updated and can continue to be used for an interim period. These special ledgers are considered part of the *compatibility scope*, which means that they will be supported for an interim period, but not beyond 2025. In addition to these ledgers, a *reconciliation ledger* stored the results of any allocations or settlements in Controlling that crossed company code boundaries and had to be reflected in General Ledger Accounting at period close by running transaction KALC to generate the appropriate journal entries. Moving to the universal journal makes the reconciliation ledger and transaction KALC obsolete because there is only one document in Accounting and Controlling. Here, however, the COFIT table is no longer updated and the legacy reports offered for Cost Element Reporting are no longer supported.

▶ *SAP ERP General Ledger Accounting* (formerly known as *new General Ledger Accounting*) available from SAP ERP onwards enabled you to extend the basic account, company code, business area approach by activating additional scenarios to support Profit Center Accounting, Cost of Goods Sold Reporting, Consolidation Preparation, Segment Reporting, and so on. Activating these scenarios extends table FAGLFLEXA to store details of the profit centers and partner profit centers, functional areas and partner functional areas, trading partners and partner trading partners, segments and partner segments, and so on. What the scenarios enable is essentially drill-down reporting for these dimensions within the general ledger. Technically, you were creating additional aggregates for each of the scenarios that you added to the general ledger. The reconciliation ledger became obsolete if you activated real-time integration with CO so that any allocation or settlement that crosses a company code boundary (or a profit center boundary, a functional area boundary, and so on) would trigger a posting in the general ledger to reflect the change. This was progress compared to classic General Ledger Accounting, but there were limits to the number of dimensions that you could safely add to aggregate table FAGLFLEXA. With the universal journal, you no longer need to activate the various reporting scenarios separately—the columns are automatically updated if you maintain the proper assignments in your master data and you can add further dimensions to the coding block and extend the operating concern for Profitability Analysis as required.

One of the common misconceptions about the universal journal is that it is the only table used for General Ledger Accounting. In truth, the old document header table (BKPF) and document line item table (BSEG) continue to exist alongside the universal journal, as shown in Figure 2.3. The BSEG table continues to be used for open item clearing and related tasks, but the entries can be summarized to remove entities such as the product sold or the cost centers, where the detailed information is only needed in the universal journal (ACDOCA). However, since the BSEG is used for clearing, you will need to retain the material for goods receipt/invoice receipt clearing.

Data Model for Journal Entries in the Universal Journal

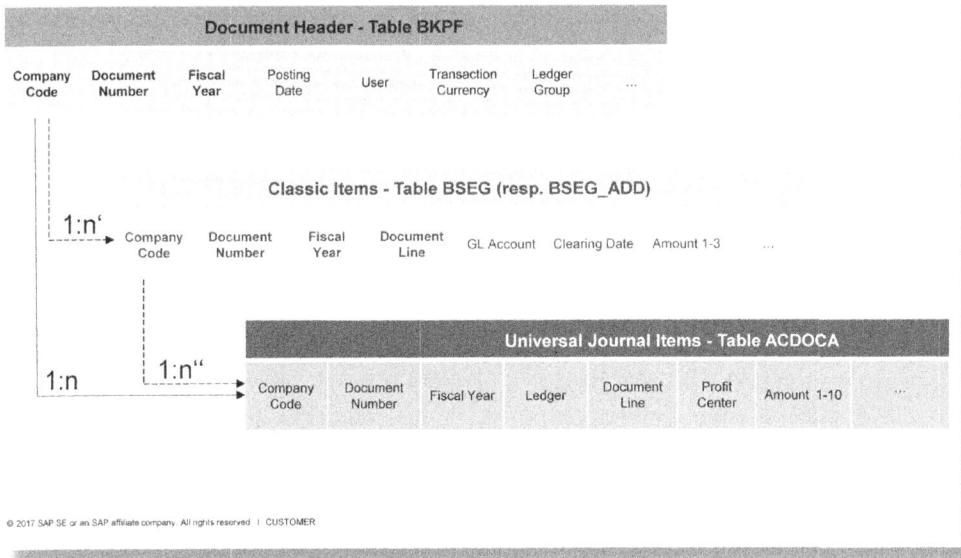

Figure 2.3: Data model for journal entries

2.1.2 Structure of Asset Accounting

SAP S/4HANA Finance includes new Asset Accounting. The new asset accounting functions were first introduced as the business functions FIN_AA_CI_1 in EhP6 and FIN_AA_PARALLEL_VAL in EhP7. The original motivation was the need to switch the leading accounting principle as it became increasingly common for US customers to switch their leading valuation from US GAAP (generally accepted accounting principles) to IFRS (International Financial Reporting Standards). If you refer back to Figure 1.3, you will notice that the *ledger* is one of the key fields in the universal journal. While Asset Accounting has always supported different valuations by offering different depreciation areas for a single asset, the new approach means that the different asset valuations for IFRS and the local GAAPs are stored in separate ledgers which are independent of each other. In earlier versions of the software, the second valuation was stored as a *delta* (or difference) to the first valuation and was updated at period close. It is now possible to update the separate ledgers in real time whenever the depreciation area has been flagged to enable real-time postings.

Asset Accounting was always integrated with General Ledger Accounting in the sense that journal entries were created for the acquisition, retirement, and revaluation of an asset, or to account for the depreciation of the fixed asset in the general ledger. However, Asset Accounting was a *sub-ledger* that stored detailed information relating to asset valuation, and General Ledger Accounting stored aggregated information about the assets in the *general ledger* (GLT0 or FAGLFLEXA tables). The account, the profit center, and any of the items we listed for the general ledger were not included in the line item table for Asset Accounting (table ANEP), and the asset-related fields were not available in Financial Accounting or Controlling. The only reporting dimension **common** to General Ledger Accounting and Asset Accounting other than the period and year is the company code. Reconciliation between the applications involved finding the postings in the general ledger that applied to fixed assets (those of account type A) and comparing them against the sum of the items in the Asset Accounting application. If you created a manual journal entry to an asset account, then the two would not match because this manual posting would not exist in the asset accounting table. Now, there is no separate subledger for Asset Accounting and the asset is simply an additional dimension in the general ledger and sits alongside the company code, cost center, profit center, and so on in the posting string, which makes it substantially easier to report across applications than in the past, as we will see when we look at the trial balance in Section 2.3.1.

2.1.3 Account assignments in Controlling

Although Cost Center Accounting, Order Accounting, and Project Accounting are generally considered to be separate applications in Controlling, the basic principle of assigning costs to an account assignment (a cost center, order, WBS (work breakdown structure) element, and so on) is the same in each application.

In general, Controlling involves two types of posting for actual costs:

- ▶ The first type of posting is a *primary cost posting*. This simply means that the general ledger posting also includes an assignment to the cost center, order, or project responsible for the costs—for example, payroll postings, travel expenses, and asset depreciation might be assigned to a cost center, and material expenses to an order or project. Each G/L account used to record these postings is linked with a sister *primary cost element* in Controlling that captures such costs. There is a one-to-one relationship between the primary cost postings and the appropriate profit and loss entries in the general ledger but the posting line items in the two applications are not necessarily at the same level of granularity. This is because the general ledger items are often configured such that the cost center, order, or project is summarized (in other words, **removed**) in order to reduce data volumes. This is frequently the case for the material items in the invoice, which are often summarized so that the 999 line item limit for the BSEG table is not exceeded.

▶ The second type of posting is a *secondary cost posting*. This means that these costs are allocated or settled further. In our example, the payroll, travel, and depreciation costs assigned to the cost center might be allocated to orders and projects using time recording, order confirmation or an overhead surcharge, resulting in the cost center being credited and the order or project debited under a *secondary cost element*. The order and project costs might be settled to market segments, resulting in the order or project being credited and the market segments debited, again under a secondary cost element. There was never a one-to-one relationship between these secondary cost elements and the G/L accounts because they were aggregated to a single reconciliation account for the relevant business transaction, irrespective of whether you use transaction KALC or the real-time integration functions in SAP ERP General Ledger Accounting. As you move to SAP S/4HANA, the results of the allocations and settlements will be stored under the secondary cost elements, so be sure to adjust any consolidation systems that access account information accordingly.

The easiest way to think of the shift to SAP S/4HANA is to understand that with *primary cost postings* the information on the account assignment extends the journal entry to explain where and why costs were incurred, so we see that salaries were posted to a *cost center* and raw material costs to a *production order*. *Secondary cost postings*, by contrast, record the relationships between the *senders* and *receivers* of any allocations or settlements. These relationships can result in updates to the affected profit centers, functional areas, and so on, resulting in journal entries that record the impact of the shift on the related *partner objects*. In Chapter 1, we discussed the removal of the totals tables for primary costs (COSP) and secondary costs (COSS). With the introduction of the universal journal, these totals records exist only as *compatibility views* until SAP rewrites all programs to select from the universal journal directly. This reimplementation effort also enables the introduction of the ledger to support different accounting principles and additional currencies by adding new fields that could not easily be accommodated in the legacy tables.

However, Controlling does more than simply collect primary costs and revenues, and record secondary costs. Separate tables continue to exist for statistical key figures (COSR), activity prices (COST), variances (COSB), and commitments (COOI). In Chapter 3, we will look at how the calculation of activity prices, variances and commitments is gradually being rearchitected to accommodate the new structures.

2.1.4 Margin Analysis

Profitability Analysis (CO-PA) was generally also considered a separate application within Controlling. SAP ERP supports two types of Profitability Analysis: *Margin Analysis* (formerly known as *account-based Profitability Analysis*) and *costing-based Profitability Analysis*. However, for performance reasons, most organizations only used costing-based Profitability Analysis prior to SAP HANA. Margin Analysis is now the preferred choice in SAP S/4HANA.

- *Margin Analysis* captures the revenues, sales deductions and cost of goods sold under primary cost elements, and the result of allocations and settlement under secondary cost elements. The difference compared to Cost Center Accounting, Order Accounting, or Project Accounting is that the account assignment is not a one-dimensional cost center or order, but a multidimensional market segment or group of characteristics, such as the product sold, the customer who bought the product, the sales office, the distribution channel, and so on. The operating concern is configurable and therefore, every organization uses its own special set of CO-PA characteristics. As you move to the universal journal, a column is created for each of the characteristics in your operating concern and reporting dimensions such as the customer, product, and sales office are on an equal level with company code, profit center, and functional area.

- *Costing-based Profitability Analysis*, by contrast, uses the same operating concern with the same characteristics, but transforms the accounts/cost elements into *value fields*. Because there is a technical limitation which means that only 200 value fields are supported (in earlier releases it was 120), there are typically far fewer value fields than there are accounts and value fields exist for items without an account assignment, such as statistical freight costs or sales deductions. Because it is common practice to summarize (or remove) not just the cost center but also the material number in invoices, there is often a different granularity between the lines in General Ledger Accounting and the lines in Profitability Analysis. Costing-based Profitability Analysis continues to be supported in SAP S/4HANA Finance but because of the value fields, the data cannot be subsumed into the universal journal and table CE1 (the line-item table for costing-based Profitability Analysis) continues to exist alongside the universal journal. There is no migration service to switch from a costing-based model to an account-based model because the two models are fundamentally different approaches (accounts vs key figures).

To illustrate the new approach, Figure 2.4 shows the Product Profitability app. The dimensions on the left include fields for the market segments (BILL-TO PARTY, COUNTRY, CUSTOMER GROUP, INDUSTRY, PRODUCT SOLD, PRODUCT SOLD GROUP, SALES DISTRICT, SALES ORDER, and so on), but also dimensions from General Ledger Accounting, including COMPANY CODE, G/L ACCOUNT, LEDGER, and so on. This is an example of how information from the formerly separate applications is brought together in SAP S/4HANA. You will notice that this report does not show all the G/L accounts, but rather an aggregated view, displaying BILLED REVENUE, RECOGNIZED REVENUE, and so on. These aggregations are similar to the value fields used in costing-based Profitability Analysis but are created using *semantic tags*. We will look at how to map your accounts to these semantic tags in Chapter 6. If you want to see which G/L accounts are behind each semantic tag, G/L ACCOUNT is part of the list of DIMENSIONS on the left and can be pulled into the rows of the report to show which G/L accounts make up the billed revenue posting.

DIMENSIONS	COLUMNS	Product Sold Group	ZYOUTH	ZRACING	ZMTN	ZCRUISE
> Measures	Product Sold Group	Product Sold Group	Youth	Racing	Mountain	Cruise
Bill-To Party		Billed Revenue	$ 9,004,750.00	$ 50,218,708.00	$ 24,508,279.00	$ 20,401,606.00
Bus. Transac. Type		Sales Deduction	$ 0.00	$ 0.00	$ 0.00	$ 0.00
Company Code		Revenue Adjustment	$ 0.00	$ 0.00	$ 0.00	$ 0.00
Company Code C...		Recognized Revenue	$ 9,004,750.00	$ 50,218,708.00	$ 24,508,279.00	$ 20,401,606.00
Condition Contract		COGS - Variable	$ -5,089,849.68	$ -27,941,573.97	$ -14,536,322.19	$ -13,041,631.94
Country		Contrib Margin I	$ 3,914,900.32	$ 22,277,134.03	$ 9,971,956.81	$ 7,359,974.06
Customer	ROWS	COGS - Fixed	$ 0.00	$ -3,734,401.01	$ -1,393,870.36	$ -1,109,400.29
Customer Group	Measures	Price Differences	$ 0.00	$ 0.00	$ 0.00	$ 0.00
		Contrib Margin II	$ 3,914,900.32	$ 18,542,733.02	$ 8,578,086.45	$ 6,250,573.77
		Billed Quantity	88,566 PC	16,116 PC	15,821 PC	29,004 PC
		Margin per Unit	44.20 $ /PC	1,382.30 $ /PC	630.30 $ /PC	253.76 $ /PC

Figure 2.4: Product Profitability app

2.1.5 Structures in the Material Ledger

The use of the Material Ledger in SAP S/4HANA is a source of some confusion. In SAP S/4HANA Finance, the use of the Material Ledger is **optional**, but with SAP S/4HANA, the use of the transactional Material Ledger becomes **compulsory**. As we saw with Margin Analysis, SAP ERP supports two approaches to the Material Ledger (the transactional Material Ledger and Actual Costing), although when most organizations talk about the Material Ledger, they generally mean that they use the second option, Actual Costing:

▶ The *transactional Material Ledger* is a subledger like Asset Accounting but structured by company code, valuation area, and material. From a Material Ledger perspective, materials have *price determination 2*, which simply means that inventory-related transactions are captured in different currencies and according to different valuation approaches (group valuation, legal valuation, and profit center valuation). You can continue to work with the moving average price that is calculated with each transaction update and you do **not** require a costing run at period close. The use of the transactional Material Ledger becomes **compulsory** with SAP S/4HANA on-premise edition 1511, although it has been available since SAP R/3 Release 4.0.

▶ *Actual Costing*, by contrast, is used in geographies and industries where there is a legal or business requirement to assign purchase price variances, production variances, and so on to the goods sold and goods in inventory at period close. This option requires you to execute one or more costing runs to calculate actual costs at period close. Actual Costing continues to be supported as an **option** in SAP S/4HANA and can be activated as an additional scope item in the cloud. The data cannot be subsumed entirely into the universal journal and the actual costing tables continue to exist alongside the universal journal. Indeed, SAP S/4HANA 1610 includes a new optimized version of Actual Costing with a simpler data structure and less closing steps.

Figure 2.5 shows the Manage Material Valuation app, where you can see that the inventory values for the bearing are available in two currencies—the company code currency (CCDE CRCY) and the group currency (GROUP CRCY).

Figure 2.5: Manage Material Valuations app

2.1.6 Other subledgers

You will notice in Figure 2.1 that while the asset subledger and material subledger merge with the general ledger, some key subledgers remain separate. *Accounts Receivable* and *Accounts Payable* continue as separate subledgers for open item management and the clearing of payments. All you will find in the general ledger is the *reconciliation account* for the supplier or the customer. This is partly to do with the clearing logic in Accounts Payable and Accounts Receivable, where multiple accounting principles and multiple currencies actually get in the way if you are trying to clear an open item for a given amount. *Contract Accounts Receivable and Payable* also remains separate to store all details for utility billing and so on. Some industry solutions also have their own subledgers, such as SAP Bank Analyzer or SAP Insurance Analyzer for financial service organizations, or the SAP Customer Activity Repository (CAR) in Retail. These continue to integrate with the general ledger at the level of the account and some key reporting dimensions.

Of course, there are more differences between the applications than the reporting dimensions listed above. Historically, Financial Accounting worked with three currencies, while Controlling offered only two currencies. Accounting principles were also handled differently in each application (ledgers in General Ledger Accounting, charts of depreciation in Asset Accounting, versions in Controlling, currency types in the Material Ledger). Many of these differences are also being addressed in SAP S/4HANA Finance and we will discuss the relevant changes in the sections that follow.

2.2 General Ledger Accounting

We looked at the new table (ACDOCA) for storing transaction data in Chapter 1. However, it makes sense to look at some of the reports delivered to get a sense of what the universal journal enables simply because the data is in a long string rather than in separate chunks for each application. Of course, this does not mean that the whole of financial reporting can be performed using one table. There are still separate reports for viewing the open items in Accounts Payable and Accounts Receivable and reports for individual stakeholders—such as cost center managers and project managers—that select by cost center, WBS element, and so on, but we will see in the examples that follow how one simple report, the trial balance, can satisfy many reporting requirements if you use the appropriate drill-downs.

2.2.1 Trial balance

The screen shown in Figure 2.6 displays the trial balance—a list of accounts together with the opening balance, closing balance, and the debits and credits for the current accounting period for each account (to save space, we have only shown the report dimensions here). In the default view, the rows of the report are sorted by COMPANY CODE and G/L ACCOUNT. In this example, we have structured the accounts by financial statement version and included the LEDGER in the general selection parameters. We have focused on the reporting dimensions rather than the figures, because what is so powerful about the new report is the ability to drill down not just by segment, profit center, functional area, business area, etc.—as was possible with the drill-down reports in General Ledger Accounting—but by any of the list of reporting dimensions that we see on the left side of the screen. The list shown here is not exhaustive, and is much longer if you scroll further down the screen.

There are many new options, including the ability to view fixed assets and other asset-related fields from Asset Accounting, the cost centers, activity types, orders, WBS elements, etc. from Controlling, the CO-PA characteristics representing the market segments, and the inventory-related fields from the Material Ledger. This means that instead of navigating to a separate report you can easily perform a drill-down from the trial balance by selecting one of the DIMENSIONS on the left and moving it under either COLUMNS or ROWS to access the information you need. Of course, these options do not just apply to the trial balance. The additional dimensions are offered throughout SAP Fiori.

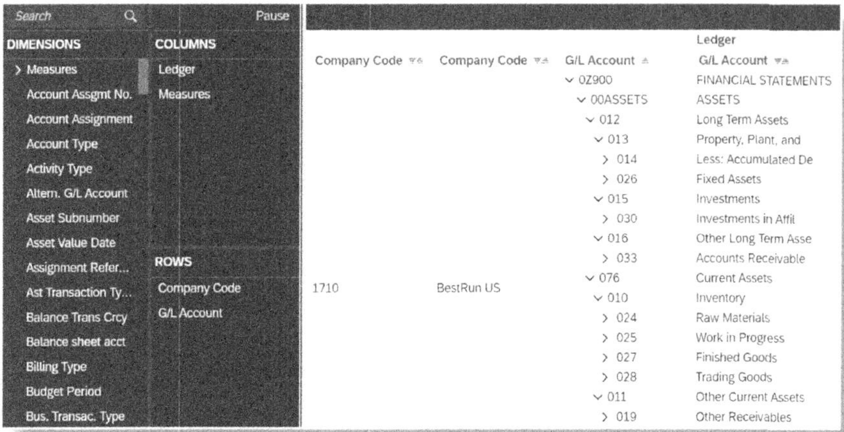

Figure 2.6: Trial Balance app with company code and G/L accounts

Figure 2.7 shows a very simple example where we have removed the COMPANY CODE from the rows, and under DIMENSIONS, we have scrolled down to COST CENTER (not visible in Figure 2.6) and pulled in this dimension to create a different set of rows in the report. This action has triggered a drill-down, so that we now see the COST CENTER and the G/L ACCOUNT in the rows of the report. In the past, you had to navigate to a separate report in Cost Center Accounting to see the same costs by cost center.

In our example, we have put the cost center before the G/L account, so all the costs shown are assigned to cost centers. If we switched the sequence of the dimensions to have the G/L account first, then we might have additional postings to an account that would show as NOT ASSIGNED. This is because most accounts also capture postings to orders, projects, and so on. To see these account assignments, we would have to change our drill-down dimensions again and add orders or projects alongside, or instead of, the cost center. As we work our way through the applications that feed into the universal journal, we will look at how each of these dimensions are populated for reporting.

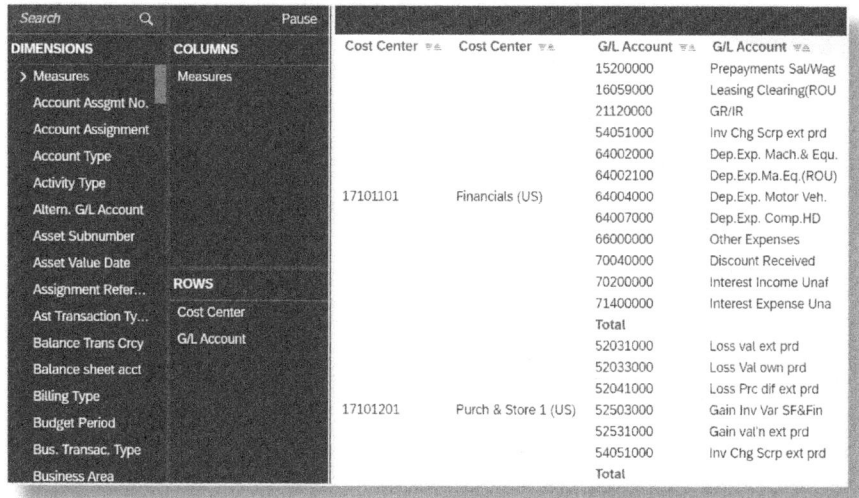

Figure 2.7: Trial Balance app with cost centers and G/L accounts

As you think through the possibilities for reporting on top of the universal journal, it makes sense to think about the different reporting dimensions and how they are filled by the various applications. Essentially, the universal journal is a *sparsely filled matrix*, meaning that some fields, such as those for the period and fiscal year, are filled by every transaction posted but that many are empty for any given transaction. If you have worked with Profitability Analysis in the past, you will already be familiar with the idea of *unassigned costs*. What is special about an SAP HANA database is that all the unfilled columns are automatically *compressed*, meaning that it is not a problem if the database includes fields that are only rarely filled because they do not occupy space in the database.

> ▶ Reporting dimensions such as company code, business area, profit center, segment, and so on are filled by **every** business transaction. All financial transactions have to take place within a company code. All costs and revenues are automatically assigned to profit centers, using the derivation rules in the assigned cost centers, orders, and projects. To assign the balance sheet items to the correct profit centers, you have to set up the appropriate document splitting rules. This ensures that the report always contains a figure for these entities.

▶ Other reporting dimensions are only filled by **some** business transactions—for example, the asset fields are only filled by the asset transactions, the material fields are only filled by goods movements, and the cost centers, orders, and projects are only filled if these are available as account assignments in the business transaction. The trading partner is only filled during an intercompany transaction. If the field is not filled, you will simply see NOT ASSIGNED in the report line.

2.2.2 Reporting dimensions in General Ledger Accounting

The universal journal contains all account assignments from General Ledger Accounting, so if you scroll to the appropriate section of the ACDOCA table, you will recognize the fields shown in Figure 2.8. These are the same as the general ledger scenarios (Segment Reporting, Profit Center Reporting, Cost of Goods Sold Reporting, and Consolidation Preparation) but the fields are always available in the universal journal and you do not have to activate them separately as scenarios. This is a good example of the difference between SAP S/4HANA Finance and the former applications.

▶ With SAP S/4HANA Finance, there is no totals table and these fields are **always** filled, provided that you have made the correct assignments to your profit centers, business areas, and functional areas in your master data.

▶ What happened previously during the activation step was that the system would generate the relevant fields in the former totals table FAGLFLEXA. Any change to the assignment in the reporting dimensions meant that you had to correct the totals in table FAGLFLEXA.

Note that for every reporting dimension in General Ledger Accounting you also have the equivalent *partner dimension*, so you will see dimension pairs (profit center and partner profit center, functional area and partner functional area, and so on). We will see this in more detail when we look at allocations because an allocation from cost center to cost center can also impact the associated profit centers, functional areas, and so on and this allocation updates the appropriate partner information.

Note that these fields are part of the general ledger. If you have handled Profit Center Accounting via a separate set of tables or used Special Ledger to handle functional areas for Cost of Goods Sold Reporting in the past, these interfaces will be supported until 2025 and the data will be updated in these tables. These applications are considered part of the compatibility scope and will not be supported after this date. However, if you are starting afresh, it makes sense to use the universal journal to handle these reporting dimensions from the beginning rather than creating additional ledgers. Full details of the difference between Profit Center Accounting in the universal journal and classic Profit Center Accounting can be found in in SAP Note 2425255[2].

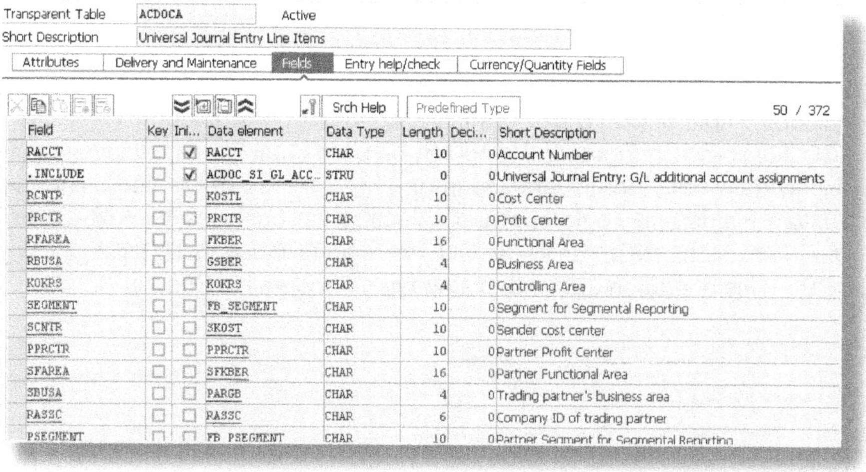
Transparent Table ACDOCA Active
Short Description Universal Journal Entry Line Items
Attributes | Delivery and Maintenance | Fields | Entry help/check | Currency/Quantity Fields
Srch Help | Predefined Type 50 / 372

Field	Key	Ini...	Data element	Data Type	Length	Deci...	Short Description
RACCT	☐	☑	RACCT	CHAR	10	0	Account Number
.INCLUDE	☐	☑	ACDOC_SI_GL_ACC...	STRU	0	0	Universal Journal Entry: G/L additional account assignments
RCNTR	☐	☐	KOSTL	CHAR	10	0	Cost Center
PRCTR	☐	☐	PRCTR	CHAR	10	0	Profit Center
RFAREA	☐	☐	FKBER	CHAR	16	0	Functional Area
RBUSA	☐	☐	GSBER	CHAR	4	0	Business Area
KOKRS	☐	☐	KOKRS	CHAR	4	0	Controlling Area
SEGMENT	☐	☐	FB_SEGMENT	CHAR	10	0	Segment for Segmental Reporting
SCNTR	☐	☐	SKOST	CHAR	10	0	Sender cost center
PPRCTR	☐	☐	PPRCTR	CHAR	10	0	Partner Profit Center
SFAREA	☐	☐	SFKBER	CHAR	16	0	Partner Functional Area
SBUSA	☐	☐	PARGB	CHAR	4	0	Trading partner's business area
RASSC	☐	☐	RASSC	CHAR	6	0	Company ID of trading partner
PSEGMENT	☐	☐	FB_PSEGMENT	CHAR	10	0	Partner Segment for Segmental Reporting

Figure 2.8: Account assignment part of the universal journal table

In the case of the cost center, the line item table COEP is no longer updated during actual postings from Financial Accounting and all new reporting applications use the ACDOCA table directly. If you work with substitutions and validations to switch an account assignment or check master data combinations, these rules will work as before. The only substitutions that will not work are those based on the reconciliation ledger, so you will not be able to manipulate accounts during secondary cost postings.

Statistical postings continue to be recorded in COEP and you can identify statistical postings in the reports for the cost centers, orders and WBS elements by selecting the Is Statistical flag in the navigation block. However, you will not be able to access statistical postings from the trial balance or financial statements, since only real account assignments are supported for these areas.

---

2 SAP Note 2425255: "Profit Center Accounting in the universal journal in SAP S/4HANA, on-premise edition" (*https://launchpad.support.sap.com/#/notes/2425255*)

There are, of course, more reporting fields in the universal journal table. If you scroll through the table, you will also find the fields needed for Public Sector Accounting, Joint Venture Accounting, and Real Estate Management, with further fields being added with each release.

The universal journal also includes placeholders for coding block extensions (INCL_EEW_COBL) filled using the customer include CI_COBL, as shown in Figure 2.9. You can find details of how to implement this customer include in SAP Note 2143232[3] and related notes.

The cloud edition offers new options for extending the universal journal to include custom fields. These are included in the placeholder INCL_EEW_ACDOC, shown in Figure 2.9, and can be used in all Fiori applications that display data from the universal journal. These fields are created using the Custom Fields and Logic app and selecting the business context journal entry item to fill INCL_EEW_ACDOC or coding block to fill INCL_EEW_COBL. This approach will be explained in more detail in Chapter 6.

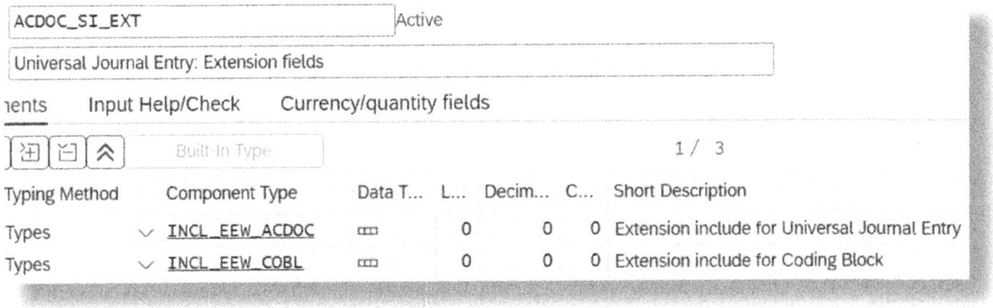

Figure 2.9: Placeholders for extension fields in the universal journal

2.2.3 Accounts and cost elements

In Figure 2.7, we drilled down by G/L account and cost center. One of the other key aspects of the merging of Financial Accounting and Controlling is that we no longer transform G/L accounts into cost elements, but rather merge the two. Figure 2.10 shows the master data for a G/L account/cost element. In the past, the ACCOUNT TYPE field offered the options BALANCE SHEET and PROFIT AND LOSS. The ACCOUNT TYPE— PRIMARY COSTS OR REVENUE, shown in Figure 2.10, applies to all profit and loss accounts

---

[3] SAP Note 2143232: "How to add a customer field to coding block without modification" (*https://launchpad.support.sap.com/#/notes/0002143232*)

that used to have a separate cost element or revenue element. You still typically have some profit and loss accounts without a sister cost element and these have the account type NON-OPERATING EXPENSE OR INCOME. The difference is that non-operating accounts cannot be assigned to a cost center, order, project, etc. (although they can be used to record work in process for an order or project). If you flag an account as PRIMARY COSTS OR REVENUE account type, you have to assign the relevant accounting item to a cost center, order, or project if it is a cost item, or to a combination of CO-PA characteristics if it is a revenue item, a sales deduction item or represents the cost of goods sold. If you are setting up accounts in a greenfield project, be sure to activate the correct account assignments via the *field status groups* for each G/L account and set up default account assignments just in case the material costs cannot be automatically assigned within the business transaction.

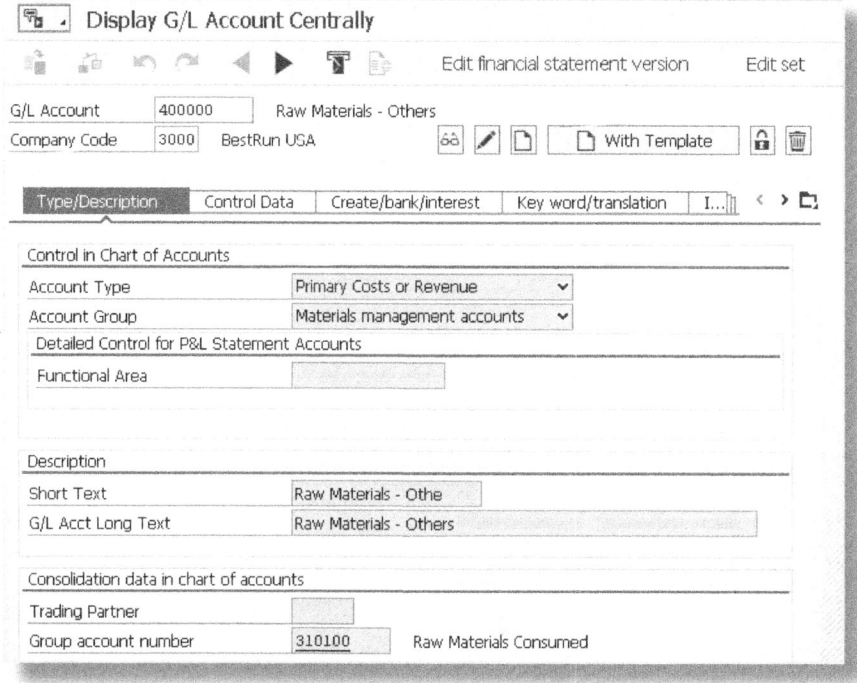

Figure 2.10: G/L account for primary costs or revenues

While the account and cost element are technically merged in the ACCOUNT field in the universal journal, you can still find the familiar COST ELEMENT CATEGORY setting by navigating to the CONTROL DATA tab in Figure 2.10. Figure 2.11 shows that in this case, the material costs are Primary Costs.

Note that you can only post material costs under account 400000 if you also update a cost center, order, project, or other CO object.

While these links make reporting simpler, note that in a few cases, the system still treats the account dimension as an account and a sister cost element.

▶ When you design your authorizations, you have to make sure that you have authorization for both the account (authorization object F_SKA_BUK) and the cost element (authorization object K_CSKB) before you can change the master data.

▶ When you design your period close processes, you need to be aware that each account must be allowed/locked in Financial Accounting and that the relevant business transactions (primary posting, allocation, settlement) must be explicitly allowed in Controlling. SAP plans to merge these settings in a future edition.

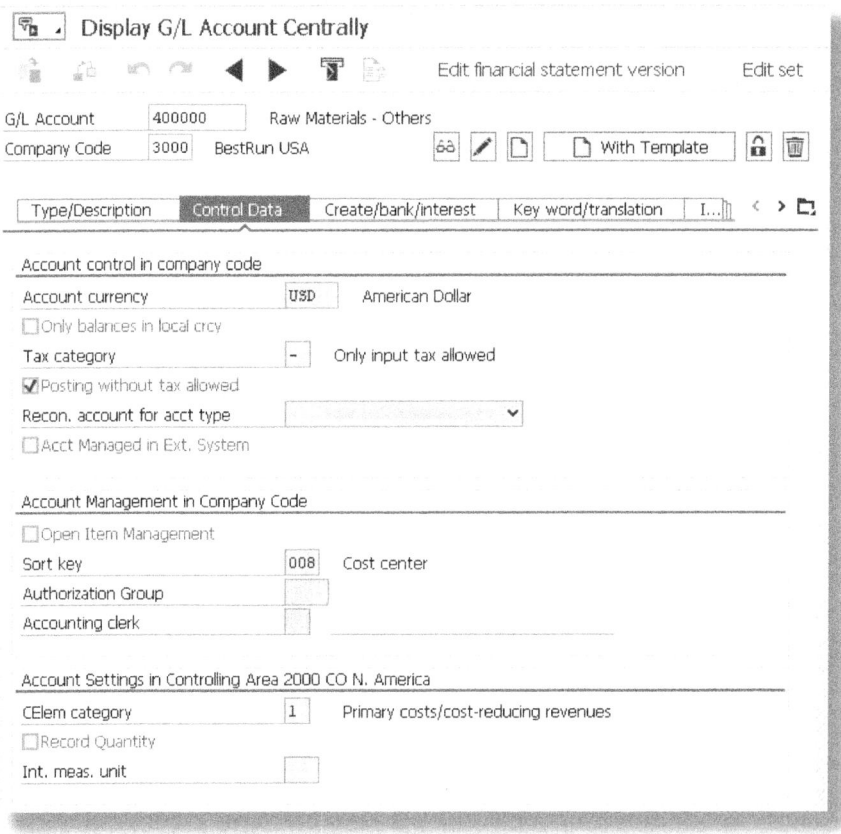

Figure 2.11: G/L account showing the cost element category

In addition, where project and order costs are to be capitalized as work in process or assets under construction, separate accounts exist that do not match one-to-one with the cost elements used to calculate work in process.

2.2.4 Types of ledger

If we now return to the business reasons for moving to SAP S/4HANA Finance, one reason is often the need to handle multiple *accounting principles*. In fact, customers have been doing this for years by using different number ranges in their charts of accounts to separate common accounts, IFRS-specific accounts, and accounts that only apply to local accounting principles and then selecting the appropriate account groups during an allocation or in reporting (you may hear this referred to as the Mickey Mouse approach, with the common accounts being the mouse's head and the special accounts the mouse's ears).

The *ledger approach* was originally introduced with the Special Ledger and then adopted in the SAP ERP ledger. As we saw in Chapter 1, the ledger is now one of the key fields of the universal journal, providing a clean way for you to segregate data according to the various accounting principles; for example, you might have one ledger for valuation according to your common accounting principle (such as IFRS) and another for valuation according to the various local accounting principles required in your organization (such as US GAAP, Japanese GAAP, French GAAP, etc.). You might perhaps also need a third ledger for tax reporting. From an architectural point of view, this means that a new posting line is created in the universal journal to reflect the valuation required within each accounting principle. Generally speaking, the business transaction itself will be captured once; so there will be one goods movement, one supplier invoice, one time confirmation, and so on. However, the values associated with this business transaction might vary by accounting principle, so it may be possible to capitalize the freight costs in the supplier invoice in one approach but not in the other. For many of the period close transactions, a different amount may apply for each accounting principle, so the depreciation approach for a fixed asset or the approach to revenue recognition could differ with each accounting principle.

You can reach the ledger settings by following the IMG path FINANCIAL ACCOUNTING • FINANCIAL ACCOUNTING GLOBAL SETTINGS • LEDGERS • LEDGER • DEFINE SETTINGS FOR LEDGERS AND CURRENCY TYPES. Figure 2.12 shows how several standard ledgers have been set up to meet the various reporting requirements. Normally, one ledger is set up to offer consistent reporting using the same accounting principle for all assigned company codes (0L in this example), and one or more additional ledgers (2L, HG and US in this example) are set up to support the various local reporting requirements, with a separate accounting principle for each assigned company code. The settings shown here are from a demo system, with HG for German GAAP and US for US-GAAP, but ledger 2L would normally handle both local approaches. It only makes sense to have a separate ledger for each accounting principle if both US-GAAP and IFRS are required in **all** company codes. Figure 2.13 shows how the accounting principles are then assigned to the combination of company code and ledger.

Ledger	Ledger Name	Leading	Ledger Type	Extn. Ledger Type	Underlying Ledger
0L	Ledger 0L	✓	Standard Ledger	Standard journal e	
2L	Ledger 2L		Standard Ledger	Standard journal e	
HG	German GAAP		Standard Ledger	Standard journal e	
OE	Committment/Order Entry		Extension Ledger	Line items with te	0L
US	US GAAP		Standard Ledger	Standard journal e	

Figure 2.12: Ledger settings

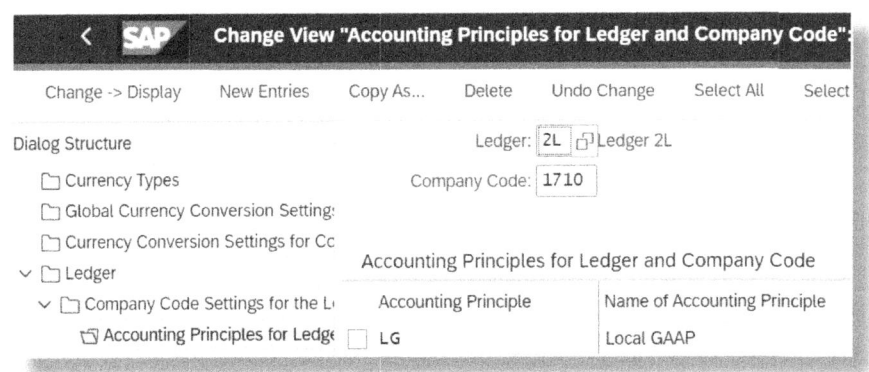

Figure 2.13: Assignment of accounting principles to ledger and company code

If, in the past, you used *group valuation* to eliminate intercompany profit, or *profit center valuation* to treat postings between profit centers with arm's length price conditions, you will remember that these valuations were always considered part of the leading ledger 0L. This approach is known as the *multi-valuation ledger* and is retained in the universal journal in that the column for group valuation and the column for profit center valuation become additional columns in the ledger line as you migrate. At the time of writing, this is still the preferred approach, the reasons for which are outlined in SAP Note 2882025[4].

Alternatively, in a greenfield project, you can set up additional *single-valuation ledgers* to represent each valuation approach. Figure 2.14 shows the two options, with ledger L1 being used to represent all three valuations as different columns (multi-valuation ledger) and ledgers L2, L3, and L4 being used to capture the legal valuation, group valuation, and profit center valuation separately (*single-valuation ledger*). However, at the time of writing, there are gaps in asset accounting if you choose to use single-valuation ledgers.

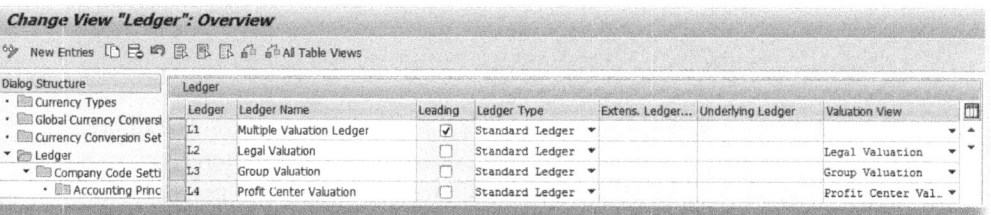

Figure 2.14: Ledger settings for group, legal, and profit center valuation

SAP S/4HANA Finance provides the option to create additional *extension ledgers* that reference the underlying main ledgers. These allow you to create manual journal entries for special purposes, enabling you to refine your profit center postings after an acquisition or to create correcting entries following an audit by making the appropriate manual journal entries. Reporting is always based on a combination of extension ledger and underlying ledger.

The extension ledgers can also be used to capture predictive accounting information and statistical journal entries. Ledger 0E in this example is used to capture sales order entries that are not yet GAAP-relevant. By combining the entries in these ledgers with the underlying ledger, you can provide a view of your future profit and loss statement. We will examine this approach in more detail when we look at predictive accounting in Chapter 3.

---

[4] SAP Note 2882025: "Multiple valuation approaches/transfer prices in SAP S/4HANA" (*https://launchpad.support.sap.com/#/notes/2882025*)

2.2.5 Currency handling

The other key setting associated with the ledgers relates to the *currencies*. In SAP S/4HANA Finance edition 1503, you could assign the group currency, a local currency for the company code, and one additional currency to each ledger. This was extended in the 1602 edition to cover eight additional currencies, meaning that you can add a functional currency, an index currency, and so on to each ledger if you need it in that country.

Figure 2.15 shows the familiar currency settings: 00 for document currency, 10 for company code currency, 20 for controlling area currency, 30 for group currency, 40 for hard currency, and so on, along with the familiar currency combinations: 11 for group valuation (eliminated intercompany profits) in company code currency, 31 for group valuation in group currency, and 32 for profit center valuation in group currency where you see the link back to the original currency type in the BASE CURRENCY TYPE column.

In SAP S/4HANA it is also possible to create new currencies, shown here as Y2, Y3 and Y4; we have set up a functional currency Y2 and then combined it with the valuation options for group valuation and profit center valuation by entering Y2 in the BASE CURRENCY TYPE column. This is useful if you have an entity that is operating using Canadian dollars as the local currency in Canada but doing most of its business with the USA and therefore has a requirement to report in US dollars as the functional currency in parallel.

Currency Type	Description	Short Description	Valuation View	Base Currency Type	Maintenance level
00	Document Currency	Doc Crcy	Legal Valuation		Global
10	Company Code Currency	CCde Crcy	Legal Valuation		Global
11	CoCode Crcy, Group Valuation	CoCo, Grp	Group Valuation	10	Global
12	CoCode Crcy, PrCtr Valuation	CoCo, PrC	Profit Center Val.	10	Global
20	Controlling Area Currency	CArea Crcy	Legal Valuation		Global
30	Group Currency	Group Crcy	Legal Valuation		Company code.
31	Group Crcy, Group Valuation	Grp, Grp	Group Valuation	30	Company code.
32	Group Crcy, PrCtr Valuation	Grp, PrCtr	Profit Center Val.	30	Company code.
40	Hard Currency	Hard Crcy	Legal Valuation		Company code.
50	Index-Based Currency	Index Crcy	Legal Valuation		Company code.
60	Global Company Currency	GloCo Crcy	Legal Valuation		Company code.
70	CO Object Currency	COObjCrcy	Legal Valuation		Global
Y2	Function Currency in legal	Func Crcy	Legal Valuation		Company code.
Y3	Function Currency in Gr Val	FuncCr Gr	Group Valuation	Y2	Company code.
Y4	Function Currency in PrCtr Val	FuncCr PC	Profit Center Val	Y2	Company code.

Figure 2.15: Currency types and associated settings

With subsequent editions of SAP S/4HANA, the challenge is to adapt the business processes to update **all** the currency columns with the appropriate logic. At the time of writing, the currencies that are not carried in the operational processes are filled as the journal entry is created using the exchange rate on this key date. So, a currency not included in an allocation is converted as the journal entry is created for the resulting allocation.

Asset Accounting and Actual Costing currently support three currencies, and Controlling supports two currencies. This is particularly critical in Controlling, where many processes (distribution, assessment, settlement, etc.) select the collected values from the sender and pass them on to one or more receivers. This approach always works in two currencies (global and local), but in some processes the values for the third currency are converted on the fly, resulting in inaccuracies if the exchange rates have changed in the meantime. Again, SAP is working to fix these issues and you can follow progress by checking for updates in SAP Note 2894297[5].

2.3 Asset Accounting

New Asset Accounting was introduced as an optional business function (FIN_AA_PARALLEL_VAL) in SAP Enhancement Package 7 for SAP ERP 6.0, which means that you can potentially already use it even if you are not yet using SAP S/4HANA. With SAP S/4HANA Finance, new Asset Accounting becomes compulsory, so be sure to include time for it in your project plan. Even if you are using ERP General Ledger Accounting and are not yet ready to go to SAP S/4HANA Finance, consider activating new Asset Accounting if you are on a modern Enhancement Package —as documented in SAP Note 1776828[6]—because it offers some key functional benefits and will make the move to SAP S/4HANA easier later.

2.3.1 Reporting dimensions in Asset Accounting

The first thing that changes is that the data model in Asset Accounting is simplified in order to merge with the universal journal. Figure 2.16 shows the asset-related fields in the universal journal. What we see here is the transactional data formerly stored in tables ANEK, ANEP, ANEA, ANLP, and ANLC that is now part of the ACDOCA table. The naming convention for the compatibility views in Asset Accounting is FAAV_ANEK and so on for the

---

[5] SAP Note 2894297: "Handling of Currencies in Controlling in SAP S/4HANA" (*https://launchpad.support.sap.com/#/notes/2894297*)

[6] SAP Note 1776828: "Asset Accounting (new): Implementation for new customers" (*https://launchpad.support.sap.com/ – /notes/0001776828*),

old structures and FAAV_ANEA_ORI and so on for access to the old tables. Statistical data (for example, for tax purposes) previously stored in ANEP, ANEA, ANLP, ANLC is now stored in table FAAT_DOC_IT. Plan data previously stored in ANLP and ANLC is now stored in FAAT_PLAN_VALUES.

Transparent Table	ACDOCA		Active			
Short Description	Universal Journal Entry Line Items					
Attributes	Delivery and Maintenance	Fields	Entry help/check	Currency/Quantity Fields		

				Srch Help	Predefined Type			16
Field	Key	Ini...	Data element	Data Type	Length	Deci...	Short Description	
.INCLUDE	☐	☑	ACDOC_SI_FAA	STRU	0	0	Universal Journal Entry: Fields for Asset Accounting	
AFABE	☐	☐	AFABE_D	NUMC	2	0	Real depreciation area	
ANLN1	☐	☐	ANLN1	CHAR	12	0	Main Asset Number	
ANLN2	☐	☐	ANLN2	CHAR	4	0	Asset Subnumber	
BZDAT	☐	☐	BZDAT	DATS	8	0	Asset value date	
ANBWA	☐	☐	ANBWA	CHAR	3	0	Asset Transaction Type	
MOVCAT	☐	☐	FAA_MOVCAT	CHAR	2	0	Classification of Transaction Type	
DEPR_PERIOD	☐	☐	PERAF	NUMC	3	0	Posting Period of Depreciation	
ANLGR	☐	☐	ANLGR	CHAR	12	0	Group asset	
ANLGR2	☐	☐	ANLGR2	CHAR	4	0	Subnumber of group asset	
SETTLEMENT_RULE	☐	☐	BUREG	NUMC	3	0	Distribution rule group	

Figure 2.16: Asset-related fields in the universal journal

We can see how these fields are used if we return to the trial balance and drill down by COST CENTER, G/L ACCOUNT and FIXED ASSET to explain the postings for depreciation expenses, as shown in Figure 2.17. You can easily drill down further to cover the ASSET SUBNUMBER, ASSET VALUE DATE, and ASSET TRANSACTION TYPE. By doing this, we have combined account-related information from the general ledger with asset-related information, showing that what was once a separate sub-ledger for Asset Accounting is now simply an additional reporting dimension in the universal journal.

In the past, you would have seen this information in the asset reports, which included asset balances by asset class, by cost center, by plant, and so on, but not in the general ledger or in the cost center reports, whereas here we see the three elements combined in a single report. Gradually, we start to see how a single report radically simplifies the reporting environment and potentially removes many spreadsheets with lookup tables from your reporting processes.

Accounting and Controlling

Figure 2.17: Trial Balance app, with Cost Center, G/L Account and Fixed Asset

You can most easily see how the posting logic changes in granularity by looking at the journal entry for a depreciation posting, as shown in Figure 2.18. Here, you see a separate balance sheet line for each asset and the corresponding expense line with the assignment to a cost center and the derived functional area. In SAP ERP this document offered only an aggregated view of the asset-related postings to the general ledger.

CoCd	Itm	Account	SG	Description	Amount LC	LCurr	Amount	Curr.	Tx	Ref date	Clrng doc.	Cost Ctr	BusA	Func. Area	Profit Ctr	Segment
1710	141	17006000		000000300014 0000	621,00-	USD	621,00-	USD							US10_PC10	Z_SEG0
1710	142	64006000		Furniture-Dep.Exp	621,00	USD	621,00	USD				US10_ADM1		Z9400	US10_PC10	Z_SEG0
1710	143	17006000		000000300015 0000	288,00-	USD	288,00-	USD							US10_PC10	Z_SEG0
1710	144	64006000		Furniture-Dep.Exp	288,00	USD	288,00	USD				US10_ADM1		Z9400	US10_PC10	Z_SEG0
1710	145	17006000		000000300017 0000	151,00-	USD	151,00-	USD							US10_PC10	Z_SEG0
1710	146	64006000		Furniture-Dep.Exp	151,00	USD	151,00	USD				US10_ADM1		Z9400	US10_PC10	Z_SEG0
1710	147	17006000		000000300018 0000	355,25-	USD	355,25-	USD							US10_PC10	Z_SEG0
1710	148	64006000		Furniture-Dep.Exp	355,25	USD	355,25	USD				US10_ADM1		Z9400	US10_PC10	Z_SEG0
1710	149	17006000		000000300019 0000	307,00-	USD	307,00-	USD							US10_PC10	Z_SEG0
1710	150	64006000		Furniture-Dep.Exp	307,00	USD	307,00	USD				US10_ADM1		Z9400	US10_PC10	Z_SEG0
1710	151	17006000		000000300021 0000	145,00-	USD	145,00-	USD							US10_PC10	Z_SEG0
1710	152	64006000		Furniture-Dep.Exp	145,00	USD	145,00	USD				US10_ADM1		Z9400	US10_PC10	Z_SEG0
1710	153	17006000		000000300022 0000	75,00-	USD	75,00-	USD							US10_PC10	Z_SEG0
1710	154	64006000		Furniture-Dep.Exp	75,00	USD	75,00	USD				US10_ADM1		Z9400	US10_PC10	Z_SEG0

Figure 2.18: Document display for depreciation postings

53

What does not change is the asset itself. The assignment from the asset to the account and the time-dependent link to the associated cost center is the key to this report. Clean master data is vital to fill the reporting dimensions of the universal journal, and therefore, it is important to check these settings to ensure that they are correct and that the correct profit center and segment can be derived.

> **Convert batch input programs for transaction AB01 into BAPIs**
>
>  If you are planning to create new assets via batch input, please note that batch input programs for AB01 are no longer supported in new Asset Accounting. If you are using customer-defined programs with batch input, you must convert these to BAPIs before you can generate new assets.

2.3.2 Ledgers and depreciation areas

Historically, Asset Accounting has always used *depreciation areas* to handle different valuations and you will be used to seeing multiple depreciation areas associated with a single asset in the *Asset Explorer*. What changes with new Asset Accounting is that depreciation area 01 is no longer hard-wired to the leading ledger and you can now easily assign the depreciation areas to the relevant ledgers. Technically, the depreciation areas are managed as full ledgers which are updated in real time, rather than as delta ledgers that are updated at period close, which makes for a much cleaner reporting process. There is now a step in the IMG that enables you to link the depreciation area with the relevant ledger and to determine whether the posting takes place in real time or periodically. Note, however, that at the time of writing, this brings its own constraints. Because you cannot add a ledger to the universal journal and fill it with historical data, you cannot add a depreciation area in Asset Accounting that is linked with the universal journal retrospectively.

It is also possible to treat assets as assets according to some accounting principles but to exclude them from other ledgers (one-sided postings).

If you have used SAP ERP General Ledger Accounting, you are probably already familiar with the idea of an *entry view*, which shows the data supplied by the delivering application, and the *general ledger view*, which shows the enriched data (where the profit center and segment are filled). New Asset Accounting picks up this same idea so that the invoice for a purchased asset delivers its data as before but posts initially to a technical *clearing account*. Figure 2.19 shows the DATA ENTRY VIEW for a sample asset acquisition from an external vendor. This entry document triggers the creation of multiple accounting documents, one for each active accounting principle. The accounting-principle specific documents clear the technical clearing account (199909) to give a zero balance. You can then manually adjust one of the accounting principles—for example, to account for freight costs differently in each accounting principle.

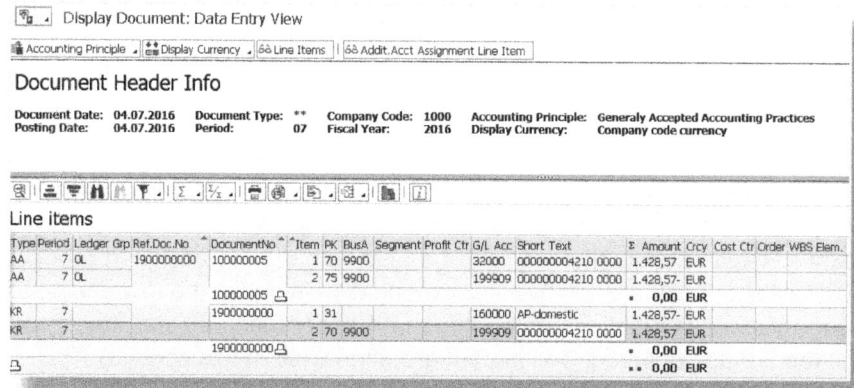

Figure 2.19: Data entry view showing clearing account 199909

2.4 Cost Center Accounting, Order Accounting, and Project Accounting

New General Ledger Accounting offered an option to include the cost center in FAGLFLEXA but orders, projects, business processes, networks, and other account assignments required organizations to report separately in Controlling. We have already looked at the drill-down by cost center in the trial balance in Section 2.2.1 but this is only half the story. We also need to understand how these costs are charged on to other cost objects in the system. We will also look at the role of the object number and partner object number with SAP S/4HANA Finance.

2.4.1 Reporting dimensions in Cost Center Accounting, Order Accounting, and Project Accounting

We began to discuss this topic in Section 2.2.1, where we showed how to drill down from the trial balance to the cost centers. The same basic principles apply to costs assigned to orders, work breakdown structure (WBS) elements, networks, network activities, business processes, and any of the objects that have previously been considered CO objects. It is also possible to capture statistical postings to orders and projects and report on these by selecting the IS STATISTICAL flag in the new reports.

Cost objects and cost object hierarchies are the major exception in terms of backward compatibility. They will **not** be supported going forward, so you will find that all functions for cost object hierarchies have been removed from the PRODUCT COST BY PERIOD menu and that the GENERAL COST OBJECT CONTROLLING menu has been removed from the SAP EASY ACCESS MENU. For cost object hierarchies that are used primarily for reporting, the recommendation is to use *summarization hierarchies* instead. For those used to capture costs that will later be distributed to the assigned product cost collectors and orders, the recommendation is to use the *distribution of usage variances* functions in the Material Ledger menu instead (these do not require use of Actual Costing but are often used in this context).

In Figure 2.20, note that the universal journal continues to contain the object number and the partner object number for reasons of backwards compatibility, but it also breaks out the object number to fill the new ACCAS (ACCOUNT ASSIGNMENT) and ACCASTY (OBJECT TYPE) fields so that we now have a separate column containing KS for cost center, OR for order, PS for project, and so on. In reporting, you use the object type in combination with the related field, such as AUFNR for the order number and PS_POSID for the work breakdown structure (WBS) element to select the relevant lines for reporting. What this means is that it is now substantially easier to create reports on the account assignments because you no longer have to unpack the CO object number as was the case in the classic line item reports and as costs were extracted to SAP BW. You will also notice that every object has its equivalent *partner object*. This means that you can easily report the way an allocation cycle charges costs from one cost center to the next, or time recording is used to charge cost center costs to a network, order, or project.

Accounting and Controlling

Transparent Table	ACDOCA		Active				
Short Description	Universal Journal Entry Line Items						
Attributes	Delivery and Maintenance	Fields	Entry help/check		Currency/Quantity Fields		

Srch Help | Predefined Type | 222 / 372

Field	Key	Ini...	Data element	Data Type	Length	Dec...	Short Description
OBJNR_HK	☐	☐	OBJNR_HK	CHAR	22	0	Object Number of Origin Object
AUFNR_ORG	☐	☐	AUFNR_HK	CHAR	12	0	Origin Order Number
UKOSTL	☐	☐	USP_KOSTL	CHAR	10	0	Origin cost center
ULSTAR	☐	☐	USP_LSTAR	CHAR	6	0	Origin activity
UPRZNR	☐	☐	USP_PRZNR	CHAR	12	0	Source: Business Process
ACCAS	☐	☐	ACCAS	CHAR	30	0	Account Assignment
ACCASTY	☐	☐	J_OBART	CHAR	2	0	Object Type
LSTAR	☐	☐	LSTAR	CHAR	6	0	Activity Type
AUFNR	☐	☐	AUFNR	CHAR	12	0	Order Number
AUTYP	☐	☐	AUFTYP	NUMC	2	0	Order category
PS_POSID	☐	☐	PS_POSID	CHAR	24	0	Work Breakdown Structure Element (WBS Element)
PS_PSPID	☐	☐	PS_PSPID	CHAR	24	0	Project Definition
NPLNR	☐	☐	NPLNR	CHAR	12	0	Network Number for Account Assignment
NPLNR_VORGN	☐	☐	VORNR	CHAR	4	0	Operation/Activity Number
PRZNR	☐	☐	CO_PRZNR	CHAR	12	0	Business Process
KSTRG	☐	☐	KSTRG	CHAR	12	0	Cost Object
BEMOT	☐	☐	BEMOT	CHAR	2	0	Accounting Indicator
QMNUM	☐	☐	QMNUM	CHAR	12	0	Notification No
ERKRS	☐	☐	ERKRS	CHAR	4	0	Operating concern
PACCAS	☐	☐	PACCAS	CHAR	30	0	Partner Account Assignment
PACCASTY	☐	☐	CO_POBART	CHAR	2	0	Partner object type
PLSTAR	☐	☐	PAR_LSTAR	CHAR	6	0	Partner activity
PAUFNR	☐	☐	PAR_AUFNR	CHAR	12	0	Partner order number

Figure 2.20: Fields for CO account assignments in the universal journal

If you compare Figure 2.21 with Figure 2.7, you will notice that we are again looking at an account/cost center combination, but this time, we are looking at how those costs are charged to a partner receiver (in this case, an order) via an activity type. The material cost posting in Figure 2.6 was external and offset against an open item for a vendor payment. but here we have an internal posting, where one cost center is credited and another receiver debited under what used to be known as a secondary cost element. In many cases, the charge is from cost center to an order or project and therefore, the partner cost center is unassigned. However, for the DAA machine costs item, we can see both the debit and credit sides of the allocation as the cost center CORPORATE SERVICES charges costs to PUMP ASSEMBLY.

We see this pattern whenever a direct activity allocation is posted (as here, either via time recording or order confirmation), overheads are applied, allocation cycles are run, or orders and projects are settled. There will always be a *sender* and a *receiver* (or indeed senders and receivers) and the value flow will be captured in an account. This sender-receiver relationship takes us back to Figure 2.8, where we looked at the account assignment pairs—profit center and partner profit center, functional area and partner functional area, and so on. A simple allocation credits one cost center and debits

57

another cost center but also potentially triggers a shift in profit centers, functional areas, and so on based on the cost center master data. These dimensions are also updated in the universal journal. What this means is that an allocation is no longer a posting that happens in Controlling and is subsequently represented in Financial Accounting, either by running transaction KALC or initiating a journal entry of type COFI, but that the allocation is simply a special type of journal entry of document type CO. The old reconciliation ledger (table COFIT) is no longer needed in SAP S/4HANA and all controlling documents are effectively accounting documents posted under the appropriate secondary cost element/G/L account.

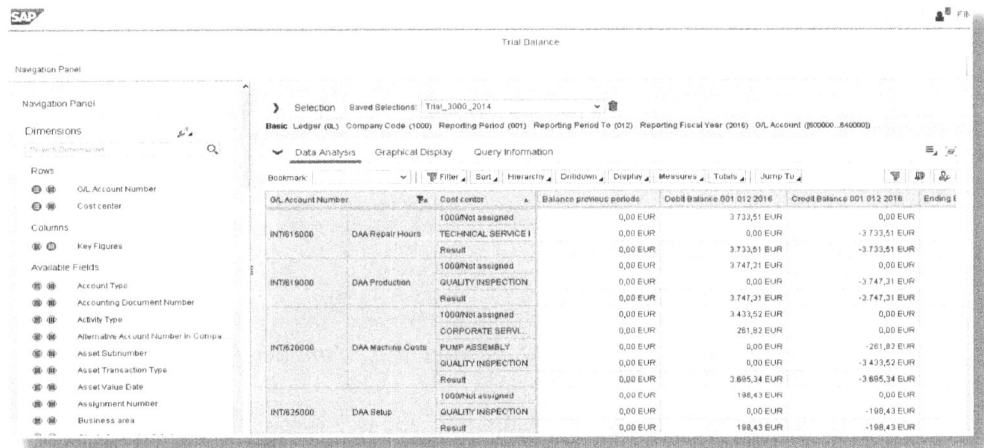

Figure 2.21: Trial Balance app, showing the allocation for machine time

2.4.2 Cost elements and the general ledger

One of the fundamental changes with SAP S/4HANA Finance is that the secondary cost elements no longer exist in isolation but are themselves G/L accounts. The old transaction KA06 (Create Secondary Cost Element) now redirects you to transaction FS00 (Change G/L Account), as does the old transaction KA01 (Create Primary Cost Element). During migration, secondary cost elements are migrated to the G/L account tables (SKA1, SKB1, and SKAT) for all company codes assigned to the CO area. Figure 2.22 shows the G/L account master data for a secondary cost element for the allocation of machine costs (Cost Element Category 43). Each of the sender-receiver relationships that can occur as a result of an allocation are represented as before by a cost element category, giving you 43 for internal activity allocation (as shown in Figure 2.22), 21 for internal settlement,

41 for overhead rates, and 42 for assessment. The fundamental change with SAP S/4HANA Finance is that the document that records this value flow (cost center to order in Figure 2.21) credits the cost center and debits the order under a G/L account of type secondary cost element. It also updates any affected profit centers, segments, functional areas, and so on in a single sweep rather than generating a CO document and a reconciliation document in FI if the reporting dimensions change.

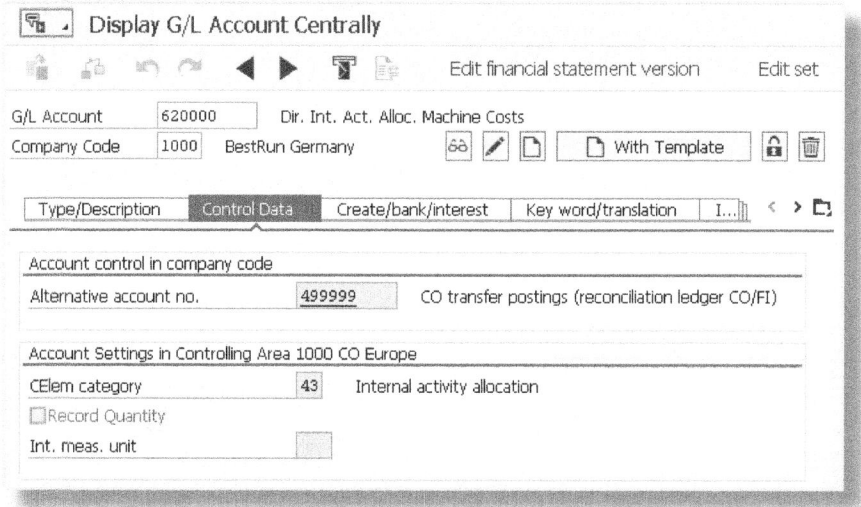

Figure 2.22: G/L account for a secondary cost element showing a cost element category

This link simplifies the closing process by ensuring that you do not need to reconcile to ensure the consistency of the FI and CO data. As you think about a *soft close*, consider activating an additional business function CO_ALLOCATIONS so that you can allocate overhead in real time. This will ensure that as you post material costs to a project, for example, the system checks the conditions in the costing sheet and assigns material overhead as appropriate, generating a double posting—one for the material costs and one for the overhead. The same principle applies to direct activity allocations and repostings where the appropriate overhead is calculated as a double posting to follow up from the allocation.

We have shown how all primary cost elements and most secondary cost elements are simply G/L accounts of the appropriate account type. The cost elements used to record work in process, results analysis, earned value, and so on must be considered an exception to this logic. Here, the calculated work in process is updated using a work in process cost element of cost element category 31 (RESULTS ANALYSIS) but settlement updates a WIP account of account type NON-OPERATING EXPENSE OR INCOME.

2.4.3 Allocations

With a move to SAP S/4HANA Finance you can continue to use all distribution cycles, assessment cycles, indirect activity allocation cycles, etc. as before. SAP has also begun to rework these applications under the term universal allocation. This includes:

- Plan assessments and distributions (OP1809)
- Actual assessments and distributions to cost centers (OP1809)
- Top-down distribution in Margin Analysis (OP1909, FPS1)
- Actual assessment to Margin Analysis (planned for CE2011)

The universal allocation approach delivers new applications to maintain the cycles (Manage Allocations), run the allocations (Run Allocations) and analyze the results (Allocation Result). Instead of the multiple transactions in SAP ERP (KSU1-3 for cost center assessments, KSV1-3 for cost center distributions, and so on), the new user interface distinguishes between using the ALLOCATION CONTEXT (Cost Centers, Profit Centers, Profitability Analysis, etc.) and the ALLOCATION TYPE (Distribution, Overhead Allocation, Top-Down Distribution, etc.) fields. Behind the scenes, the new applications select directly from the universal journal and can handle multiple accounting principles and currencies. Figure 2.23 shows the Manage Allocations app. In this example, the ALLOCATION CONTEXT is COST CENTERS and the ALLOCATION TYPE is OVERHEAD ALLOCATION (formerly "assessment"). You can switch between planned and actual costs in the same user interface by selecting ACTUAL/PLAN. We have selected cycle WC1 for overhead allocation and segment SEG1 to allocate the posted amounts for electricity and utilities from one sender cost center to several receiver cost centers in accordance with fixed percentages.

While the new application is more intuitive than the existing transactions, note that there is also an Excel upload icon alongside the create, copy and delete functions. This enables you to maintain the cycles in a spreadsheet and then add them into the system prior to period close. This is particularly useful when working with manually entered percentages or amounts as tracing factors.

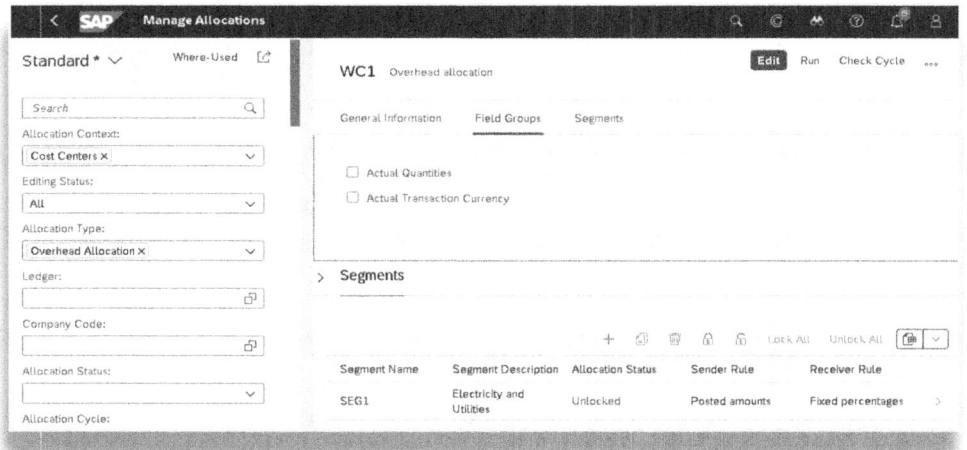

Figure 2.23: Manage Allocations App—segment details for cost center allocation

Once you have defined the senders, receivers and tracing factors for your cycle, you can run the allocation using the Run Allocations app shown in Figure 2.24. Here, we see the status for various allocation cycles and can navigate to the results to see the senders and receivers of the allocation.

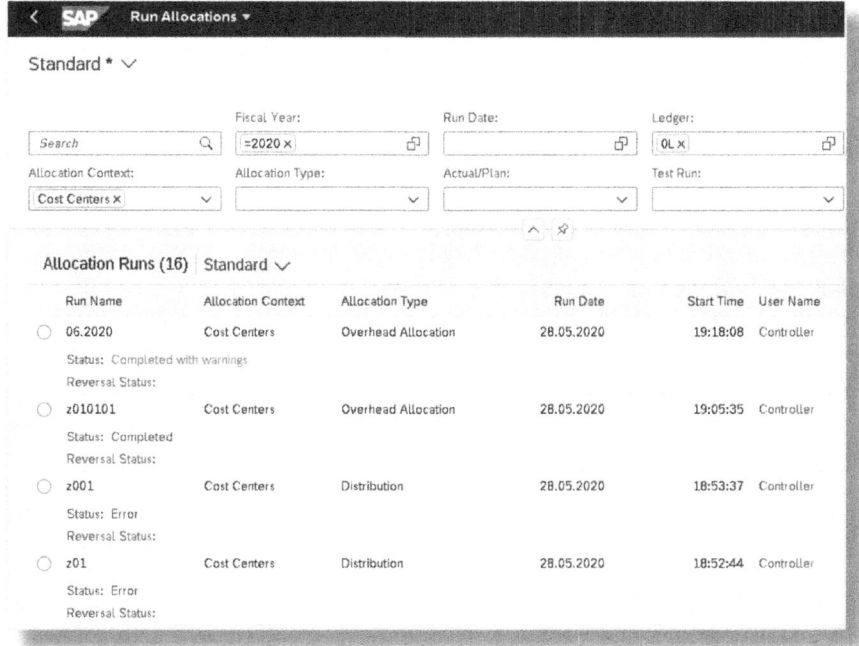

Figure 2.24: Run Allocations app

In SAP ERP, the senders and receivers of a distribution or assessment must be within a controlling area, but can cross company codes. Some organizations define validations to prevent accidental cross-company allocations, but others ignore this implicit barrier and allocate costs across company codes using the classic transactions. Currently, universal allocation only works within one company code. In SAP ERP allocations update the sender and receiver cost objects, but not the affected trading partners, unless a modification is implemented. This modification relies on the totals records and is no longer supported in SAP S/4HANA.

At the time of writing, the classic assessment and distribution cycles continue to be offered alongside the Manage Allocations app because this does not yet support iterative or cumulative cycles or allow cross-company postings.

2.4.4 Ledgers and versions

Note that in Figure 2.23 and Figure 2.24 all allocations are performed with reference to a LEDGER, rather than to a version. This is a very conscious move to make the ledger available across all the applications in Controlling. You will also find the ledger group on the selection screens in the manual posting transactions, such as KB11N and KB41N. As we discussed in Section 2.2.4, we can now use the **ledger** to handle all differences associated with the different accounting principles and the different valuation approaches. Note that SAP is currently reworking its transactions to enable ledger-specific settlement, activity price calculation, and so on.

However, for compatibility reasons, you still have to assign a version for group and profit center valuation (available from edition 1605) and for parallel cost of goods manufactured (business function FIN_CO_COGM) available from edition 1610.

With SAP S/4HANA Finance, the versions are still used for planning, and for storing target costs, variances, and results analysis data. We will come back to the version used in planning and how to calculate target costs and variances in Chapter 3.

2.5 Margin Analysis

We have just looked at how cost centers, orders, projects, business processes, networks, etc. are recorded in the universal journal for reporting purposes. Margin Analysis (formerly known as account-based Profitability Analysis) is based on the same idea, but the account assignment is **multidimensional**, being a combination of the various characteristics selected in your operating concern (typically, the product, customer, sales organization, and so on). If you have already worked with costing-based Profitability Analysis, the configuration steps will look similar in that you select the characteristics that you want to report against and set up derivation rules for those characteristics (such as product group, customer group, and region) that cannot be read straight from the invoice or delivery document but must be **derived** from the associated master data using look up tables and so on. What changes as Profitability Analysis becomes part of the universal journal is that you work with **accounts/cost elements** rather than value fields, so you have to make sure that all the relevant revenue accounts, sales deduction accounts, and cost of goods sold accounts that you want to see in your financial statements are defined as primary cost elements of the appropriate category (see Figure 2.11).

One of the major changes is the way in which cost of goods sold is handled, because this account becomes a cost element in Margin Analysis and derives the CO-PA characteristics at the time of delivery rather than invoicing. We will explain this in more detail in Section 2.5.2 when we explore changes to the COGS posting.

You must also check secondary cost elements (see Figure 2.22) that you use to settle or allocate to market segments to ensure that they provide sufficient transparency and that you are not just using a single settlement cost element to clear all orders and projects when you really want to distinguish the type of costs that are being selected for settlement.

2.5.1 Reporting dimensions in Margin Analysis

A standard operating concern can have up to 60 characteristics (this limit still holds with SAP S/4HANA Finance) and as you activate the operating concern or migrate, the system generates a column in the universal journal for each of these characteristics. You can identify these postings by the entry EO in the new ACCASTY (account assignment) field. Many are already available as standard characteristics, but each industry generally has its own handful of characteristics (such as brand and category in the consumer goods industry) that are added to the operating concern and for which a column is generated in the universal journal. While it is generally considered best practice to have a single operating concern, if you do have multiple operating concerns, the system generates a column for every different characteristic but only fills lines for that operating concern.

Figure 2.25 shows the fields for the CO-PA characteristics in the universal journal. If you used account-based Profitability Analysis in the past, you will know that there used to be settings to reduce the number of characteristics used in account-based Profitability Analysis compared to costing-based Profitability Analysis. Those settings are now obsolete and **all** characteristics in the operating concern are automatically in the universal journal. Table CE4 (with the characteristics) continues to exist for compatibility reasons, so classic reports, such as KE30, will continue to read it, but the new reports read directly from the universal journal. Remember also that the currency settings for Profitability Analysis are driven by the ledger, so you always have group currency and local currency and the option to add additional currencies as we discussed in Section 2.2.4.

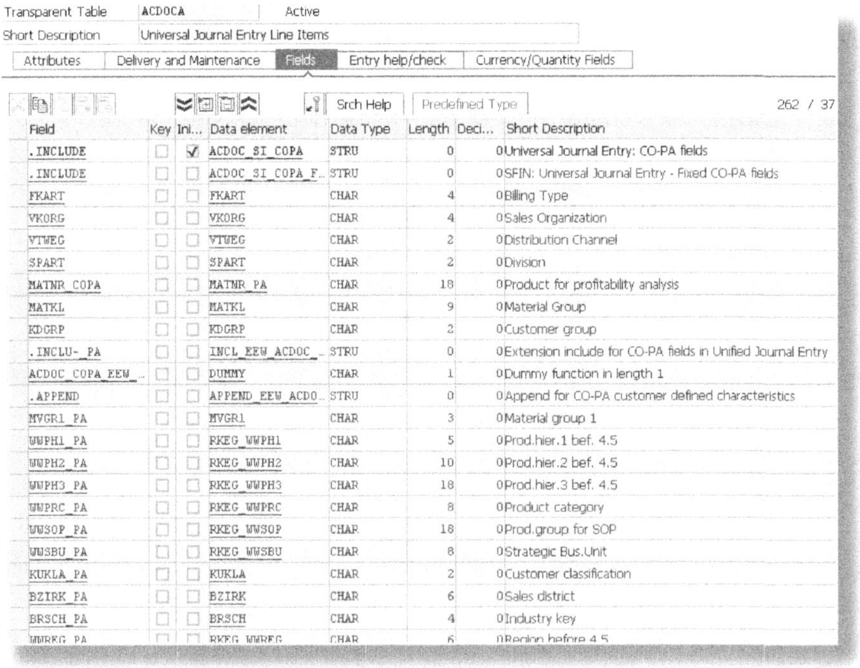
Transparent Table ACDOCA Active
Short Description Universal Journal Entry Line Items
Attributes | Delivery and Maintenance | Fields | Entry help/check | Currency/Quantity Fields
Srch Help | Predefined Type 262 / 37

Field	Key	Ini...	Data element	Data Type	Length	Deci...	Short Description
.INCLUDE	☐	☑	ACDOC_SI_COPA	STRU	0	0	Universal Journal Entry: CO-PA fields
.INCLUDE	☐	☐	ACDOC_SI_COPA_F...	STRU	0	0	SFIN: Universal Journal Entry - Fixed CO-PA fields
FKART	☐	☐	FKART	CHAR	4	0	Billing Type
VKORG	☐	☐	VKORG	CHAR	4	0	Sales Organization
VTWEG	☐	☐	VTWEG	CHAR	2	0	Distribution Channel
SPART	☐	☐	SPART	CHAR	2	0	Division
MATNR_COPA	☐	☐	MATNR_PA	CHAR	18	0	Product for profitability analysis
MATKL	☐	☐	MATKL	CHAR	9	0	Material Group
KDGRP	☐	☐	KDGRP	CHAR	2	0	Customer group
.INCLU-_PA	☐	☐	INCL_EEW_ACDOC_...	STRU	0	0	Extension include for CO-PA fields in Unified Journal Entry
ACDOC_COPA_EEW_...	☐	☐	DUMMY	CHAR	1	0	Dummy function in length 1
.APPEND	☐	☐	APPEND_EEW_ACDO...	STRU	0	0	Append for CO-PA customer defined characteristics
MVGR1_PA	☐	☐	MVGR1	CHAR	3	0	Material group 1
WWPH1_PA	☐	☐	RKEG_WWPH1	CHAR	5	0	Prod.hier.1 bef. 4.5
WWPH2_PA	☐	☐	RKEG_WWPH2	CHAR	10	0	Prod.hier.2 bef. 4.5
WWPH3_PA	☐	☐	RKEG_WWPH3	CHAR	18	0	Prod.hier.3 bef. 4.5
WWPRC_PA	☐	☐	RKEG_WWPRC	CHAR	8	0	Product category
WWSOP_PA	☐	☐	RKEG_WWSOP	CHAR	18	0	Prod.group for SOP
WWSBU_PA	☐	☐	RKEG_WWSBU	CHAR	8	0	Strategic Bus.Unit
KUKLA_PA	☐	☐	KUKLA	CHAR	2	0	Customer classification
BZIRK_PA	☐	☐	BZIRK	CHAR	6	0	Sales district
BRSCH_PA	☐	☐	BRSCH	CHAR	4	0	Industry key
WWREG_PA	☐	☐	RKEG_WWREG	CHAR	6	0	Region before 4.5

Figure 2.25: Fields for market segments in the universal journal

As you think about the fields that you want to include in the universal journal, it also makes sense to think about what can be filled when. Usually, the richest information comes from the billing document, where you have full details of the customer, the product, and so on in the invoice. It is common to use summarization to remove the material detail from the invoice in the accounting document because it is not needed for open item management. By contrast, the universal journal can handle the detail of thousands of material lines. Derivation rules can populate additional fields for these material lines as before. For reporting purposes, what you effectively see is the document view **as posted**. If you need to change these assignments later, you can reassign characteristic values retrospectively using the reorganization function delivered with edition 1610. You can use this to make corrections if your organizational structure changes, or to adjust the CO-PA characteristics after the fact.

2.5.2 Cost of goods sold reporting and Profitability Analysis

Prior to SAP S/4HANA Finance, one of the other arguments in favor of costing-based Profitability Analysis was that it enabled you to break out the cost of goods sold (COGS) posting and the variance posting into separate value fields to provide more transparency in the cost breakdown. Now, new configuration settings enable you to pick up the cost of goods sold posting and repost it to several subaccounts based on the weighting of the different cost components in the standard cost estimate. To configure this split, choose the following path in the IMG: FINANCIAL ACCOUNTING (NEW) • GENERAL LEDGER ACCOUNTING (NEW) • PERIODIC PROCESSING • INTEGRATION • MATERIALS MANAGEMENT • DEFINE ACCOUNTS FOR SPLITTING THE COST OF GOODS SOLD.

Figure 2.26 shows a sample Cost Splitting Profile with SOURCE ACCOUNT: 52546000 (the COGS account). The costs are to be split based on the STRATEGY TYPE: RELEASED COST ESTIMATES (i.e., the cost estimate used to set the standard price for the material). Note also that this preliminary COGS split can be adjusted later to reflect the results of running actual costing at period close by selecting the SPLIT REVALUED CONSUMPTION WITH ACTUAL COST COMPONENT SPLIT flag.

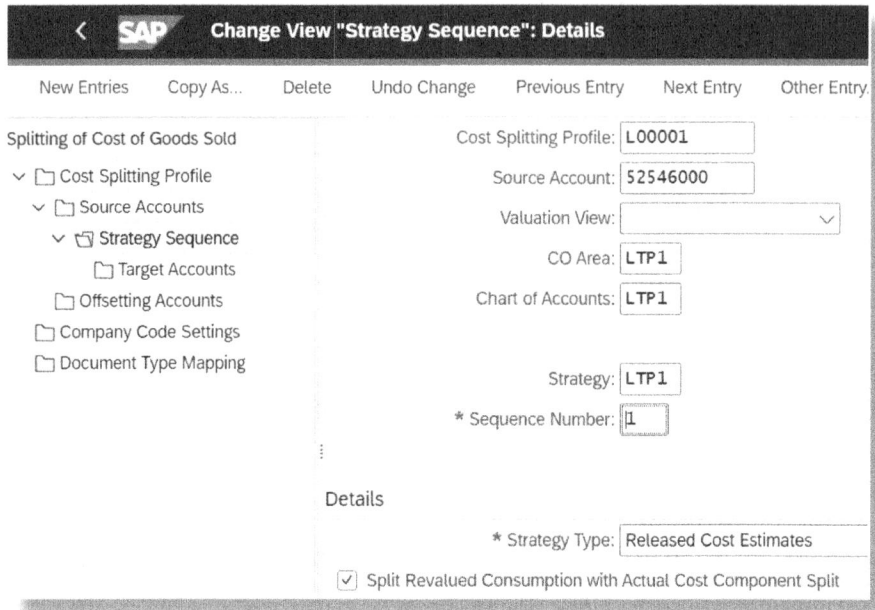

Figure 2.26: Cost Splitting Profile with strategy for COGS splitting

Figure 2.27 shows the target accounts for a sample splitting scheme for breaking out the cost of goods sold into four subaccounts. To implement this approach, you can leave the account assignment for the COGS posting unchanged (though make sure that the account is flagged as a cost element) but you have to create new accounts of account type primary costs for each of the cost components that you want to include in the split. This does not have to be a 1:1 assignment—you can also assign multiple cost components to one account.

Figure 2.28 shows a COGS posting based on these settings. Note that the account assignment is always to the market segment in Margin Analysis. We see that the delivery is posted as before and then reversed. The total COGS value is then split according to the configuration in Figure 2.27 to create four new posting line items under the appropriate accounts/cost elements.

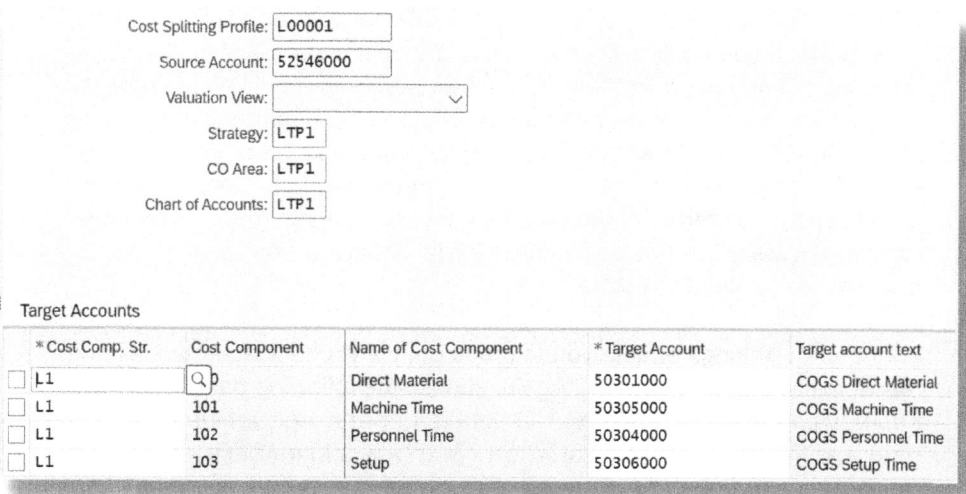

Figure 2.27: Cost Splitting Profile with Target Accounts for COGS splitting

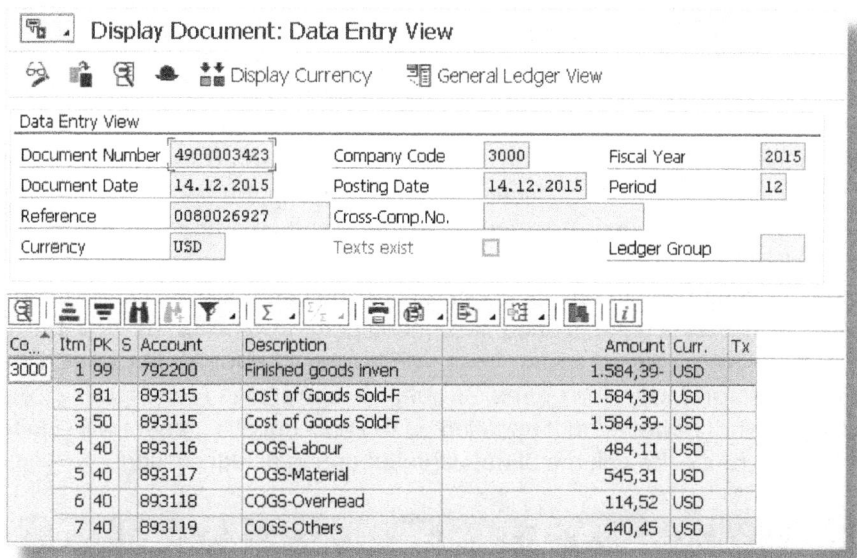

Figure 2.28: Cost document for COGS splitting

While this might seem like a new way of implementing the valuation strategy with which you could assign the standard cost component split to value fields in costing-based Profitability Analysis, there is a critical difference—note in Figure 2.27 that we can use exactly **one** cost component structure (COST COMP. STR.). In an account view, we can explain the cost of goods sold either in terms of the cost of goods manufactured (the main cost component split) or in terms of the primary cost components (the auxiliary cost component split) but not both. With Margin Analysis, you have to opt for **one** cost component structure.

Further new settings enable you to break out the production variances and repost to several subaccounts. Again, choose the following path in the IMG: FINANCIAL ACCOUNTING (NEW) • GENERAL LEDGER ACCOUNTING (NEW) • PERIODIC PROCESSING • INTEGRATION • MATERIALS MANAGEMENT • DEFINE ACCOUNTS FOR SPLITTING PRICE DIFFERENCES.

If you use Actual Costing to update the cost of goods sold with the purchase and production variances at period close, you can include these variances in Margin Analysis by changing the parameters in the posting step of the costing run in order to update consumption. The use of the posting step in the costing run replaces the procedure of using transaction KE27 (Periodic Valuation) to update the invoice documents with the actual costs from either the periodic costing run or the alternative valuation run in costing-based Profitability Analysis. If you work with actual costing, be aware that the delivery document is now assigned to market segments and that these are considered CO account assignments by Actual Costing. You can choose whether to update the cost of goods sold at the G/L account level or for individual market segments under IMG menu path: CONTROLLING • PRODUCT COST CONTROLLING • ACTUAL COSTING/MATERIAL LEDGER • MATERIAL UPDATE • ASSIGN MOVEMENT TYPE GROUPS OF MATERIALS (see Figure 2.29). Bear in mind, however, that updating by CO account assignment will significantly increase the volume of data created during actual costing.

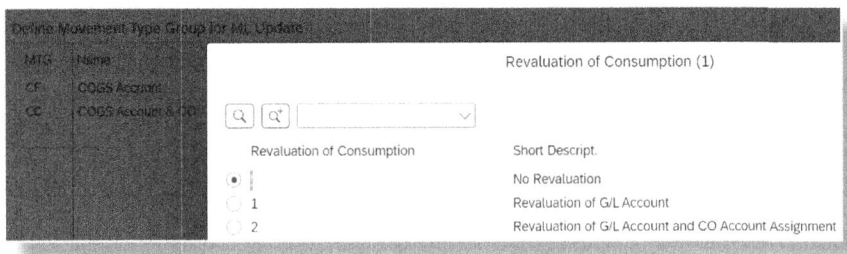

Figure 2.29: Settings for the COGS update in Actual Costing

In the past, you were also only able to capture the delivery quantity in the delivery unit of measure. The universal journal also includes new columns for extra quantities if you need them for your sales reporting. To access the configuration, follow menu path: CONTROLLING • GENERAL CONTROLLING • ADDITIONAL QUANTITIES • DEFINE ADDITIONAL QUANTITY FIELDS in the IMG. You can then use a BADI to convert the delivery quantity into the unit of measure of your choice. A sample BADI FCO_HOME_COEP_QUANTITY is delivered to illustrate how the process works but you will probably create your own BADI to fill the new quantities according to your business requirements. You can find this in the same part of the IMG under ADDITIONAL QUANTITIES • BADI: INTERFACE FOR ADDITIONAL QUANTITIES.

2.5.3 Allocations in Margin Analysis

We have now looked at how to assign revenues and cost of goods sold to the market segments, but the ability to assign further costs using assessment cycles, settlement and top-down distribution are equally important. The existing assessment cycles, settlement rules and top-down distribution transactions continue to work as before, but as we saw in Section 2.4.3, SAP is gradually reworking the allocations to deliver a modern user interface and support multiple ledgers, currencies, and so on. This process has begun for top down distribution.

Figure 2.30 shows the Manage Allocations app, this time with the ALLOCATION CONTEXT Margin Analysis and the ALLOCATION TYPE Top Down Distribution. If you compare this screen with transaction KE28 (top-down distribution), you will see that the idea of the allocation with a sender and receiver guides the design of the app. The difference is simply that the sender is a high-level market segment (such as a region or company code) and the receiver is a more granular market segment (such as all the products sold, customers served or a combination of the two). In Figure 2.31 we have selected an allocation cycle for top-down distribution and tabbed to the receivers. The same approach will be taken in future for allocations from sender cost centers to market segments.

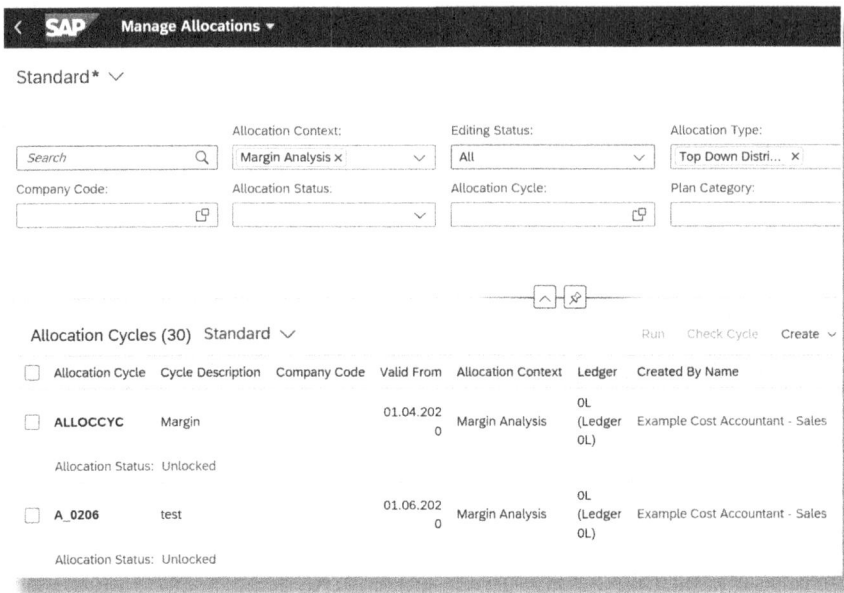

Figure 2.30: Manage Allocations app, showing cycles for Top-Down Distribution

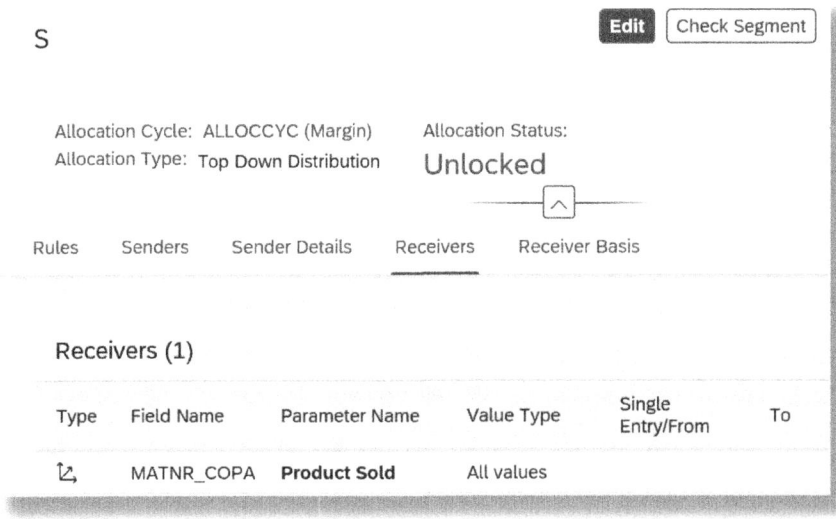

Figure 2.31: Manage Allocations app, showing Product Sold as Receiver

2.5.4 Predictive accounting

Besides the use of value fields rather than accounts, costing-based Profitability Analysis was also previously characterized by the ability to capture information relating to the future, such as the value of incoming sales orders, and statistical information, including statistical sales conditions. It is now possible to handle both options in Margin Analysis. We will start by looking at incoming sales orders as an example of predictive accounting. Figure 2.32 shows the Incoming Sales Orders app, where we see the journal entries created for the sales orders. As the incoming sales order is being created, a financial document is also created in the extension ledger 0E (see Figure 2.12). Not only is this document stored in a separate ledger, it also has a prefix PA to ensure that it is easy to recognize that this is not a GAAP-relevant posting, but only an indication of future business. Note also the detailed document information in the items list, where we see that the journal entry has been assigned to all the market segments (sales order, sales organization, product sold, customer, and so on) which will be used later when the final revenue and cost of goods sold are captured. The dates in this list are also important. The incoming sales orders values are shown immediately whereas the presumed revenue and cost of goods sold are based on the planned delivery and invoice dates.

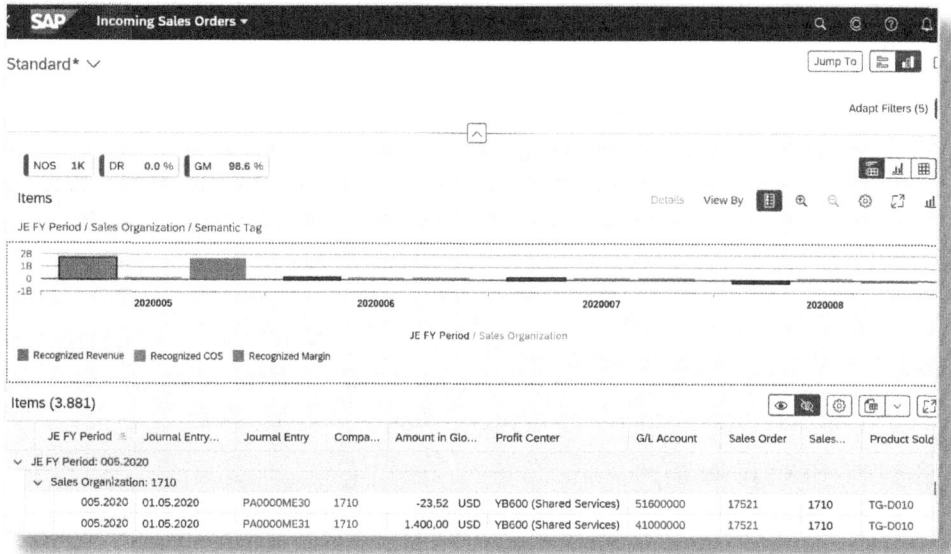

Figure 2.32: Predictive accounting—Incoming Sales Orders app

Figure 2.33 shows the Gross Margin app. This differs from the previous application in that the figures shown refer to when the order is expected to be invoiced (presumed revenue) and delivered (presumed COS).

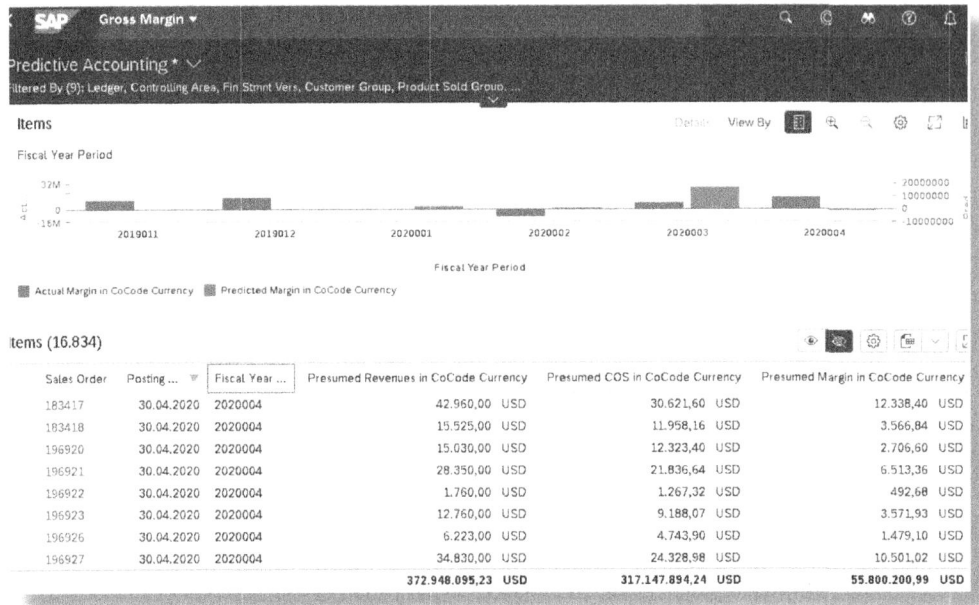

Figure 2.33: Predictive Accounting—Gross Margin app

As the sales order is being fulfilled, the values for the incoming sales order are **reduced** until the predictive values are finally reduced to zero and the accounting documents show the revenues and cost of goods sold. Changes to the sales order quantities or prices will also result in changes to the predicted values.

You will find the settings to activate Predictive Accounting in the IMG under menu path: FINANCIAL ACCOUNTING • PREDICTIVE ACCOUNTING. As you look at the new options, bear in mind that in SAP S/4HANA 1909, Predictive Accounting only processes the following SD document categories:

- ▶ Sales order (C)
- ▶ Return (H)
- ▶ Order without charge (I)
- ▶ Credit memo request (K)
- ▶ Debit memo request (L)

It is not yet possible to create predictive accounting documents in the following scenarios:

- Third-party direct shipment
- Intercompany sales (within selling company)
- Service sales scenarios

Some customers were also reluctant to move to account-based Profitability Analysis immediately because they had been making extensive use of statistical sales conditions, allowing for costs such as freight or warranty costs where a relationship exists with the sales price conditions, but the values are not to be invoiced to the customer but simply allowed for as additional costs.

Figure 2.34 shows a price condition table where condition ZWAR has been included for statistical warranty costs (STATISTICAL flag). To create a predictive document for the statistical costs you need to use the new RELEVANT FOR ACCOUNTING flag. If this flag is set, the system will generate a journal entry in the extension ledger for the statistical condition, provided that the appropriate account determination is entered in the accounting column (ZWR in this example).

Step	Cou...	Con...	Description	From...	To Step	Man...	Re...	Stati...	Rele...	Print Type	Subtotal	Require...	Alt.Calcul...	Alt.Cond...	Account...
110	1	RA01	% Disc.from Gross	100	0	✓				X		2	0	0	ERS
110	2	RA00	% Discount from Net	0	0	✓				X		2	0	0	ERS
110	3	RC00	Quantity Discount	0	0	✓				X		2	0	0	ERS
110	4	RB00	Discount (Value)	0	0	✓				X		2	0	0	ERS
110	5	RD00	Weight Discount	0	0	✓				X		2	0	0	ERS
111	0	HI01	Hierarchy	0	0					X		2	0	0	ERS
112	0	HI02	Hierarchy/Material	0	0					X		2	0	0	ERS
120	0	VA01	Variant Price	0	0					a		2	0	0	ERS
125	0	ZWAR	Stat. Warranty Costs	1	100			✓	✓	a		2	0	0	ZWR

Figure 2.34: Statistical price conditions

The accounting documents for an invoice based on such price conditions will again separate the GAAP-relevant values (what is billed to the customer) from the statistical conditions. The billed revenue based on the price conditions will be stored in a normal accounting document and an additional statistical accounting document will be generated that contains the values for the warranty costs under a separate ledger.

If you are setting up extension ledgers to handle incoming sales orders and statistical sales conditions, it makes sense to create two separate ledgers. The values from the predictive accounting documents for the incoming sales orders will gradually be reduced as the orders are fulfilled and invoiced, while the values for the statistical sales conditions will not be reduced automatically. Statistical sales conditions will only be included in the invoice document and not with the incoming sales orders.

2.5.5 New options to derive CO-PA characteristics

While the CO-PA characteristics were always derived immediately for the revenues and cost of goods sold, other contribution margins were only possible in SAP ERP when overhead costs had been transferred using allocation, settlement, and so on. In SAP S/4HANA you can continue to run assessment cycles to move costs from your cost centers to the market segments or to run settlement to move them from the orders and projects at period close; but it's also worth investigating the new options for *real-time derivation* for cost centers, orders, and projects. The idea is that instead of waiting for period close and running an allocation to bring costs from the marketing cost center to the region it serves, you can set up derivation rules to update the region **immediately** when the costs are posted to the relevant cost center.

These derivations are set up using the familiar derivation rules (transaction KEDR). When the costs are posted to the cost center, the relevant CO-PA columns in the universal journal are filled accordingly. Figure 2.35 shows a sample derivation rule that takes the cost center and derives the country based on conditions defined on the CONDITION tab. Depending on the logic required, this might be a master data lookup or a full user exit-based derivation.

Accounting and Controlling

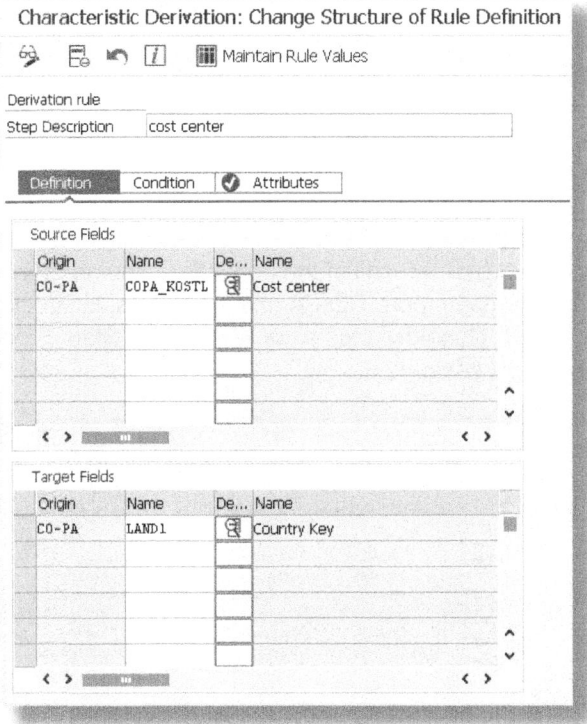

Figure 2.35: Derivation rule for deriving the country from the cost center

For very simple relationships, this can mean that you do not need an allocation at period close at all, but can immediately extend the line in the universal journal to include the relevant characteristics. If you have a *disaggregation,* where the costs on the cost center are to be assigned to multiple market segments (as might be the case if the marketing cost center was working for many product groups or products), then you have to use an allocation cycle as before to credit the cost center and debit each of the lines for the products at period close. This wait may also make sense from a business perspective if you need to use the final sales volumes for the various products as a basis for the allocation.

This approach works extremely well for commercial project costs, where the CO-PA characteristics, such as customer and product, can easily be derived from the associated sales order item, meaning that you do not have to settle at all. Again, this only works if you have a single settlement receiver in CO-PA. If you want to settle to multiple receivers, you have to settle using distribution rules containing the relevant receiver objects as before.

Figure 2.36 shows the Project Profitability app with double assignment to the PROJECT and PRODUCT SOLD as a result of the derivation. The reporting dimensions on the left include many more CO-PA characteristics, including CUSTOMER, CUSTOMER GROUP, DIVISION, etc., all of which were filled using derivation rather than traditional settlement.

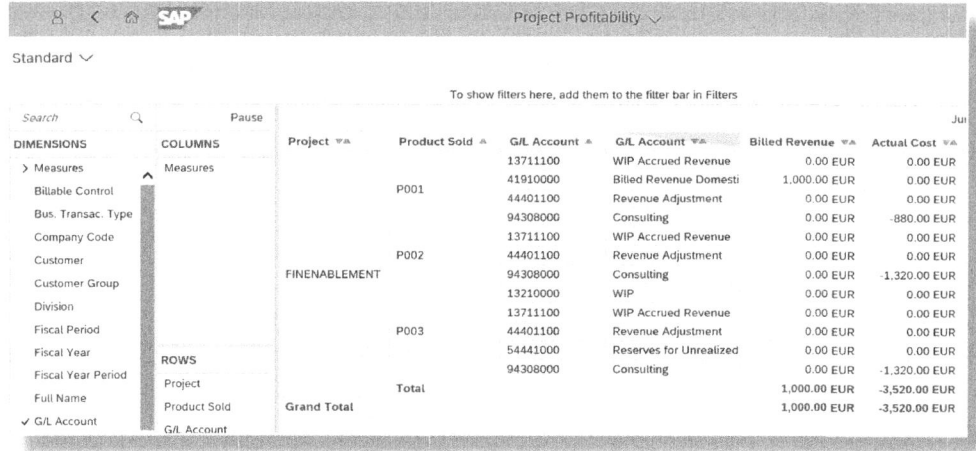

Figure 2.36: Project Profitability app

2.5.6 Event-based revenue recognition

In addition to deriving CO-PA characteristics when revenue and cost postings are made to the project, SAP is changing the timing of the postings for work in process and accrued revenues.

In SAP ERP, revenue recognition used results analysis to calculate the revenues in excess of billings when valuation was based on the percentage of completion method, and to calculate work in process when valuation was based on the completed contract method. These values were then settled to Profitability Analysis.

With SAP S/4HANA 1610 a new approach was introduced to recognize revenues immediately when the relevant costs are posted. This means that with each posting that records time or materials to a project, a part of the revenue is recognized in accordance with the planned costs and revenues. Figure 2.37 shows the resulting posting to the project, with the new posting lines for revenue adjustments and WIP for accrued revenue (business transaction TBRR).

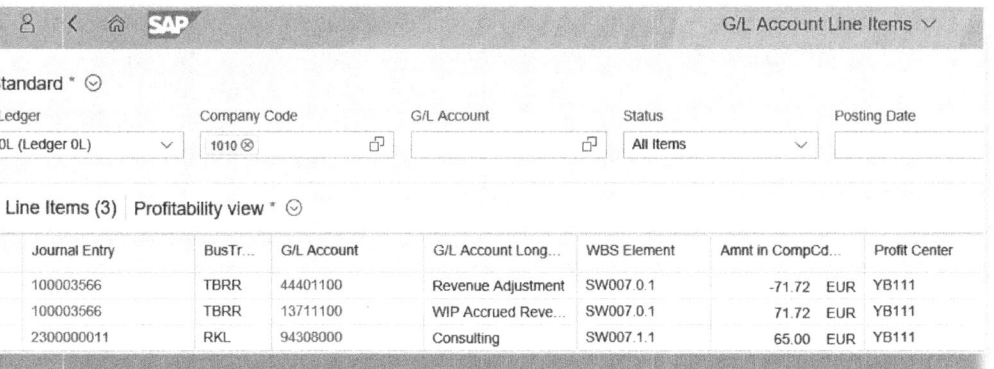

Figure 2.37: Journal entries for event-based revenue recognition

2.5.7 The case for costing-based Profitability Analysis

If you used costing-based Profitability Analysis in the past, there is no reason to deactivate it immediately. The interfaces will continue to update table CE1 (for costing-based Profitability Analysis) as before and you can switch off the update via the controlling area settings when you are ready to do so. Some customers have kept the two approaches running in parallel in order to build up comparison data, with a view to deactivating costing-based Profitability Analysis in the longer term. In some cases, there may still be good reasons for continuing to use costing-based Profitability Analysis.

▶ Account-based Profitability Analysis captures record types F (billing), B (direct posting from FI), C (order and project settlement) and D (allocations), so if you are using other record types, such as A (sales order entry), you can choose whether to continue using costing-based Profitability Analysis or to use the new options delivered with Predictive Accounting.

▶ Account-based Profitability Analysis is inherently reconciled with General Ledger Accounting, so the cost estimate will always be the one used to value the goods movement. If you capture multiple cost estimates to represent different planning assumptions, you may want to continue using costing-based Profitability Analysis.

The approaches are different and complement one another. The account approach is inherently reconciled with General Ledger Accounting so there is always one revenue line item with the associated CO-PA characteristics, whereas the costing-based approach gives you more freedom in that you can capture different assumptions and statistical costs in your profitability model. If you run only costing-based Profitability Analysis without account-based Profitability Analysis, then allocations and settlements are not assigned to profitability segments (account assignment type EO) but only to reconciliation objects (account assignment type AO). These simply ensure that all secondary cost postings balance but do not give you the full details you need for analysis.

2.6 Material Ledger and Actual Costing

Just as there are two types of Profitability Analysis, there are two types of Material Ledger in SAP S/4HANA:

- The first option is to use the Material Ledger as an *inventory subledger* that captures inventory values in multiple currencies. This option is **compulsory** in SAP S/4HANA and is activated during migration, writing the inventory values in multiple currencies to the universal journal.

- When most people talk about the Material Ledger, they mean *Actual Costing*. This approach is used to track goods movements, invoices, and order settlements and then calculate a *weighted average cost* (the periodic unit price) using one or more costing runs at period close. This option continues to be supported in SAP S/4HANA for industries that regularly use Actual Costing, such as chemicals, pharmaceuticals, and food, and countries that require Actual Costing, such as Brazil, but the use of Actual Costing is **not** compulsory in SAP S/4HANA.

Figure 2.38 shows the fields for the Material Ledger in the universal journal. Note that the fields include all types of special stocks relating to the material.

Accounting and Controlling

Field	Key	Ini...	Data element	Data Type	Length	Deci...	Short Description
.INCLUDE	☐	☑	ACDOC_SI_ML	STRU	0	0	Universal Journal Entry: Fields for Material Ledger
KALNR	☐	☐	CK_KALNR	NUMC	12	0	Cost Estimate Number for Cost Est. w/o Qty Structure
VPRSV	☐	☐	VPRSV	CHAR	1	0	Price control indicator
MLAST	☐	☐	CK_ML_ABST	CHAR	1	0	Material Price Determination: Control
KZBWS	☐	☐	KZBWS	CHAR	1	0	Valuation of Special Stock
XOBEW	☐	☐	XOBEW	CHAR	1	0	Vendor Stock Valuation Indicator
SOBKZ	☐	☐	SOBKZ	CHAR	1	0	Special Stock Indicator
VTSTAMP	☐	☐	VTIMESTAMPL	DEC	21	7	Valuation Time Stamp
MAT_KDAUF	☐	☐	MLMAT_KDAUF	CHAR	10	0	Sales Document Number of Valuated Special Inventory
MAT_KDPOS	☐	☐	MLMAT_KDPOS	NUMC	6	0	Sales Document Item Number of Valuated Special Inventory
MAT_PSPNR	☐	☐	MLMAT_PSPNR	NUMC	8	0	WBS Element (internal) of Valuated Special Inventory
MAT_PS_POSID	☐	☐	MLMAT_PS_POSID	CHAR	24	0	WBS Element (external) of Valuated Special Inventory
MAT_LIFNR	☐	☐	MLMAT_LIFNR	CHAR	10	0	Vendor of Valuated Special Inventory
BWTAR	☐	☐	BWTAR_D	CHAR	10	0	Valuation Type
BWKEY	☐	☐	BWKEY	CHAR	4	0	Valuation Area
HPEINH	☐	☐	MLHPEINH	DEC	5	0	Price Unit in Local Currency
KPEINH	☐	☐	MLKPEINH	DEC	5	0	Price Unit in Group Currency
OPEINH	☐	☐	MLOPEINH	DEC	5	0	Price Unit in Another Currency
VPEINH	☐	☐	ML4PEINH	DEC	5	0	Price Unit in Fourth Currency
MLPTYP	☐	☐	CK_PTYP_ORG	CHAR	4	0	Original process category
MLCATEG	☐	☐	CKML_KATEGORIE	CHAR	2	0	Category in Material Update Structure
QSBVALT	☐	☐	CKML_ALPROCNR	NUMC	12	0	Procurement alternative/process
QSPROCESS	☐	☐	CKML_F_PROCNR	NUMC	12	0	Production Process

Figure 2.38: Fields for the Material Ledger in the universal journal

2.6.1 Changes to Inventory Accounting in edition 1511

As you think about the impact of collecting inventory data in the universal journal, you should also be aware that from SAP S/4HANA 1511, the data model for Inventory Management (MM-IM) changes radically. With the switch to the Material Ledger, the inventory valuation tables in MM that used to be accessed directly from the ACCOUNTING view material master, such as EBEW and EBEWH (Sales Order Stock Valuation), MBEW and MBEWH (Material Valuation), OBEW and OBEWH (Subcontractor Stock Valuation), and QBEW and QBEWH (Project Stock Valuation), are replaced and the stock values read directly from the Material Ledger. What we see here is an example of the *principle of one* applied to inventory valuation, where we used to have two documents, one in MM-IM (Inventory Management) and one in ML (Material Ledger), and now have a single document.

79

The removal of aggregates that began in Finance continues in Inventory Management, so where totals tables were used to store the inventory figures for a plant, a storage location, or to store the values of special stocks—such as project stock, sales order stock, consignment stock, stock in transit, and so on—we now find these values being aggregated on the fly from the new transactional table MATDOC. Pure aggregate tables that store the values by stock type have been removed completely, while others remain where they are needed to store genuine master data (such as the name and description, the weight, the assignment to a profit center, and so on) but aggregate the total inventory figures on the fly. These are known as *hybrid tables* on account of their dual purpose in former releases.

- There is a new document table MATDOC which records all goods movements. Just as we learnt in Chapter 1 when we looked at the case for removing aggregate tables in Finance, this new table accelerates processing because you can now record a goods movement simply by inserting a new document into the database without locking the associated master data tables.

- Tables such as MARC (Plant Data for Material), MARD (Storage Location Data for Material), and MCHB (Batch Stocks) still exist to store product attributes which do not change regularly. However, they are no longer used to store aggregated stock values and instead, the data is aggregated on the fly from the new table MATDOC.

- The tables for vendor stock, sales order stock, project stock, and stock in transit have been removed completely and all inventory values are aggregated on the fly from the new table MATDOC.

- The extra history tables that used to exist for all the inventory tables MARCH, MARDH, MCHBH, and so on have been removed.

If you have not worked with the Material Ledger before, Figure 2.39 shows the material master for a raw material using the transaction-based Material Ledger (PRICE DETERMINATION 2). Inventory values are stored in three currencies: company code currency, group currency, and in this case, a hard currency. We will use this example to understand the implications of the new Inventory Management:

- Fields such as DIVISION, VALUATION CLASS, VALUATION CATEGORY, PRICE CONTROL, etc. are *product attributes* and will continue to be stored in the old master data tables.

- The STANDARD PRICE and PERIODIC UNIT PRICE fields are stored in the Material Ledger. Note that if you use transaction-based price determination, you can still use a moving average price that recalculates the price with every goods movement and invoice receipt. However, it is not recommended to use a statistical moving average price alongside a standard price, as the statistical moving average price can only be calculated if the tables are briefly locked during the goods movement.
- Inventory levels are calculated on the fly from the new MATDOC table.

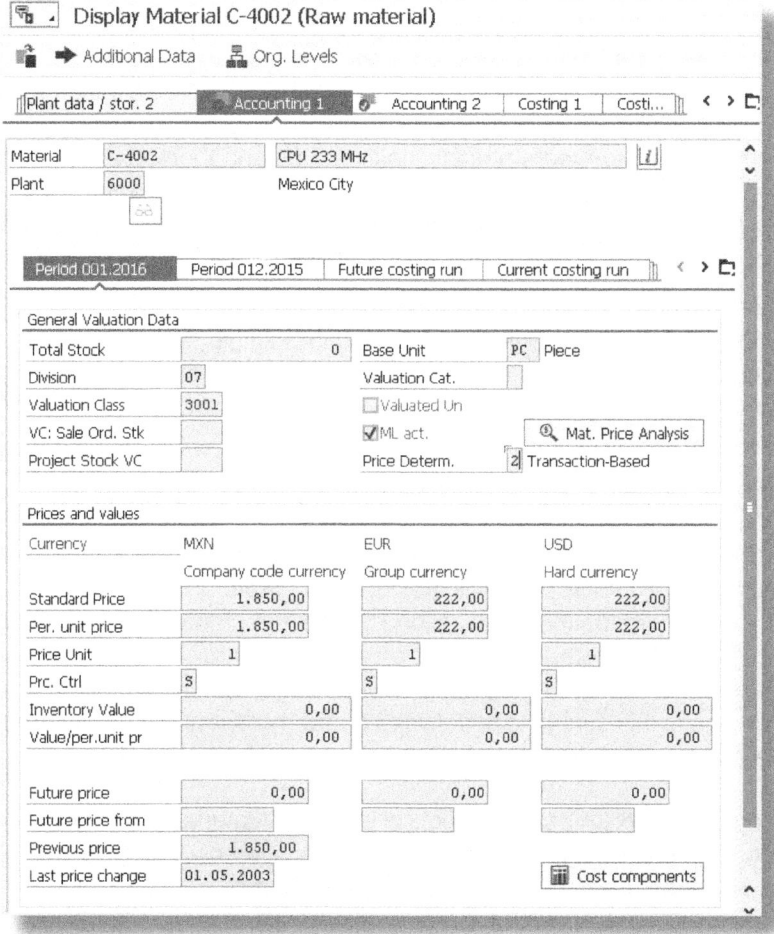

Figure 2.39: Material master using transaction-based Material Ledger

2.6.2 Changes to Actual Costing in edition 1610

If you are using Actual Costing, SAP S/4HANA brings some major simplifications. The first is the combination of the periodic costing run and alternative valuation run into one actual costing cockpit, as shown in Figure 2.40. You can switch between the two approaches using the settings in APPLICATION. The ACTUAL COSTING application is used for the former periodic costing run and ALTERNATIVE VALUATION application is used for the former alternative valuation run. The steps have also been combined, and are as follows:

- ▶ SELECTION remains the same and determines the plants to be included in the costing run. Normally, you include all plants in a company code.

- ▶ PREPARATION covers the determination of the sequence for costing in the periodic run and cumulation for the alternative valuation run. If you work with time buckets larger than a single period, you no longer need to create periodic costing runs and then an alternative valuation run to cumulate the separate runs; you can simply create a costing run for a longer time frame and use this to cumulate the postings required for actual costing on the fly.

- ▶ SETTLEMENT covers single-level valuation, multi-level valuation, WIP valuation and COGS revaluation in a single step. The system no longer separates single-level and multilevel price determination, meaning that the material account determination transactions PRV and KDV have become obsolete.

- ▶ POST CLOSING covers the accounting postings to update inventory, WIP and COGS. As we saw in Section 2.5.2, as of SAP S/4HANA 1809, this step also triggers the revaluation of the cost component split for the COGS. You will also need to create a new material account determination Transaction PRL for the credit postings to the cost center. There is no longer a delta posting run within the alternative valuation run. Instead, you need to create one posting run and have this cumulate to deliver a quarterly or year-to-date view by entering the appropriate periods in the selection parameters.

The second change that you will notice is in the Material Price Analysis transaction, shown in Figure 2.41. Here we can see how the price determination structure (the columns quantity, valuation unit, preliminary valuation, price differences, exchange rate differences, actual valuation and price) and the cost component structure (the columns direct material, machine time, personnel, setup, material overhead, production overhead, freight and intercompany profit) have been combined in one view.

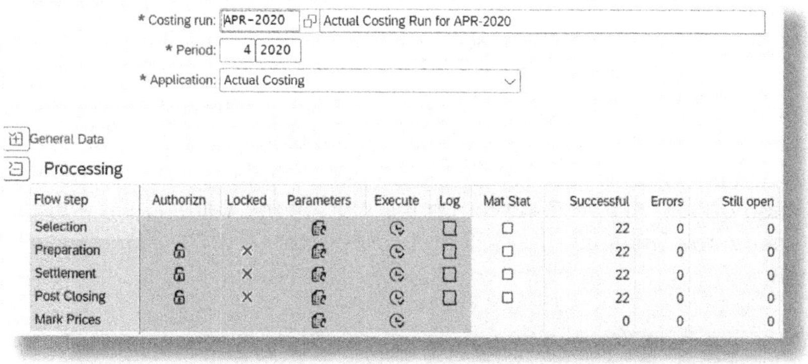

Accounting and Controlling

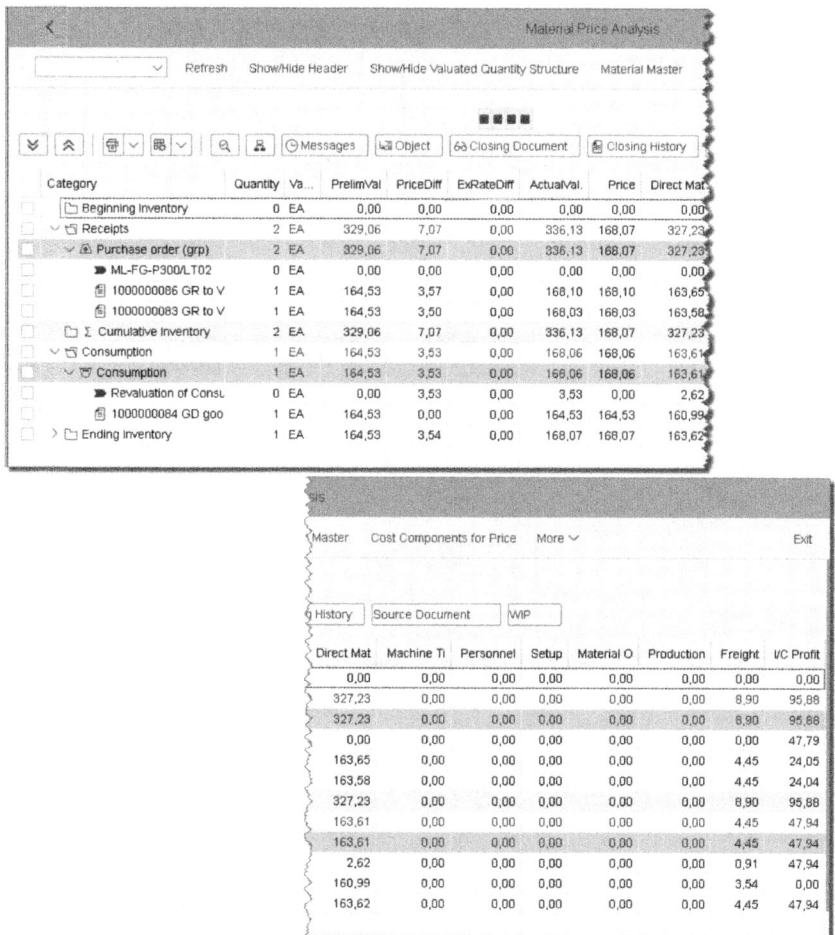

Figure 2.40: Costing cockpit for Actual Costing

Figure 2.41: Material Price Analysis

83

Behind the scenes, new tables have been introduced for the actual costing documents (MLDOC) and the cost component split (MLDOCCCS).

In addition to the architectural changes, the Display Material Value Chain app, shown in Figure 2.42 and Figure 2.43, enables you to use the values captured in actual costing to follow the flow of materials from raw material to finished goods. Figure 2.42 shows the start of the value chain and the usage of the raw material RAW122 and cost center 0010101301/activity 11 in production.

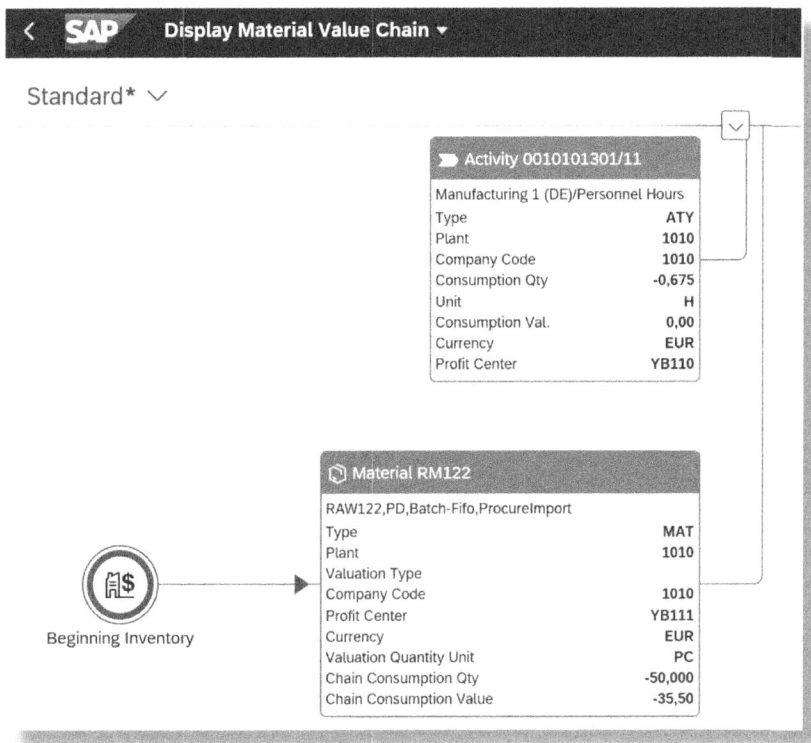

Figure 2.42: Material Value Chain app, Showing Raw Materials and Activities Used

Figure 2.43 shows the next step in the value chain where further activities are consumed in production in order to deliver the finished product, material FG126. This app provides a significant benefit over the simple material price analysis shown in Figure 2.41 in that it is easy to navigate through the entire flow of materials in actual costing and view details of the costs incurred at each step.

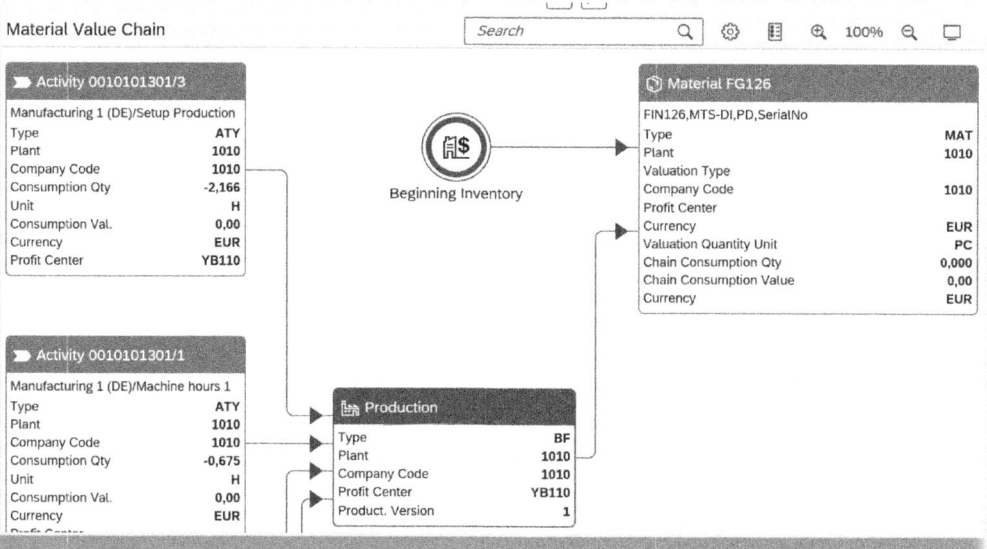

Figure 2.43: Material Value Chain app, showing usage of activities in final product

Now that we have looked at the main aspects of SAP Accounting, we will turn our attention to planning. Many organizations consider this a key part of Controlling and we will look at how this plan can be used to prevent excess spending during the creation of journal entries.

85

3 Planning and S/4HANA Finance

SAP S/4HANA Finance brings a new approach to financial planning. Planning was part of the finance solution in SAP ERP and included separate planning transactions for cost center planning, order planning, project planning, market segment planning, profit center planning, general ledger planning, and so on, each of which updated totals records. The various plans were connected by further transactions that transferred, for example, the planned costs for the cost center to profit center planning. SAP S/4HANA Finance provides a single planning table that combines the various dimensions in a common model, just as we saw for the universal journal.

3.1 The case for a single planning model

If you have already conducted planning within core ERP, you will be familiar with the planning transactions for cost center planning (transaction KP06), order planning (transaction KPF6), project planning (transaction CJR2), market segment planning (transaction KEPM), profit center planning, general ledger planning (transaction GP12N), and so on. These are essentially detailed plans for the account assignments we discussed in Chapter 2 (cost center, order, WBS element) and the CO-PA characteristics, together with aggregations of these plans by profit center, company code, and so on.

In SAP ERP, these planning applications updated the totals tables, meaning that cost center planning, order planning, project planning, and CO-PA planning updated tables COSP and COSS, and general ledger planning and profit center planning updated table FAGLFLEXP. The new architecture for capturing actual costs also required changes to the storage of the planned costs and this led to the creation of a single planning line item to mirror the actual line items in the universal journal. A full description of the transition from the classic planning transactions to the single planning model is given in SAP Note 2142447[7].

---

[7] SAP Note 2142447: "Cost Center Planning by Cost Element" (*https://launchpad.support.sap.com/#/notes/0002142447*)

Many ideas concerning the actual line items apply equally to a planning model, as we saw in Figure 1.8. Just as we expect payroll costs to be assigned from the cost center to the assigned profit center, functional area, etc., users entering plan data expect to capture wage costs per cost center and have the system update the affected functional areas, profit centers, company codes, and so on. It is the same story when we think about entering material costs for a project or order. Similarly, when planning secondary costs by entering the activity usage on the project, we expect the relevant partner objects to be updated. Only by doing this can we ensure that the plan and the actual costs are available for the same reporting dimensions. In SAP ERP, this meant using transfer programs, taking data from the cost center plan and aggregating to profit center level, and so on.

In planning, we sometimes plan at the most detailed level, such as the order, project, or a CO-PA characteristic, and sometimes at a higher aggregation, such as the company code or the profit center. To this extent, the planning application will always aggregate the detailed planned data to the higher aggregations. The reverse process of breaking down targets set at the higher level to cost centers, and so on (a process known as *disaggregation*), is also possible and you can plan not just by reporting dimension but also by node. For example, you might plan wages and salaries rather than the original accounts, something that could never happen for a journal entry which always refers to an account.

The planning model is a combination of a new planning table ACDOCP (available as of SAP S/4HANA 1610) and a multidimensional planning model. Initially, the technology from SAP Business Planning and Consolidation (SAP BPC) was *embedded* in SAP S/4HANA to enable you to build powerful simulations using the faster aggregations and disaggregations that are possible with SAP BW on HANA. With the arrival of SAP S/4HANA Cloud, a second planning model was introduced based on SAP Analytics Cloud for Planning, which is being successively extended with each edition.

Figure 3.1 shows the new planning table and the various options to fill it:

- ▶ The simplest approach is to perform an excel upload to fill the table with the manually entered plan data or to use an API to transfer plan data from an external planning tool, as shown on the left.
- ▶ Some applications running in SAP S/4HANA can also update the planning table directly. These include production orders and maintenance orders that can update the new planning table in parallel with the classic planning tables (COSP and COSS) and commercial

projects which update only the new planning table. We can also use universal allocation (see Section 2.4.3) to perform plan distributions and assessments that read from, and write to, the planning table.

▶ At the top, we see SAP Analytics Cloud for Planning, which runs on the SAP Cloud Platform and uses connectors in the form of data services to select data from, and write data to, SAP S/4HANA.

▶ At the bottom, we see SAP BPC optimized for S/4HANA Finance, which stores its plan data either in its own cubes or uses a virtual provider to update the planning table.

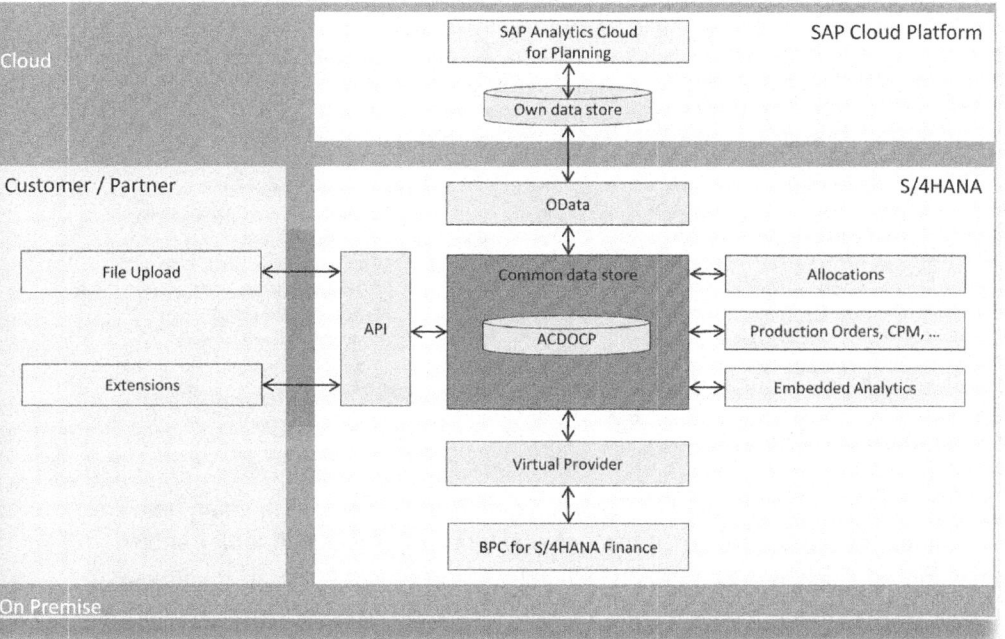

Figure 3.1: Planning model in SAP S/4HANA

The planning transactions originally delivered in SAP ERP are still available and update the totals records as before, with the exception of the planning transactions for Classic Profit Center Accounting, which are part of the compatibility scope. With SAP S/4HANA 2020 there is a plan to introduce a function to transfer data from these tables to ACDOCP when planning is complete.

Before we look at the planning options in detail, we will look at the new planning table at the center of this undertaking.

89

3.1.1 ACDOCP—a new table for planning

In Chapters 1 and 2 we introduced the universal journal and the ACDOCA table. With SAP S/4HANA 1610, there is an equivalent planning table, AC-DOCP, as shown in Figure 3.2. This stores planning data for reporting purposes once planning within SAP Analytics Cloud or SAP BPC on S/4HANA Finance has been completed (see Figure 3.1), uploaded from a spreadsheet, or recorded with the production orders or maintenance orders in SAP S/4HANA.

Key	Initi...	Data element	Data Type	Length	Decim...	Coordinate	Short Description
		ACDOCP_SI_VALUE_D/	STRU	0	0	0	ACDOCP: Value Fields
		ACDOCP_SI_FIX	STRU	0	0	0	ACDOCP: Mandatory fields for G/L
		ACDOCP_SI_GEN	STRU	0	0	0	ACDOCP: Fields for several subledgers
		ACDOCP_SI_CO	STRU	0	0	0	ACDOCP: CO fields
		ACDOC_SI_EXT	STRU	0	0	0	Universal Journal Entry: Extension fields
		ACDOC_SI_COPA	STRU	0	0	0	Universal Journal Entry: CO-PA fields
		ACDOCP_SI_PS	STRU	0	0	0	ACDOCP: Fields for Public Sector
		ACDOCP_SI_BUDGET	STRU	0	0	0	ACDOCP: Fields for budgeting
		ACDOC_SI_LOG	STRU	0	0	0	Universal Journal Entry: Fields for Logistics

Figure 3.2: Plan Data Line Items table

At first glance, you might think that you are not looking at the plan data line items at all, but rather at the universal journal (ACDOCA table) shown in Figure 2.2 because there are so many common elements. The intention is that the planning table should contain the same reporting dimensions as we discussed in Chapter 2. Note that the fields for the GL account assignments contained in ACDOCP_SI_GL_ACCASS are exactly the same as the reporting dimensions we saw in Section 2.2.2 and the CO fields in ACDOCP_SI_CO are exactly the same as the account assignments that we saw in Section 2.4.1. More specifically, where customer-specific dimensions are involved, such as COBL extensions or the CO-PA characteristics within an operating concern, it is important that the table structures are only extended in one place and that the planning table should reference the same structure as the actual line item table; we can see this in the fields contained in ACDOC_SI_EXT (extension fields) and ACDOC_SI_COPA (CO-PA fields).

3.1.2 Plan categories

While the planning table has many common fields with the actual line item table, it is also different in the sense that a plan is not meant to be a single version of the truth, but rather a model reflecting several different assumptions about how future business could evolve. The different planning assumptions are assigned to *plan categories*. To display the plan categories, follow menu path: CONTROLLING • GENERAL CONTROLLING • PLANNING • MAINTAIN CATEGORY FOR PLANNING in the IMG. Note in Figure 3.3 the distinction between the plan categories that are filled using SAP BPC or SAP SAC (PERIODIC PLANNING AND CONSOLIDATION) and those filled using applications within SAP S/4HANA, such as the PRODUCTION ORDER, for which there are two categories—PLANORD01 and PLANORD02. Similar categories exist for the planning of projects and maintenance orders, with further objects migrating to the new plan table with each edition of SAP S/4HANA.

Maintenance View for Category

Plan Category	Medium description	Application Type	Category Usage
ACT01	Actual	Periodic Planning and Consolidation	No specific usage
ACT_CONST	Actual at constant rate	Periodic Planning and Consolidation	No specific usage
BASE	Base Plan	Periodic Planning and Consolidation	No specific usage
BUDGET01	Cost Center Budget	Periodic Planning and Consolidation	Cost Center Budget
CPP1	Cash Pool Planning	Periodic Planning and Consolidation	No specific usage
FINAL	Final Consolidation	Periodic Planning and Consolidation	No specific usage
FORE01	Forecast 01	Periodic Planning and Consolidation	No specific usage
FORE02	Forecast 02	Periodic Planning and Consolidation	No specific usage
FORE03	Forecast 03	Periodic Planning and Consolidation	No specific usage
FORE04	Forecast 04	Periodic Planning and Consolidation	No specific usage
FORE05	Forecast 05	Periodic Planning and Consolidation	No specific usage
FORE06	Forecast 06	Periodic Planning and Consolidation	No specific usage

Figure 3.3: Plan categories in SAP S/4HANA

Figure 3.4 shows details of the PLAN CATEGORY: PLAN01. This controls the exchange rate type for currency conversions and includes flags to control the import of plan data, and the copying and deletion of data—functions that were controlled by the plan version in SAP ERP.

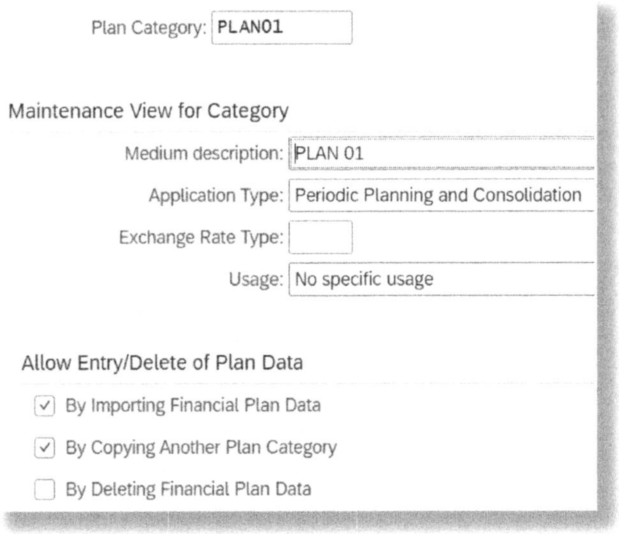

Figure 3.4: Plan category details

These parameters are used in combination with various apps: Import Financial Plan Data app, Copy Financial Plan Data app and Delete Financial Plan Data with Time Stamp app. The plan category also controls the usage of the planned data. In this example, the plan is just that—a plan or collection of planning assumptions about future business performance. However, specific plan categories can be used to identify one plan as the basis for cost center budgeting, project budgeting and public sector budgeting so that a check can be made against the contents of this plan before costs are posted.

Figure 3.5 shows the additional settings to activate availability control and budget consistency checks for cost center budgeting, and equivalent plan categories are available for project budgeting and public sector budgeting. To activate a plan category for the budget availability control, follow menu path: CONTROLLING • GENERAL CONTROLLING • PLANNING • DEFINE BUDGET CHECKS FOR CATEGORIES in the IMG.

Once you have created plan categories, the simplest way to fill the planning table is to use the Import Financial Plan Data app to load data from a spreadsheet. Figure 3.6 shows the various Microsoft Excel templates that are available to load plan data directly to the planning table. To do this, simply download the relevant template, update it with your planning data and load it to the planning table. It makes sense to use these if you are not yet ready to move to SAP Analytics Cloud for Planning or if you are using an external tool to prepare your planned data.

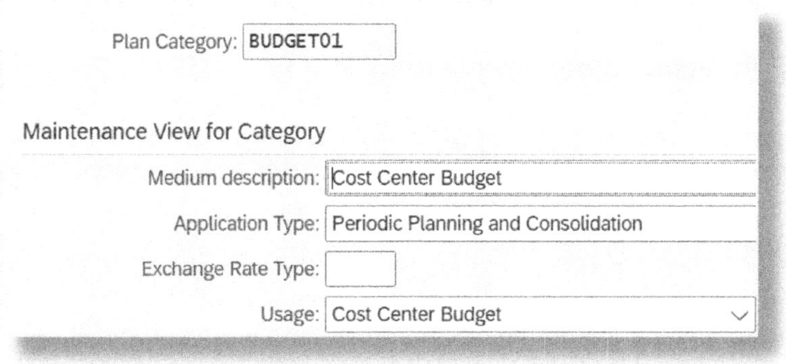

Figure 3.5: Activating budget availability control for a plan category

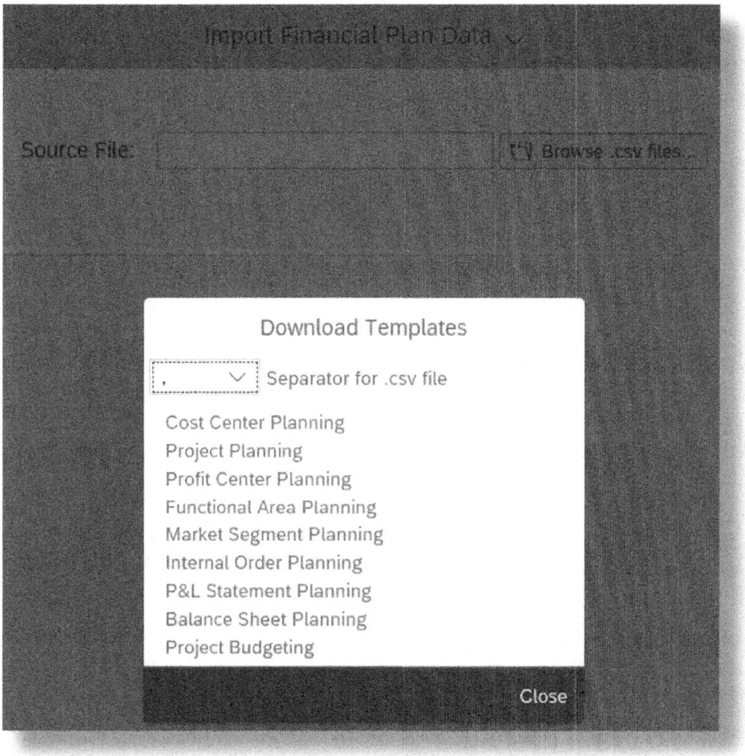

Figure 3.6: Excel templates for the upload of plan data

If you want more sophistication than a spreadsheet upload, consider using SAP Analytics Cloud for Planning.

3.2 SAP Analytics Cloud for planning

Both SAP Analytics Cloud and SAP BPC for SAP S/4HANA can be operated independently of SAP S/4HANA; but of course they also connect directly with the universal journal and the associated master data. This connectivity is at the heart of both approaches:

- SAP Analytics Cloud is SAP's strategic solution for planning. At the time of writing, this is the solution receiving the most investment. The ability to transfer planned data from SAP Analytics Cloud to SAP S/4HANA was added with SAP S/4HANA Cloud 1805 and SAP S/4HANA 1809 (SP1).

- This does not mean that SAP S/4HANA customers should not consider SAP BPC for SAP S/4HANA, which is a mature and fully functional planning solution. It can store planned data either in the planning cubes that are activated within the embedded BW or transfer them directly to the planning table, depending on the settings in the virtual infoprovider.

This chapter focuses on SAP Analytics Cloud for Planning, specifically on the delivered content packages, available at *https://sapanalytics.cloud/learning/business-content*. As befits a modern planning solution, the strengths of this approach are its powerful visualizations and collaboration tools. Figure 3.7 gives a sense of how data can be visually displayed, with various charts showing operating income, revenue and expenses over time.

The delivered business content for Financial Planning and Analysis for SAP S/4HANA Cloud covers the areas of: P&L, Balance Sheet and Cash Flow Planning. It is integrated with SAP S/4HANA in the sense that it uses the same master data, accesses transactional data from the universal journal and can write back to the planning table we saw in Figure 3.2. This financial content is complemented by additional content for the Project Planning, Sales Planning and Workforce Planning applications. Content for Financial Planning and Workforce Planning is integrated. You can transfer employee expenses calculated in Workforce Planning into P&L Planning. The various planning applications are delivered within folders comprising *stories* for the different planning and reporting tasks.

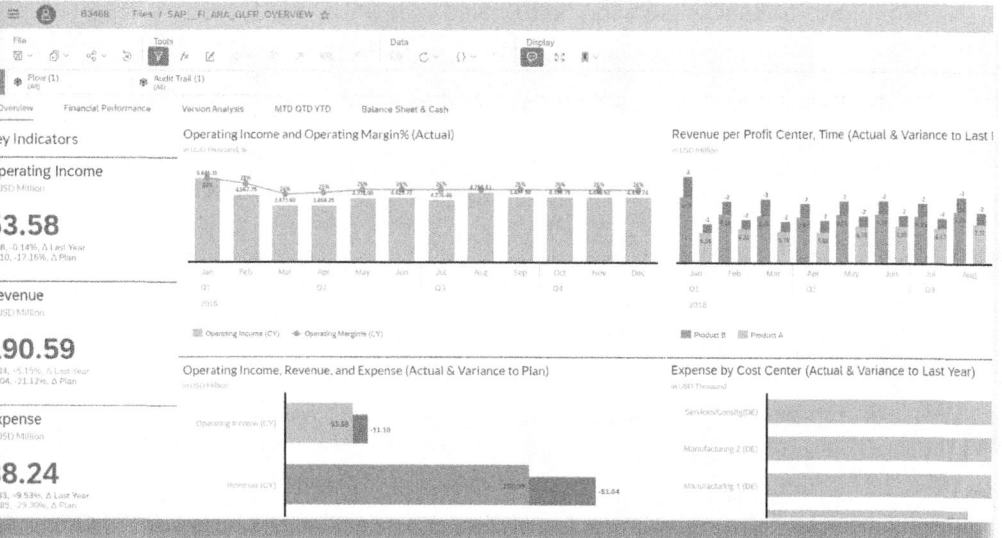

Figure 3.7: Key performance indicators to guide planning

Those familiar with the classic planning transactions in SAP ERP will find this business content delivered as the Integrated Financial Planning content, which enables users to enter plan data for cost centers, market segments, orders, projects, etc., but also to perform allocations, calculate activity rates and include the calculated cost of goods sold in their profitability planning. The Integrated Financial Planning content covers the following elements:

- Cost and activity planning (introduced with S4HC 1905)
  - Expense planning
  - Statistical key figure planning
  - Allocations (distribution and assessment)
  - Activity quantity planning (cost center outputs)
  - Activity type splitting (where one cost center provides multiple outputs)
  - Activity price planning and calculation
- Sales and profitability planning
  - Sales quantity planning (introduced with S4HC 1908)
  - Sales price planning (introduced with S4HC 1908)
  - Sales revenue and deductions planning (introduced with S4HC 1908)

- Profitability planning (introduced with S4HC 1911)
- Profit and loss planning (introduced with S4HC 1911)
- Product cost simulation (introduced with S4HC 1911)
  - Raw material planning
  - Quantity structure selection (the itemization for the cost estimate in SAP S/4HANA)
  - Product cost simulation
- Project planning (introduced with S4HC 2002)
- Internal order planning (introduced with S4HC 2002)
- Financial statement planning (introduced with S4HC 2005)
  - Balance sheet planning
  - Cash flow planning

Figure 3.8 shows the contents of the SAP_FI_BPL_BUDGETING_AND_PLANNING folder and the planning stories delivered for Integrated Financial Planning. Each of the topics listed above corresponds to a planning *story* and these stories reference the planning model.

Name	Description	Type
SAP__FI_BPL_IM_COSTCENTE...	SAP Finance: BPL - Calculate Cost Center Cost Rates	Story
SAP__FI_BPL_IM_COSTCENTE...	SAP Finance: BPL - Cost Center Budgeting	Story
SAP__FI_BPL_IM_COSTCENTE...	SAP Finance: BPL - Cost Center Planning Administr...	Story
SAP__FI_BPL_IM_FINANCIAL_...	SAP Finance: BPL - Financial Statement Planning	Story
SAP__FI_BPL_IM_FINANCIAL_...	SAP Finance: BPL - Financial Statement Planning A...	Story
SAP__FI_BPL_IM_FINANCIAL_...	SAP Finance: BPL - Financial Statement Planning A...	Story
SAP__FI_BPL_IM_FINANCIAL_...	SAP Finance: BPL - Financial Statement Reporting	Story
SAP__FI_BPL_IM_INTERNAL_...	SAP Finance: BPL - Internal Order Administration	Story
SAP__FI_BPL_IM_INTERNAL_...	SAP Finance: BPL - Internal Order Planning	Story
SAP__FI_BPL_IM_CAPEX_PLA...	SAP Finance: BPL - Investment Planning	Story
SAP__FI_BPL_IM_CAPEX_PLA...	SAP Finance: BPL - Investment Planning Administra...	Story
SAP__FI_BPL_IM_COSTCENTE...	SAP Finance: BPL - Plan Cost Center Cost Rates an...	Story
SAP__FI_BPL_IM_COSTCENTE...	SAP Finance: BPL - Plan Cost Center Expenses	Story
SAP__FI_BPL_IM_PRODUCTC...	SAP Finance: BPL - Product Cost Planning Administ...	Story
SAP__FI_BPL_IM_PRODUCTC...	SAP Finance: BPL - Product Cost Rates	Story
SAP__FI_BPL_IM_PROFITABILI...	SAP Finance: BPL - Profitability Planning	Story
SAP__FI_BPL_IM_PROJECT_P...	SAP Finance: BPL - Project Administration	Story
SAP__FI_BPL_IM_PROJECT_P...	SAP Finance: BPL - Project Planning & Budgeting	Story

Figure 3.8: Planning stories for Integrated Financial Planning

3.2.1 Cost and activity planning

The goal of cost and activity planning is to capture the expenses expected for the cost center as part of the budgeting process and to plan how these costs will flow to other cost centers as activity flows and allocations. In Section 3.3.1, we will look at how this plan data can also be used to set budgets and perform budget availability checks within SAP S/4HANA whenever actual costs are updated to the relevant cost centers.

We will begin by looking at how to plan primary costs by copying the actual costs from the previous year and making the appropriate adjustments. In Figure 3.9, we have selected the PLAN COST CENTER EXPENSES story from the list of files shown in Figure 3.8. We have prefilled the plan for 2021 using reference data from the previous year by selecting the EXPENSES: ACTUAL BASED button. As shown here, this button triggers a *data action* using a scripting language to perform a simple copy, but it can also be used to perform more complex calculations and allocations as we will see later. Further sophisticated options for copying data can be found by clicking on the EXPENSES: USING CONTROL PARAMETERS button.

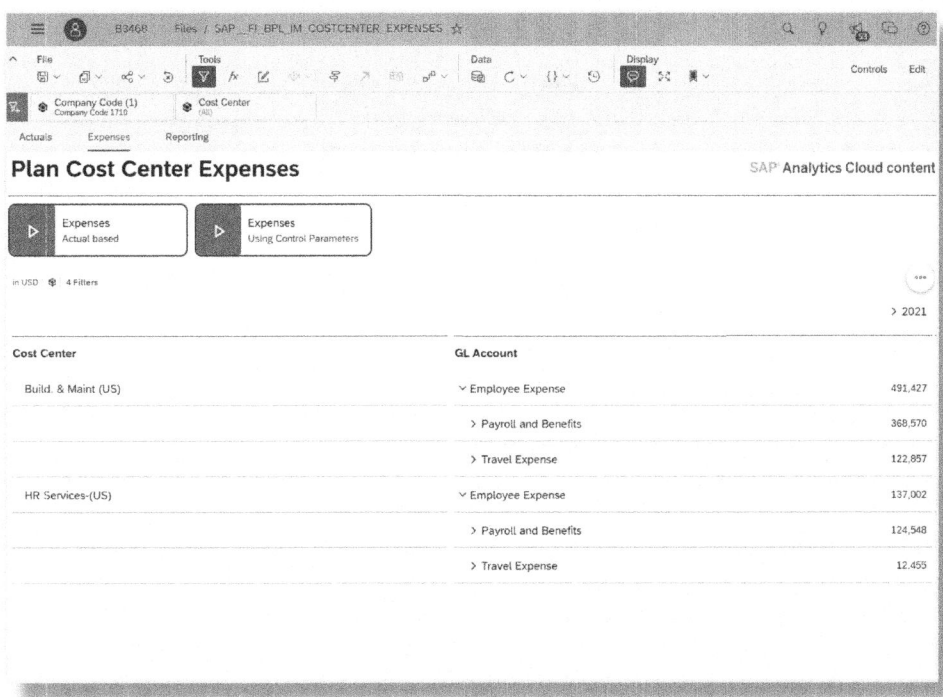

Figure 3.9: Plan Cost Center Expenses, using Actuals as reference

97

To define how these primary costs then flow to other cost centers, navigate from the EXPENSES tab (see Figure 3.9) to the REPORTING tab where you can perform simple allocations using the EXPENSES: DISTRIBUTE and EXPENSES: ASSESSMENT buttons shown in Figure 3.10. In this example, we have used assessment to allocate the payroll and travel costs for the building and maintenance cost center (COST CENTER) to a manufacturing cost center (PARTNER COST CENTER). Note that as a result of the data action, we now see debit and credit codes indicating how the costs for the building and maintenance cost center have been charged as secondary costs, matching the future cost flow for the actual costs. A distribution also results in debit and credit postings, but under the original accounts for payroll and travel.

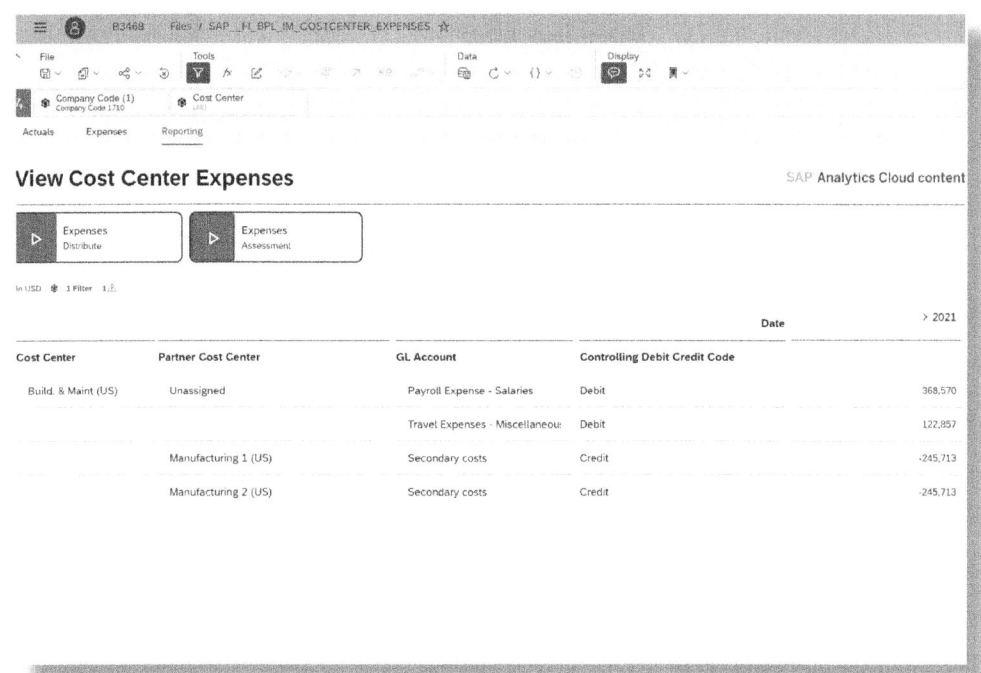

Figure 3.10: Using data actions to trigger distribution or assessment on the planned costs

We have shown here how the delivered planning stories support the basic cost center planning process and how to use distribution and allocations to move costs to other cost centers. If you are approaching this planning exercise having previously used SAP ERP, then the main disadvantage at the time of writing is that you cannot yet split the costs according to an allocation structure.

Distributions and allocations might cover the full planning process in some organizations. In others, this approach is used to move costs from support cost centers to operational cost centers, but then additional steps are required to plan the work performed by the operational cost centers. For this reason, the integrated financial planning content also covers activity quantity planning, cost splitting (where one cost center provides more than one activity type), and activity price calculation.

Figure 3.11 shows the COST CENTER ACTIVITY PRICE story, where we have associated the activity types service, machine hours, and personnel hours with the relevant cost centers, and defined hours as the unit of quantity. Note also the G/L account to be used to charge the costs during the activity allocation and a manual cost rate to be charged per unit of activity consumed in 2021. In the next section, we will see how these manufacturing activities are consumed by the products when we explain how to perform product cost simulation. These activities can also be consumed by orders and projects.

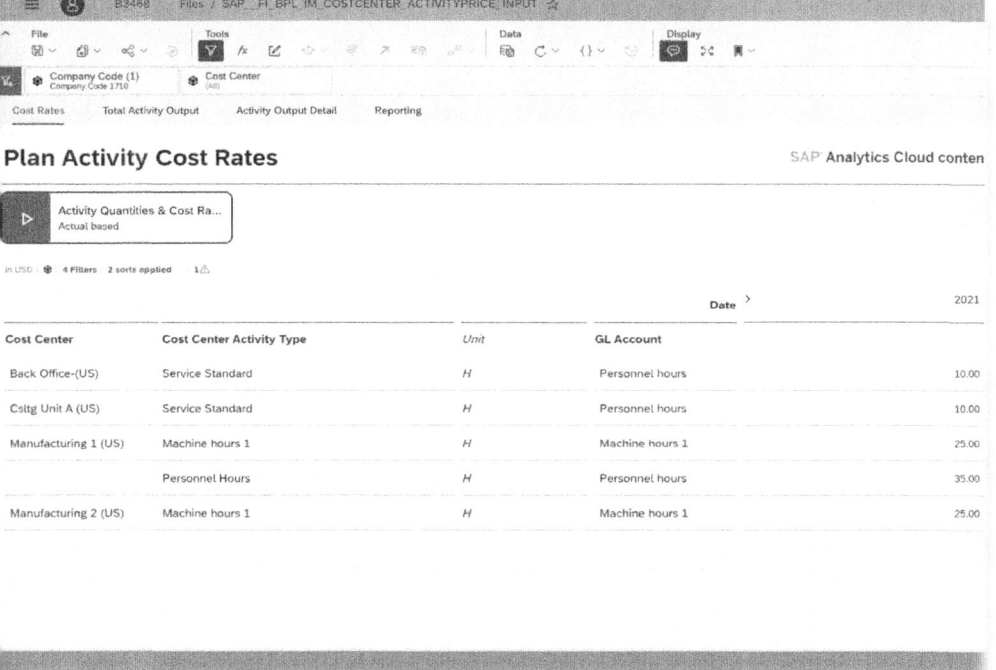

Figure 3.11: Cost centers and activity types

Some organizations enter their activity rates manually, but others go further and have the system do it for them. To do this, choose the TOTAL ACTIVITY

99

OUTPUT tab and enter the CAPACITY available and the ACTIVITY QUANTITY, as shown in Figure 3.12, where we have planned the hours of activity to be performed by the four cost centers.

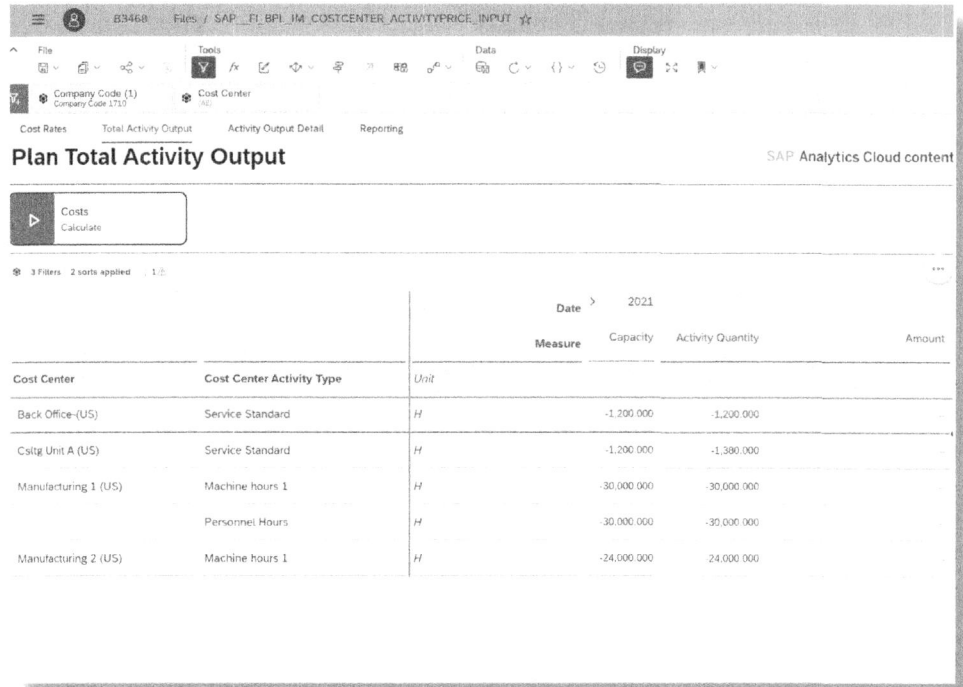

Figure 3.12: Planned Activity Output of cost centers

The next step is to plan how this output will be used by the various cost centers, as shown in Figure 3.13. Various options are available:

- ▶ To calculate activity quantities based on an assumed relationship between two key figures, choose ACTIVITY QUANTITIES: CALCULATE INVERSELY. This might be the case where the number of electricity hours is assumed to be related to the number of machine hours.

- ▶ To split activity quantities based on driver information, choose ACTIVITY QUANTITIES: ALLOCATE. This might be the case where the total number of consulting hours can be split based on the relative number of consulting hours supplied by various consulting cost centers.

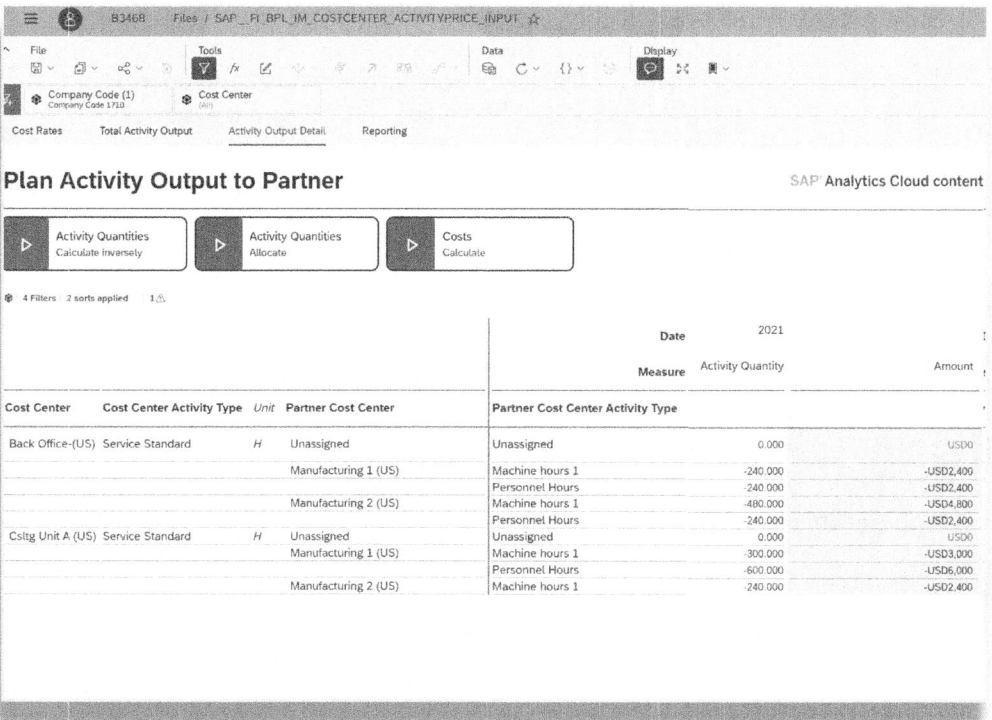

Figure 3.13: Plan Activity Output to Partner

In both cases, the calculated activity quantities are then associated with the calculated activity rate by choosing the COSTS: CALCULATE button shown in Figure 3.12. If you compare Figure 3.13 with Figure 3.10, you will notice not only the COST CENTER and PARTNER COST CENTER, but also the COST CENTER ACTIVITY TYPE and PARTNER COST CENTER ACTIVITY TYPE, because assessments and distributions work at the level of the cost centers, and activity-based calculations are more detailed and include the activity type.

If you are approaching this planning exercise using SAP ERP, then the main disadvantage at the time of writing is that you can calculate an activity price for each cost center/activity type combination, but you cannot yet break this price out into the underlying cost components (the primary cost component split).

3.2.2 Sales and profitability planning

The goal of the sales and profitability planning content is to support the sales and revenue planning process, beginning with sales price and sales quantity planning, and to support the planner with simulation capabilities based on past actual data, as we saw previously for cost center expenses. We can then use revenue and deduction calculation to include the various rebates that customers typically request. In Figure 3.14 we have planned the quantity and associated revenue for each product/customer combination.

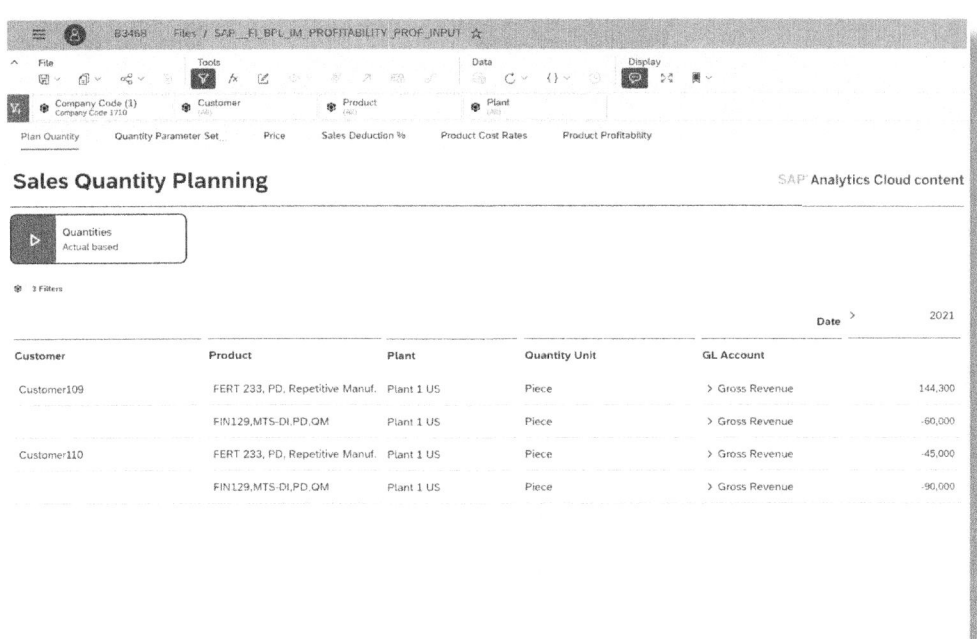

Figure 3.14: Quantity and revenue planning

We can then plan a unit price for the product and sales deductions by navigating to the PRICE and SALES DEDUCTION tabs. We can associate the cost of goods sold with the planned revenue, as shown in Figure 3.15, where we have navigated to the PRODUCT COST RATES tab to show the product costs for the two materials sold in Figure 3.14.

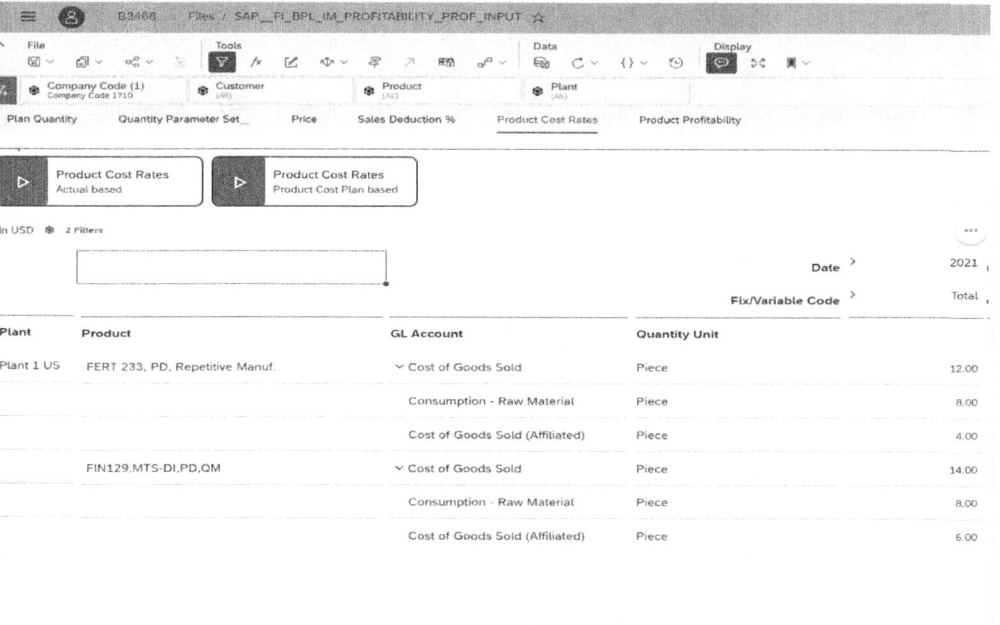

Figure 3.15: Planning Cost of Goods Sold

The cost of goods sold is calculated using product cost simulation (see Section 3.2.3) and includes the detailed cost components that we looked at in Chapter 2. These form the basis for the cost of goods sold split that is created whenever a material is delivered to the customer, which has an appropriate standard cost estimate (see Section 2.5.2).

3.2.3 Product cost simulation

The product cost simulation content relies on the standard cost estimate in SAP S/4HANA to calculate the initial standard costs based on the BOM and routing in the underlying system. The cost estimate itemization provides the *quantity structure* and is transferred to SAP Analytics Cloud where it provides the basis for raw material planning and product cost simulation, resulting in costs of goods sold that can then be used in combination with the sales quantities to simulate product profitability. This process is not completely independent of SAP S/4HANA as it assumes the existence of bills of material, routings, work centers, and so on, in SAP S/4HANA and also the existence of an initial activity price to value the production activities used in the manufacture of the product. Since cost center planning takes place in SAP Analytics Cloud, you will need to orchestrate the process to determine whether the activity price should be calculated first in SAC and then transferred to SAP S/4HANA, or whether the value of the cost estimate should be adjusted once cost center planning is completed in SAP Analytics Cloud for Planning.

The product costs used to fill the cost of goods sold in Figure 3.15 are calculated using a separate story, PRODUCT COST RATES. This includes the planning of the lot size (since the product will not always be sold in the same units that it is manufactured in) and a quantity structure which includes all the raw materials, activity usage, and overheads required to manufacture the product to be sold.

Figure 3.16 shows the product costs for the good to be sold, that were planned in Figure 3.15. Note that this is structured by the G/L accounts for the cost of goods sold that we looked at in Section 2.5.2. The quantity structure has been imported from the standard cost estimate in SAP S/4HANA and we see the activity usage (COST CENTER and COST CENTER ACTIVITY TYPE) and the material usage (COMPONENT PLANT and MATERIAL) per product lot.

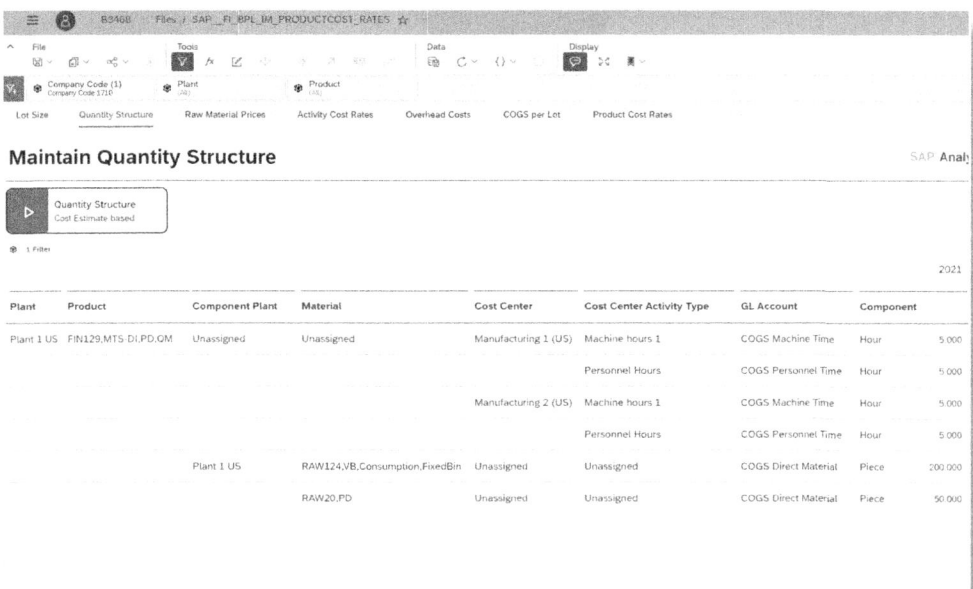

Figure 3.16: Quantity Structure for product costs

We can adjust the raw material prices, the activity cost rates and the overhead costs by making changes in the appropriate tabs, before finally calculating the product costs for the goods to be sold, as shown in Figure 3.17.

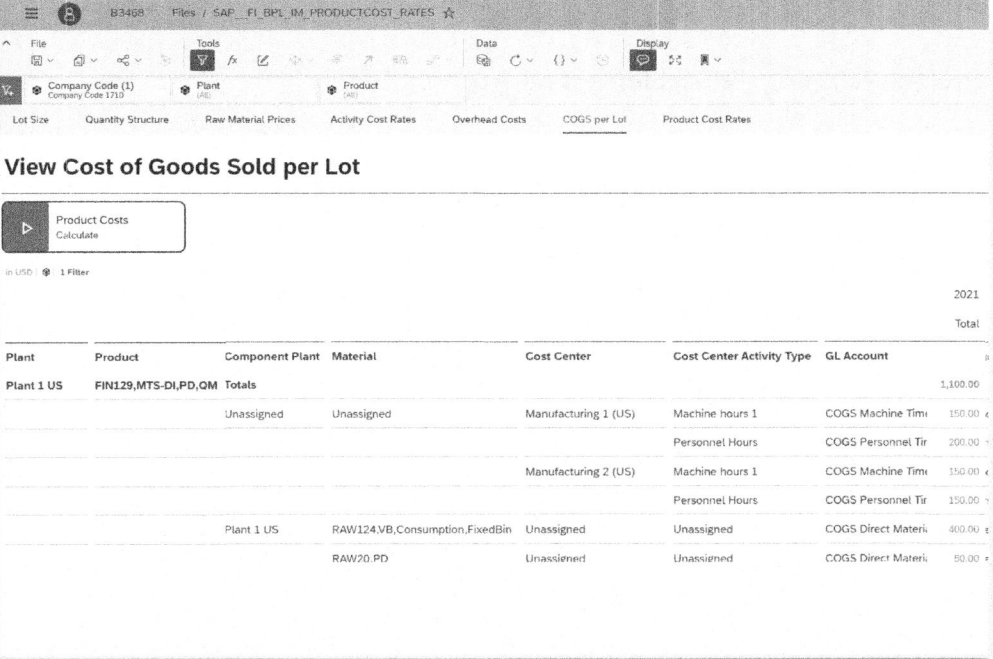

Figure 3.17: Planning of cost of goods sold

3.2.4 Project planning

SAP Analytics Cloud also supports project planning, as shown in Figure 3.18. This can be a simple exercise where expenses are planned by project, as we see here, or you can go go further to capture planned activity usage from the cost centers. Like cost center planning, this project plan can also be used to set budgets and perform active availability control by project, as we will see in Section 3.3.1. This plan can also be used as a basis for event-based revenue recognition, which we will cover in Section 3.3.2.

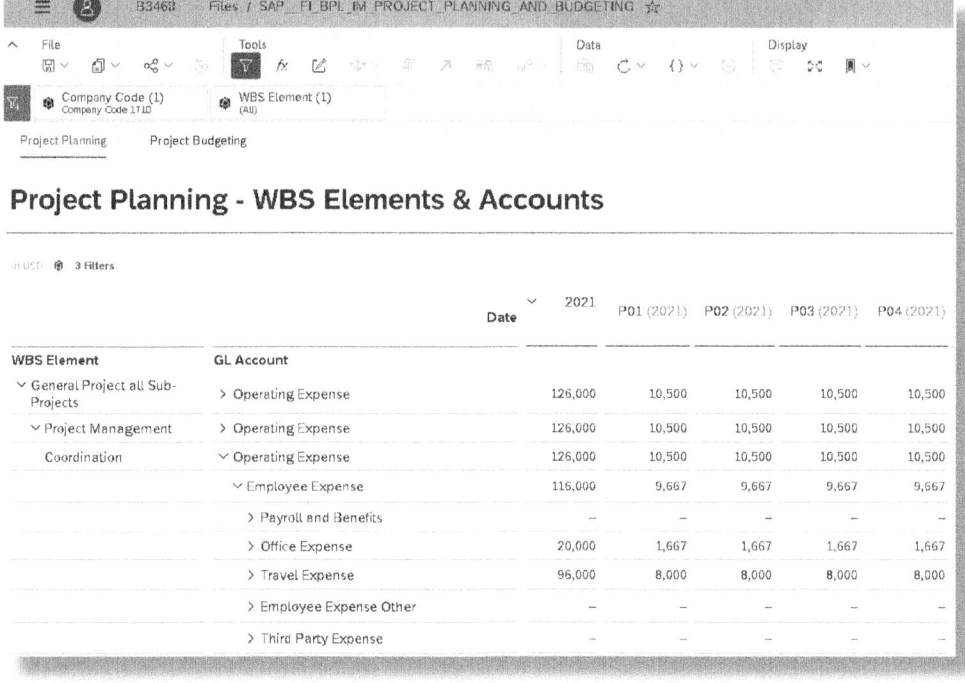

Figure 3.18: Project planning

3.2.5 Financial statement planning

The costs for cost centers and projects, the revenues for the products sold, and the cost of goods sold for the associated products roll up to deliver a profit and loss statement by company code, profit center, functional area, and trading partner. These can then be used to derive various key figures. Figure 3.19 shows how these figures are in turn used to derive a simple balance sheet.

Now that we have looked at how to capture planned data, we will move on to examine how to use that planned data in the operational processes.

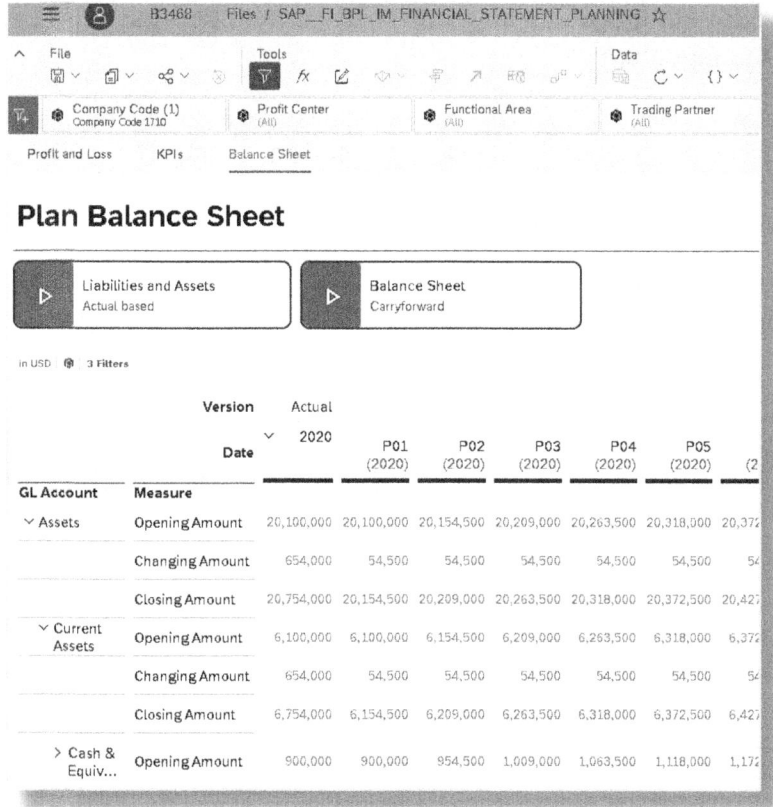

Figure 3.19: Financial statement planning

3.3 Using financial plan data in SAP S/4HANA

While many customers have been planning in data warehouses for some years, it has been common to put the data back into SAP ERP because many functions use this planned data to determine when to block spending if certain budget thresholds are exceeded or to calculate a percentage of completion for the purposes of revenue recognition in an engineer-to-order environment. We will now explore some of the options to use the financial plan data in the operational processes running directly in SAP S/4HANA.

3.3.1 Budgeting, availability control and commitments management

Plan/actual reports may be a key element of financial reporting, but many organizations also use their plans to set a **ceiling** on spending by fixing the plan as a *budget* and then setting up *availability control* to prevent any spending that exceeds this budget. Figure 3.20 shows the Cost Center Budget Report app which combines the budget, the actual costs, and the commitments to show the budget remaining for the various cost centers selected. This is essentially a passive budget control because it relies on the cost center manager managing the budget by monitoring the figures in this report.

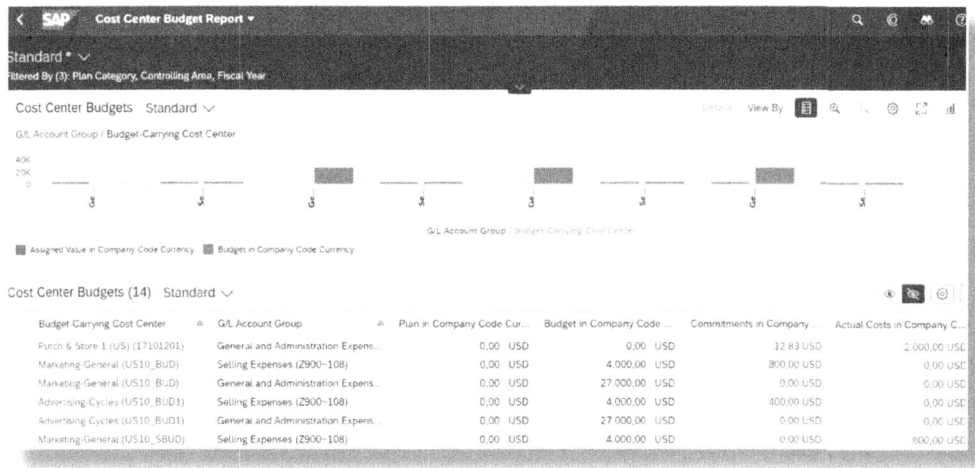

Figure 3.20: Cost Center Budget Report app

You can take this idea further and use an active budget control to have the system issue warnings or even block spending when certain thresholds have been exceeded. This option was available in SAP ERP for projects and orders but is new for cost centers in SAP S/4HANA. Besides designating a plan category to store your budget (see Figure 3.5), you need to decide which cost centers should be included in the budget availability control, since the approach makes most sense for cost centers with a manager responsible. You can perform a budget availability check for each cost center directly or designate another cost center to carry the budget for several assigned cost centers. Figure 3.21 shows the Manage Cost Centers app and the parameters to activate Budget Availability Control for the selected cost center (BUDGET AVAILABILITY CONTROL IS ACTIVE). Note that in this case, cost center 17101201 is carrying the budget, but that this field could contain a different cost center that bundle budgets for several cost centers. The BUDGET AVAILABILITY CONTROL PROFILE controls the thresholds for the budget check.

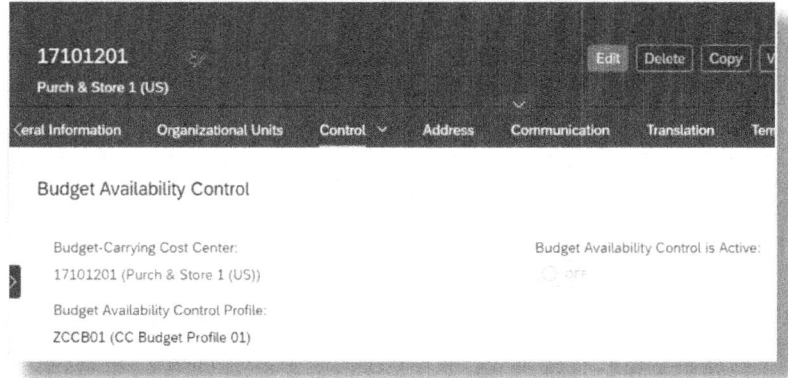

Figure 3.21: Manage Cost Centers app, showing Budget Availability Control parameters

To define the thresholds for the budget availability control, follow menu path: CONTROLLING • COST CENTER ACCOUNTING • BUDGET MANAGEMENT • MAINTAIN BUDGET AVAILABILITY CONTROL FOR COST CENTERS in the IMG. Here, you define the name of the budget availability control profile, the account groups that will be checked, and the tolerance for each account group. Figure 3.22 shows a budget availability control profile for which a warning will be issued when 90% of the annual budget has been spent, and an error declared when 100% of the annual budget has been used.

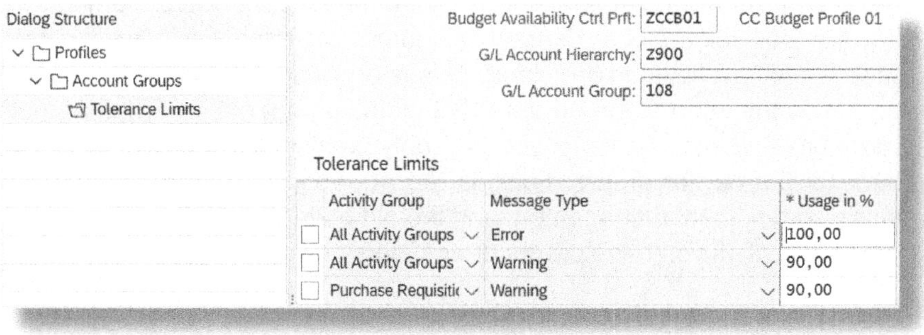

Figure 3.22: Settings for budget availability control

Budget availability control includes the actual costs already recorded for the cost center but also any *commitments* for purchase orders that are still outstanding for that cost center, that will result in future costs. Figure 3.23

shows the Commitments by Cost Center app. This displays the actual costs, the commitments, the assigned costs (actual costs plus commitments), the planned costs, and the available budget. The commitments in this report are created for open purchase orders and are stored in an extension ledger in a process that is essentially the reverse of the incoming sales order that we looked at in Section 2.5.3. In SAP S/4HANA 2008, predictive accounting documents are also available for travel requests in SAP Concur.

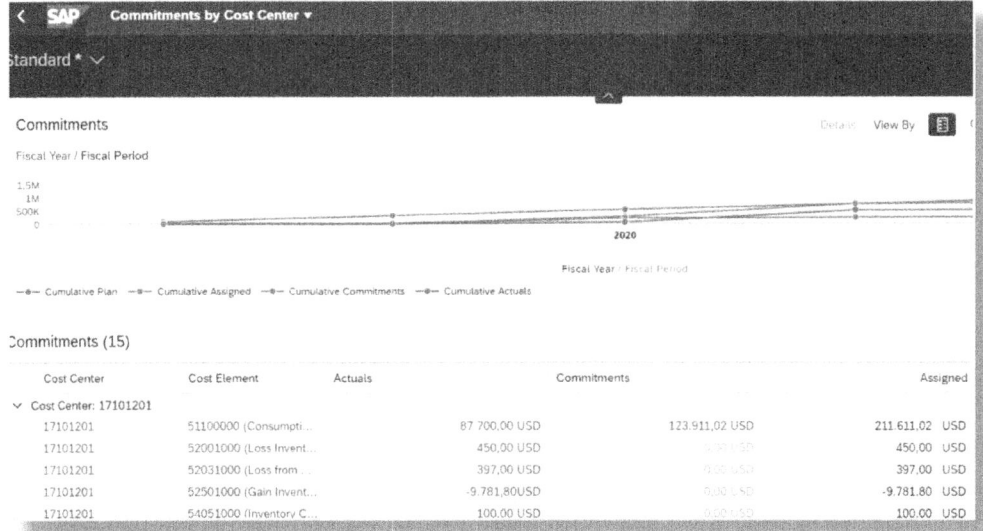

Figure 3.23: Commitments by Cost Center app

Similar functions are available to capture commitments for a WBS element and to perform a budget availability control against the WBS element, as shown in the Project Budget Report in Figure 3.24. At the time of writing, this report is only available in the cloud. This is because the availability control only reads the information on the WBS elements but not on any assigned orders or networks. Similarly, you can only create commitments for WBS elements but not for orders. For this reason, you should continue to use classic commitment management and the old budget availability checks for WBS elements if you have orders or networks assigned to your projects.

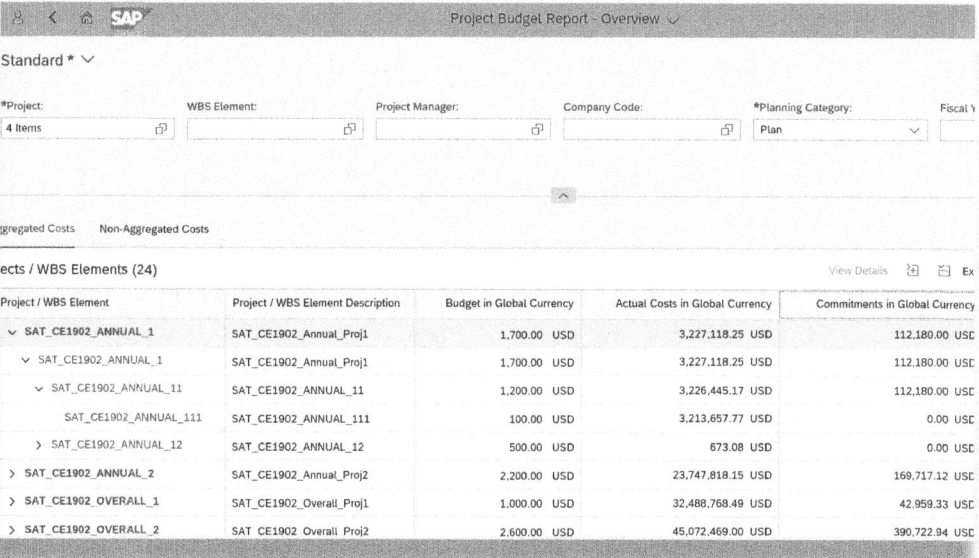

Figure 3.24: Project Budget Report app (cloud only)

3.3.2 Project planning and event-based revenue recognition

When we looked at event-based revenue recognition in Chapter 2, we implicitly assumed that planned data was available to calculate the percentage of completion. In fact, several plan categories have been delivered for use with commercial projects to deliver reports such as the one shown in Figure 3.25. The three plan categories are used as follows:

- The baseline is the original plan to deliver the original scope within the original timeframe and is typically locked once work begins on the project.
- The ongoing plan reflects adjustments to the scope of the project.
- EAC (estimate to complete) is a key figure that is regularly requested from project managers to reflect their assumptions regarding what it will cost to complete the project.

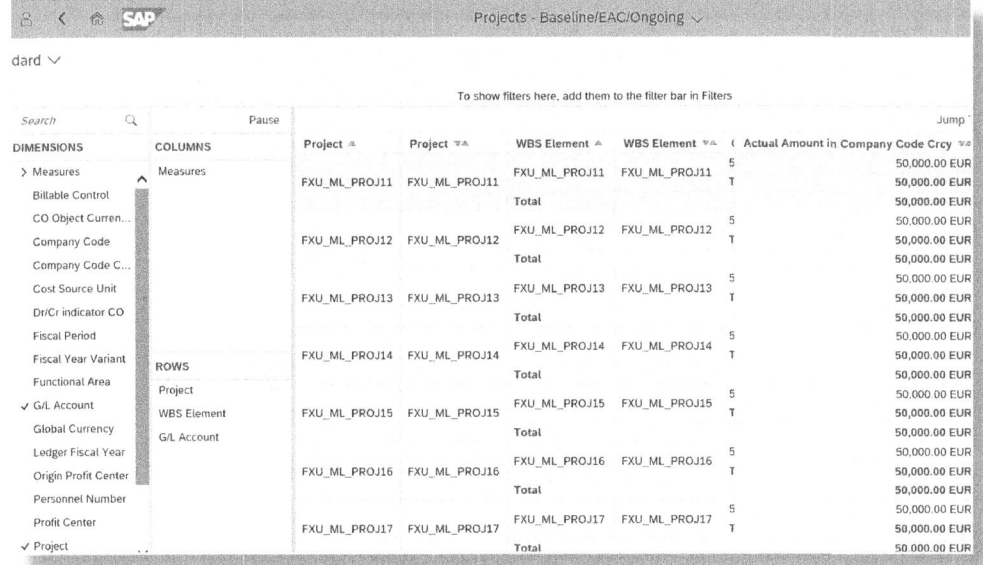

Figure 3.25: Projects—Baseline/EAC/Ongoing app

3.3.3 Production order planning and variance calculation

If you work with production orders, you have two options to calculate target costs and variances:

▶ Within the production order itself, all reporting continues to be based on the old tables, so you still see the planned data stored in the COSP and COSS tables. You can also display this data in the classic transaction KKBC_ORD alongside the target costs and production variances that are stored in the COSB table.

▶ If you use the new Production Cost Analysis app or the Display Costs by Work Center or Operation app, you read the actual costs directly from the universal journal, and planned costs from the ACDOCP table. The values shown in the target cost columns are calculated on the fly using the new planning table, and a new approach to variances is being introduced.

When we looked at the planned categories in Section 3.1.1, we showed the two plan categories delivered for planning on production orders. These are used when you work with the Production Cost Analysis app, as shown in Figure 3.26.

- ▶ The values shown in the PRODUCTION ORDER PLAN COST category reflect the various cost items for the material components and operations in the production order, plus any overhead costs. In SAP ERP, this was effectively the target cost version 1.

- ▶ The values shown in the PRODUCTION ORDER STANDARD COST category reflect the cost items from the standard cost estimate for the product manufactured, adjusted to reflect the order lot size. In SAP ERP, this was effectively the target cost version 0, although it is now calculated when the order is created rather than at the time of the final goods receipt.

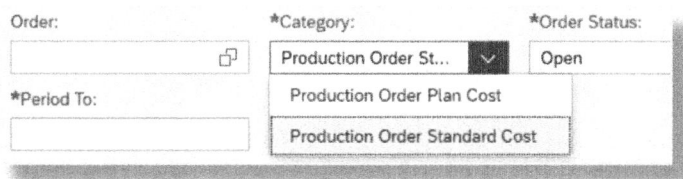

Figure 3.26: Production Cost Analysis app, showing plan categories for production costs

Figure 3.27 shows the Production Cost Analysis app and the selected production orders with their planned costs, target costs, and actual costs. The target costs have been calculated within the app by taking the planned costs and adjusting them to reflect the quantity of goods delivered to stock for the order.

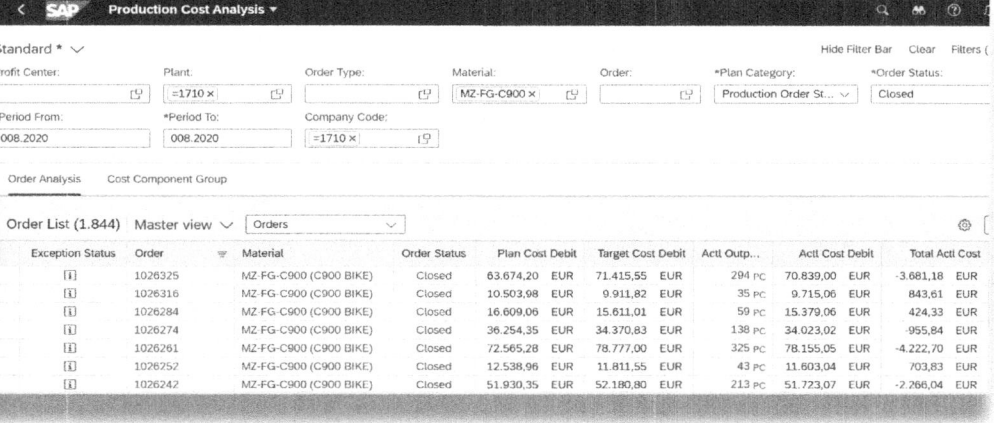

Figure 3.27: Production Cost Analysis App, showing Order List

113

The general approach is to calculate work in process and production variances in real time rather than at period close, using the new table structure; but this approach is not yet available in all areas. Note that at the time of writing, cost center variances continue to be available only in the COSB table, following the classic approach. It is also not yet possible to use this approach for Product Costs by Period.

Now that we have looked at the key aspects of Accounting, Controlling and Planning, we will explore how to migrate from the separate tables to the universal journal.

4 Migrating to SAP S/4HANA Finance

In Chapter 2, we learnt how the universal journal combines transactional data from Accounting and Controlling. If you are involved in a new SAP implementation, you can skip this chapter because your transactional data will be stored in the new structures from the start. However, if you are coming from an earlier release of SAP ERP, this chapter explains how to bring your existing transactional data, which is currently spread over several tables, into the new data model. We also look at how the migration removes the totals and index tables that we discussed in Chapter 1.

There are several parts to a migration project:

- Blueprinting and defining how the new system should behave
- Testing on a cloned system (you will generally repeat this around five times until all errors have been identified and fixed)
- The migration proper using real data in the live system
- The sign-off for the migration from your auditors

It is important to understand that this is **not** simply a technical upgrade but that the topics we discussed in Chapter 2 have a business impact: you will need business users as well as IT people to decide the configuration settings that make sense for your organization, to ensure that the correct master data is in place before you start enriching the existing data with profit centers, functional areas, and so on, and to sign-off on the consistency of the data after the migration.

4.1 Documenting a migration

In Chapter 2, we looked at the key fields for each application in the universal journal. Because the migrated data is subject to the normal **audit** requirements on financial data, it is important to understand how to identify a universal journal entry that has been migrated and to explain what type of line item you are dealing with. Indeed, you should involve your auditors in the project to ensure that your audit requirements are met during the migration. Figure 4.1 shows the migration-specific fields in the universal journal table.

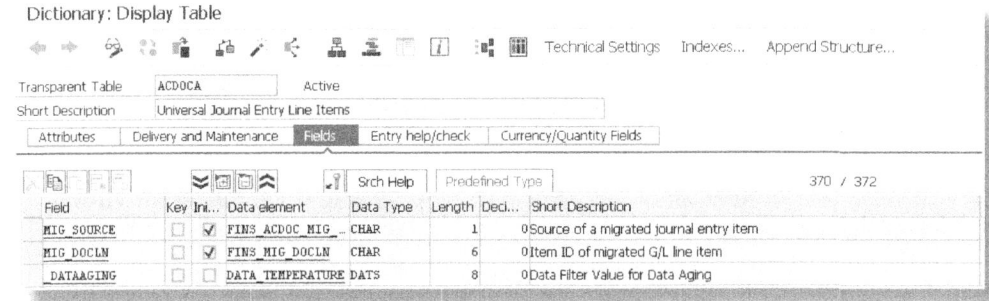

Figure 4.1: Migration-specific fields in the universal journal

The entry in the MIG_SOURCE field is used to show what sort of line item has been migrated (General Ledger Accounting only, Asset Accounting, Controlling, or Material Ledger) and whether the line item is a true line item from one of the applications or one containing the information from a former entry in the totals table. Finally, line items for reposting/correction document changes made in the course of migration where it was not possible to merge the FI and the CO document for the same business transaction retrospectively. The result will be an FI document that contains the original posting lines and a correction document that contains the CO account assignments with a reference to the original CO document number. Note that there is no migration for existing profit center documents that were not part of the general ledger. Instead, the profit center will be derived afresh using the underlying account assignment in the CO document during migration.

Figure 4.2 shows the keys that identify the original line items that have been migrated and the correction postings entered where the totals do not match the sum of the line items. If there is no entry in the MIG_SOURCE field, it means that the document was not migrated but is a new journal entry (the normal case once operations start after conversion).

There are different types of migration record depending on the data source:

- ▶ M (MATERIAL LEDGER ONLY) and A (ASSET ACCOUNTING ONLY) records represent data from the subledgers that is enriched with the assignment to an account assignment object in Controlling and the reporting dimensions in General Ledger Accounting. These are usually the most granular records.

- ▶ C (CONTROLLING ONLY) records represent data from Controlling that is enriched by the reporting dimensions in General Ledger Accounting.

Migration Source	Short Descript.
(blank)	Not created by migration
F	FI excluding NewGL, potentially including CO, ML, AA
G	FI including NewGL, potentially including CO, ML, AA
C	Controlling only
D	Accrual Engine only
I	Accrual Engine Legacy Data Transfer
E	Enrich Balances
M	Material Ledger only
A	Asset accounting only
P	Special Purpose Ledger only
R	Reposting / correction
S	Totals correction for Controlling
T	Totals correction for Material Ledger
U	Totals correction for General Ledger
V	Totals Correction for Special Purpose Ledger
N	Material Ledger at migration step M10
H	Balances upload from legacy system

Figure 4.2: Sources of migrated journal entries

- F and G (general ledger accounting) records represent either data from SAP ERP General Ledger Accounting, which includes the reporting dimensions from FAGLFLEXA, or data from classic General Ledger Accounting that has been enriched to include the relevant reporting dimensions.

- D (ACCRUAL ENGINE ONLY) records represent manual accrual postings created using the SAP ERP accrual engine. This migration path was delivered with SAP S/4HANA 1809.

- P (SPECIAL PURPOSE LEDGER ONLY) records capture journal entries moved from a special ledger.

Normally, the entries in the totals table are an aggregation of the data in the line item tables (and are therefore redundant), meaning that the migration can simply take the data from the totals tables and put it in backup tables (we saw these when we looked at the GLT0 view in Chapter 1) because the same data can be aggregated on the fly and does not need to be precalculated and stored. However, where the sum of the line items is **not** the same as the totals to be migrated, the system creates a separate document for the difference. This document effectively makes it clear for an auditor that some of the supporting line items for a totals entry are no longer in the system because they have already been archived.

This correction entry accounts for the fact that old line items might have been archived, leaving only the totals for the early years. The correction entries do not include all the reporting dimensions because they can only access the fields in the original totals records. However, they do ensure that your balance sheet and profit and loss statement for the closed periods meet the audit requirements for such data. Depending on the source of the totals difference, you will find entries for S (Controlling), U (Material Ledger) and V (General Ledger Accounting). There may also be errors in the migration process itself, which are documented with source R (reposting/correction).

Before you start, it is important to understand that the migration process will migrate **every** financial document in the system. It therefore makes sense to archive as much as possible before beginning the migration. Obviously, this will speed up the process because there will be fewer objects to handle, but it also means that you will not be faced with correcting errors in documents from previous migrations, such as those from SAP R/2 to SAP R/3 or SAP ERP or conversions from local currencies to the euro.

We will now walk through the key things that you need to know in order to prepare for a migration.

4.2 Preparation

As you move into the blueprinting stage, it is important to understand what kind of SAP S/4HANA system you are migrating to because the installation and migration steps will be different in each case. Figure 4.3 provides an overview of the paths supported. As you can see from ❶, you can move from the SAP Business Suite to the SAP Simple Finance Add-On and migrate later via ❸ to SAP S/4HANA. Alternatively, you can take the direct route via ❷ from the SAP Business Suite to SAP S/4HANA. The direct route to SAP S/4HANA is now the recommended approach.

Transition Paths to Move to SAP S/4HANA

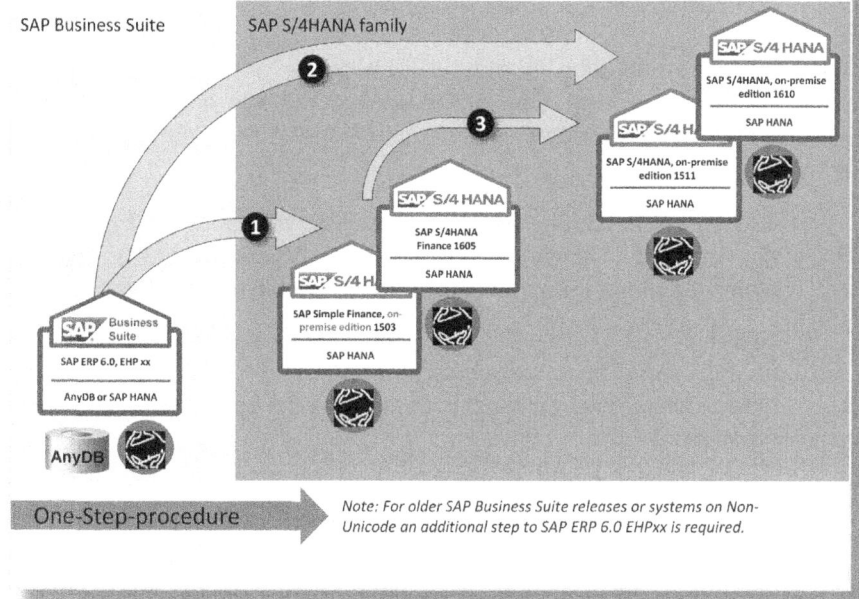

Figure 4.3: Transition paths to SAP S/4HANA

Before you start, refer to the relevant administration guides in the SAP Service Marketplace (you will need to provide log-on information to access the SAP Service Marketplace):

- ▶ "Administrator's Guide for SAP S/4HANA Finance", available at:
  https://help.sap.com/doc/d12ca04ea099443ab34b2bc8eb99844f/3.8/ en-US/SFIN_ADMIN_GUIDE_308.pdf
  Here, the migration removes totals tables and index tables, moves the financial transactions into the universal journal, and activates new Asset Accounting and new Cash Management.

- ▶ "Installation Guide for SAP S/4HANA, on-premise edition 1511", found at:
  https://uacp.hana.ondemand.com/http.svc/rc/ PRODUCTION/pdf3be8f85500f17b43e10000000 a4450e5/1511%20000/en-US/INST_OP1511.pdf

Here, the migration removes totals tables and index tables, moves the financial transactions into the universal journal, moves the material movements into table MATDOC, activates the long material number and the Material Ledger (unless it is already active), new Asset Accounting, new Cash Management, and converts vendors and customers into business partners.

Embarking on a migration journey is a challenge because there appear to be many moving parts. One of the easiest ways to find out what has changed is to search for SAP Notes containing the term "S4WTL". Some examples are:

- SAP Note 2270333—"S4TWL – Data Model Changes in FIN", available at: *https://launchpad.support.sap.com/#/notes/2270333*. This explains the major data model changes to enable the universal journal.

- SAP Note 2270419—"S4TWL – Account/Cost Element", available at: *https://launchpad.support.sap.com/#/notes/0002270419*. This SAP note explains the implications of merging the accounts and the cost element.

- SAP Note 227040—"S4TWL – Technical Changes in Controlling", which can be found at: *https://launchpad.support.sap.com/#/notes/0002270404*. This note introduces the new data structures in Controlling and explains their impact.

- SAP Note 2349278—"S4TWL – Profitability Analysis", available at: *https://launchpad.support.sap.com/#/notes/2349278*. This explains the new approach for Margin Analysis and how it compares with costing-based Profitability Analysis.

- SAP Note 2270387—"S4TWL – Asset Accounting: Changes to Data Structure", found at: *https://launchpad.support.sap.com/#/notes/0002270387*. This note introduces the new data structures in Asset Accounting and explains their impact.

- SAP Note 2352383—"S4TWL – Conversion to S/4HANA 1610 Material Ledger and Actual Costing", available at: *https://launchpad.support.sap.com/#/notes/0002352383*. This introduces the new data structures for the Material Ledger and Actual Costing.

- SAP Note 2582883—"S4TWL – Manual Accruals (Accrual. Engine)", which can be found at: *https://launchpad.support.sap.com/#/notes/2582883*. This explains the changes to the handling of manual accruals via the accrual engine.

Do your homework before you begin a migration project and make sure that you really understand the impact of the changes that are about to take place.

4.2.1 Readiness checks

Initially, the preparation process does not require you to install any software at all. The idea is to look in the system for anything that might prevent a migration or cause problems during the migration. It is important to keep your eye on the various simplification items in SAP S/4HANA and the following blog is a good place to keep abreast of changes: *http://scn.sap.com/docs/DOC-70833*.

As you work your way through the various simplification items, you need to understand how these will impact your current system. Here are a couple of examples of things to check:

- Your own use of index and totals tables:
  The *select statements* that pull data for reporting via the compatibility views will work automatically. If you are planning an upgrade, however, you need to look for *write statements* (INSERT, UPDATE, DELETE, MODIFY) on these tables because these will need to be replaced. You also have to check that no custom DDIC views have been created on top of the removed tables. You can find full details about how to handle your totals tables in SAP Note 1976487[8]. If you have added fields to your index tables, refer to SAP Note 2191738[9] for details of how to handle the extra fields.

- Addition of fields to tables COEP and BSEG:
  You have to manually extend the ACDOCA table to include any fields that your organization has added to COEP or BSEG, as described in SAP Note 2160045[10]. If you have added coding block fields to structure CI_COBL, these will be migrated automatically and do not require special treatment.

---

[8] SAP Note 1976487: "Information about adjusting customer-specific programs to the simplified data model in SAP Simple Finance" (*https://launchpad.support.sap.com/#/notes/0001976487*)

[9] SAP Note 2191738: "Error FGL_PRE_CHECK 030 in S/4HANA Pre-Transition Check" (*https://launchpad.support.sap.com/#/notes/0002191738*)

[10] SAP Note 2160045: "S/4HANA Finance: Fields of Appends to COEP and BSEG missing in table ACDOCA" (*https://launchpad.support.sap.com/#/notes/0002160045*)

4.2.2 Deprecated transactions

It is also important to check for transactions that have been removed and to understand your alternatives **before** you begin migration. For example, in Chapter 3, we discussed the need to make a choice between using the new SAP S/4HANA options for planning or continuing to use the classic planning transactions for an interim period. The business rationale was that there was to be a principle of one, so if a transaction has been removed, there will usually be an alternative which will be documented in the relevant *simplification list*.

Again, the list of deprecated transactions is different depending on the SAP S/4HANA system in question:

- ▶ SAP Simple Finance Add-On for SAP Business Suite powered by SAP HANA and SAP S/4HANA Finance—refer to SAP Note 2270335[11]
- ▶ SAP S/4HANA—refer to the details in the *simplification list* included in the SAP Help: *https://uacp.hana.ondemand.com/http.svc/rc/ PRODUCTION/pdfa4322f56824ae221e10000000a4450e5/1511%20 000/en-US/SIMPL_OP1511.pdf*

4.2.3 Data preparation

Essentially, the data preparation steps are the same as for any migration project:

- ▶ Perform period-end closing activities and reconciliation
- ▶ Create a data snapshot for comparison after migration
- ▶ Prepare all business areas, not only finance

However, in addition to the standard closing programs, you should also execute various check reports delivered by SAP:

---

[11] SAP Note 2270335: "S4TWL – Replaced Transaction Codes and Programs in FIN" (*https:// launchpad.support.sap.com/#/notes/0002270335*)

- ▶ FINS_MIG_PRECHECK_CUST_SETTNGS (SAP Note 2129306[12] explains how to check your ledger, company code, and controlling area settings)

- ▶ RACHECK_ACTIVATION_PARVAL (SAP Note 1968305[13] explains how to use new Asset Accounting if you are already using SAP ERP General Ledger Accounting)

- ▶ RASFIN_MIGR_PRECHECK (SAP Note 1939592[14] explains how to use this report and which solutions are not compatible with new Asset Accounting)

- ▶ Follow the instructions in SAP Note 2176077[15] to check your ability to use the solution in general.

4.3 Installation

To install SAP S/4HANA as we discussed in Chapter 2, the following parts are compulsory:

- ▶ SAP HANA database:
  This is the primary database for storing all data. The architectural changes are only possible if an in-memory database is used.

- ▶ SAP NetWeaver kernel:
  The SAP NetWeaver kernel provides certain functions that are required, such as CDS views to provide a virtual view of the universal journal from the viewpoint of the removed tables.

- ▶ SAP Simple Finance Add-On for SAP Business Suite powered by SAP HANA
  This add-on replaces the existing coding for the Finance modules.

---

[12] SAP Note 2129306: "Check Customizing Settings Prior to Upgrade to Simple Finance" (*https://launchpad.support.sap.com/#/notes/0002129306*)

[13] SAP Note 1968305: "S2I: New Asset Accouting Activation report should not check on inactive company codes" (*https://launchpad.support.sap.com/#/notes/0001968305*)

[14] SAP Note 1939592: "SFIN: Pre-Check Report for migrating to New Asset Accounting" (*https://launchpad.support.sap.com/#/notes/0001939592*)

[15] SAP Note 2176077: "Check report for SAP S/4HANA Finance" (*https://launchpad.support.sap.com/#/notes/0002176077*)

In Chapter 6, we will learn about the following optional parts:

- SAP Fiori:
  Used to provide the user interfaces we saw in Chapter 1.
- SAP Gateway:
  Used to handle communication between the SAP system and the mobile devices that the SAP Fiori user interfaces run on.
- SAP Smart Business:
  Used as a framework for reporting the key figures we saw in Chapter 1.

> **Checklist for SAP installation**
>
>  Because more and more information is added on the basis of each SAP S/4 Finance project, use the Excel checklist in SAP Note 2157996[16] to inform the project teams of the main concerns prior to installation.

Once you have installed the relevant software, you can find the relevant migration/conversion guides for each release, as listed here:

- SAP S/4HANA Finance:
  http://help.sap.com/saphelp_sfin200/helpdata/en/87/2f6152b82bf35fe 10000000a423f68/frameset.htm
- SAP S/4HANA:
  https://uacp.hana.ondemand.com/http.svc/rc/PRODUCTION/pdfe6 8bfa55e988410ee10000000a441470/1511%20000/en-US/CONV_ OP1511.pdf

4.4 Customizing

Once you have installed the latest software updates, you have access to the IMG shown in Figure 4.4. This is a change from the *Migration Cockpit* used to migrate to the new G/L. You do not have to wait until the end of a fiscal year—you can perform the steps listed in the IMG at any time.

---

[16] SAP Note 2157996: "SAP Simple Finance, on-premise edition: Checklist for Technical Installation / Upgrade" (*https://launchpad.support.sap.com/#/notes/0002157996*)

Figure 4.4: IMG showing preparatory activities for the migration

We will now walk you through the critical Customizing settings that you need to configure prior to a migration.

4.4.1 General Ledger Accounting

If you refer back to Figure 4.2, you will notice that there are two potential sources for general ledger data—SAP ERP General Ledger Accounting (new G/L) and classic General Ledger Accounting. Bear in mind that a conversion to the universal journal is not the same as a new G/L migration; a conversion to the universal journal converts **every** document in the system, while a new G/L migration takes place on a key date.

Figure 4.5: Customizing settings for General Ledger Accounting

Figure 4.5 shows the various checks needed prior to a migration of the General Ledger.

1. All financial applications must use the same *fiscal year variant* because every application has to have the same periods. Therefore, you have to make sure that every company code has the same fiscal year variant as the controlling area.

2. Because you are merging documents from Accounting and Controlling during the migration, you may be taking currencies such as the controlling area currency that was previously only available in Controlling and moving it to the universal journal.

3. Make sure that the settings for your ledgers are correct. If you are coming from SAP ERP General Ledger Accounting, the system migrates your existing settings. However, if you are using classic General Ledger Accounting, you have to create at least one ledger.

4. We discussed the ledger and currency settings in Chapter 2, Section 2.2.4. You have to decide whether you have use cases that require you to implement an extension ledger. With effect from edition 1602, you have the option to set additional currencies (up to eight new currencies in addition to the local currency and group currency). Therefore, draw up a list of the relevant currency settings for each of your ledgers along with the exchange rate types.

5. Prior to the migration all controlling data is stored with reference to a *version* rather than a ledger, so at the very least, you have to assign version 0 to the relevant ledger. If you are also using group valuation or profit center valuation, you have to map the versions you currently use for this valuation to the appropriate ledger.

6. Going forward you will effectively be performing reposting transactions in the general ledger. Therefore, you may wish to define additional document types to identify the journal entries for each of the Controlling business transactions. A new document type CO is delivered as a default but you may want to add others with the appropriate number ranges and authorizations. You then link these with the appropriate Controlling business transaction (such as RKU1 for reposting).

7. How you migrate your balances in the general ledger will depend on whether you have used SAP ERP General Ledger Accounting since your initial implementation or migrated to it. A migration to the universal journal migrates all the totals, those in both GLT0 (classic) and in FAGL-FLEXT (new).

8. If you are using cost of sales accounting, you have to make sure that the settings for filling your functional areas are correct.

9. Because some of the code needed within SAP S/4HANA was contained within business functions in previous releases, your administrator has to activate the following business functions prior to migration:

   - EA-FIN (Financials Extension)
   - FIN_GL_CI_1 (Enhancements to the new G/L)
   - FIN_GL_CI_2 (Enhancements to the new G/L)
   - FIN_GL_CI_3 (Enhancements to the new G/L)

In addition to the configuration settings, it makes sense to check your master data because the profit centers, functional areas, and so on in your Controlling master data determine how the documents are enriched during the migration.

If you are coming from SAP ERP General Ledger Accounting (new G/L), then you may already be using different ledgers for each of your accounting principles and *document splitting* to fill the segments and profit centers for balance sheet reporting. This information will be included in the migration and you will be able to carry on as before. If you are coming from classic General Ledger Accounting, then your system does not have these features yet.

With SAP S/4HANA 1709, new functions were delivered to support the addition of a **new ledger** and to perform document splitting for historic documents.

4.4.2 Controlling and Profitability Analysis

The Controlling settings for the migration are essentially concerned with Profitability Analysis, as shown in Figure 4.6.

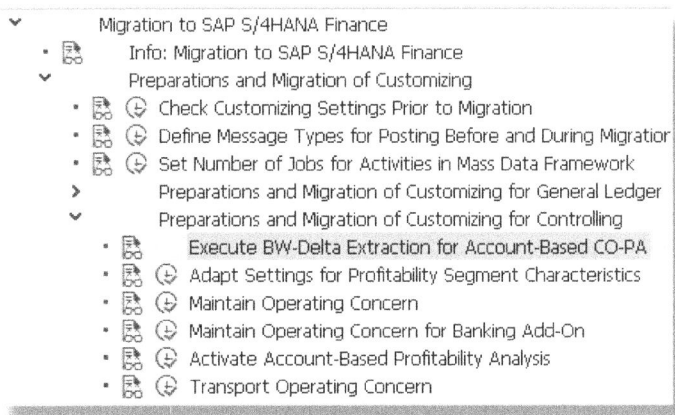

Figure 4.6: Customizing settings for Controlling

As discussed in Chapter 2, the universal journal contains columns for each of the characteristics in the operating concern. If you are already using account-based Profitability Analysis, the only thing you need to know is that **all characteristics** in the operating concern are available to you (there is no longer a transaction to reduce account-based Profitability Analysis to a subset of the characteristics in costing-based Profitability Analysis). If you are already using costing-based Profitability Analysis, provided that you flag the operating concern as relevant for account-based Profitability Analysis, the migration adds columns for each of the characteristics in your operating concern to the universal journal.

Note, however, that account-based Profitability Analysis will only be updated **going forward**. The historic data in the transactional tables for costing-based Profitability Analysis (tables CE1) will **not** be migrated to the universal journal. Therefore, following migration, you will see pre-existing revenue line items in the granularity of the general ledger (company code, profit center, and so on) rather than with an assignment to products, customers, and so on. If you are new to Profitability Analysis, then clearly you need to prepare a list of the characteristics that you want to report on and document where they come from (invoice, settlement, and so on) and what extra derivations you will be performing to enrich this data (such as deriving a product hierarchy from the product sold or setting up real time derivation to derive CO-PA characteristics from the cost center, order, or WBS element as we saw in Chapter 2).

In this situation, you will also generally have sales documents that were created prior to the migration but that have not yet been fulfilled. One of the changes with the move to Margin Analysis, which we saw in Chapter 2, is that the delivery generates a posting for the cost of goods sold with an assignment to the market segment and updates a cost element (account type P) rather than a G/L account (account type N). To avoid issues in the transition period, adjust your material account determination to assign an account of type N to account modification VAX, and an account of type P to account modification VAY.

4.4.3 Asset Accounting

As discussed in Chapter 2, new Asset Accounting is no longer an optional business function (FIN_AA_PARALLEL_VAL) as it was in SAP Enhancement Package 7 for SAP ERP 6.0, where it worked in combination with SAP ERP General Ledger Accounting—it is **compulsory** in SAP S/4HANA Finance. Figure 4.7 shows the customizing settings for Asset Accounting.

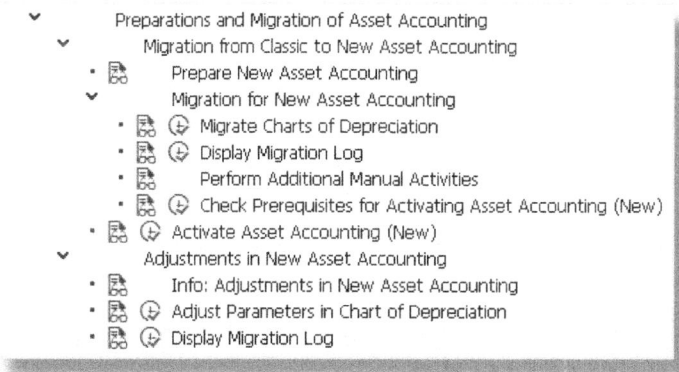

Figure 4.7: Customizing settings for Asset Accounting

As you go into the blueprinting phase, make sure that you have a clear understanding of the new posting logic in Asset Accounting:

▶ Start by listing your existing *charts of depreciation* and understanding how they map to the various accounting principles you are using (if you use more than one) and how these are represented as ledgers.

- ▶ Decide for which accounting principles you are able to post in real time and how this update to the general ledger will work.
- ▶ Determine which charts of depreciation (if any) only need to post periodically.

4.4.4 Accrual engine

Accruals are periodic postings created by the accrual engine in SAP ERP. These are created with reference to an accrual object, such as an insurance contract or employee stock options, in a separate sub-ledger (ACEPSOIT table). The goal of the migration is to enrich the associated journal entries with the details from the accrual sub-ledger. The migration process handles manual accruals created within the accrual engine, but does not touch the following accrual types which continue to use the SAP ERP accrual engine:

- ▶ Real Estate Management
- ▶ Grants Management
- ▶ Intellectual Properties Management
- ▶ Provisions for Outgoing Royalties

The migration process converts both the customizing settings for the accruals engine and the existing accruals postings. It runs separately from the Accounting and Controlling migrations, so you can perform the switch at a different time to the general migration to SAP S/4HANA Finance.

4.5 Migration steps

One of the first technical steps in the migration is that the former totals tables that we looked at in Chapter 1 are converted into SAP Core Data Service (CDS) views (the compatibility views). As we discussed in Chapter 2, **before** you run this step you need to understand which of your function modules currently update these tables (read statements do not matter) and which interfaces call these tables from outside the system (including ALE scenarios). Do not forget to also check for tools such as SLT which read these tables at database level rather than by function module.

The basic steps of the migration are essentially similar in each release:

- Merge cost elements into the chart of accounts
- Enrich data (add profit centers, functional areas, and so on)
- Migrate line items into the universal journal
- Migrate balances

These various steps are included in one migration task monitor (START AND MONITOR DATA MIGRATION) that can be accessed together with documentation of the separate steps in the various separate menu entries (see Figure 4.8). Take the time to read the documentation for each of these steps as you approach the migration.

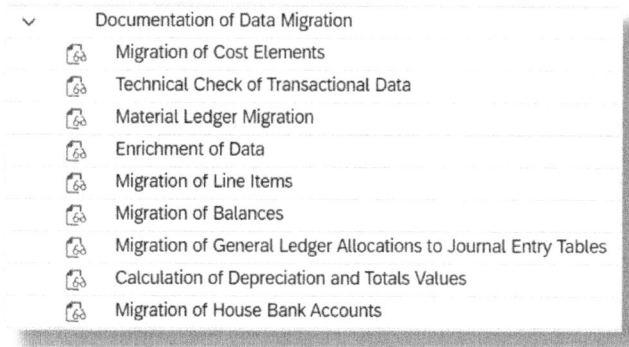

Figure 4.8: IMG for data migration

Note that because the steps of the migration are so critical, the recommendation is to perform test migrations on a **copy** of the existing system in order to identify issues before moving into the migration proper. Generally, the work with a cloned system is iterative until you have identified and solved all barriers to the conversion.

4.5.1 Migrating cost elements

As we saw in Chapter 2, during the migration the system creates new G/L accounts for all secondary cost elements and adjusts the account type and updates the cost element category for all primary cost elements. Before you start, you should check that you do not have any rogue primary cost elements without an associated G/L account. You should also check that the secondary cost elements are correct before you generate G/L accounts during the migration. If you have not already used transaction OKB9 to enter default account assignments, the system creates default account assignments based on the cost centers and orders entered in your existing cost elements. Figure 4.9 shows the result of migrating the secondary cost elements in one of the SAP demo systems (which is why the number of migrated cost elements is fairly small). You can see details of the items processed by double-clicking on the relevant line. You will find equivalent check reports for each of the steps in the migration.

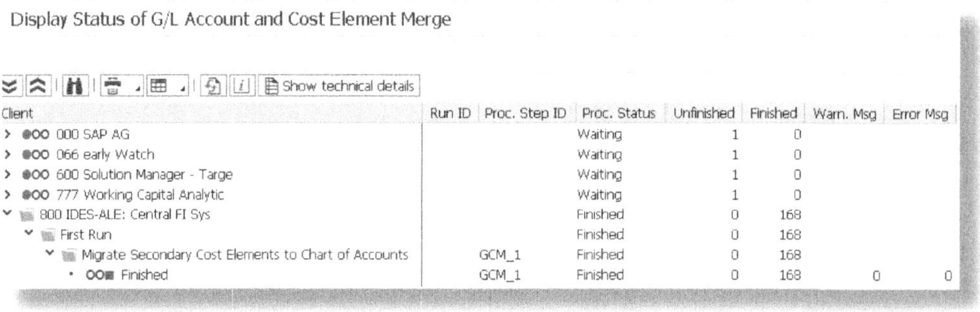

Figure 4.9: Status report for merging the G/L account and cost elements (1503 edition)

4.5.2 Enriching actual data

In Chapter 2, we talked about how the relevant reporting dimensions are written to the universal journal. Wherever possible, the migration process fills these fields as if the relevant data had always been there—this is what SAP means by the idea of enriching actual data. Therefore, going into a migration, you might have been running Profit Center Accounting as a separate ledger but the migration will need to assign profit centers to the relevant line items in the universal journal by reading the appropriate assignments in the cost centers, orders, WBS elements, and so on. In other words, the migration will freshly derive the relevant profit centers for the underlying documents rather than migrating existing profit center documents.

In Chapter 2, we looked at how the CO object is "unpacked" to fill the ACCAS and ACCASTY fields (shown in Figure 2.20) along with the relevant fields for the cost center, order, WBS element, and so on. For historical data, the migration process unpacks the object number and updates the account assignment type and the account assignment. Technically, a cost center that was stored as object number KS10000000001000, for example, fills the fields ACCOUNT ASSIGNMENT TYPE (ACCASTY)=KS, CONTROLLING AREA (KOKRS) = 1000, and COST CENTER (KOSTL) = 1000 during the migration and it is the new fields that are displayed using the Fiori reports.

4.5.3 Migrating line items

With the migration of the line items from the various transactional tables, the idea of the universal journal becomes **reality**. The system brings together, into a **single journal entry**, the line items that represent a single business transaction but were separated in the example of an asset posting into an Asset Accounting document, a Controlling document and a General Ledger Accounting document or in the example of a goods movement into a Material Ledger document, a Controlling document and a General Ledger Accounting document. It is not just a question of merging data from different storage points but also of bringing all the data relating to one business transaction to the same granularity—for example, a posting for ten assets might impact four cost centers and only two G/L accounts. The result will be ten asset line items that also include the relevant cost centers and account and offsetting account. Refer back to the migration source shown in Figure 4.1 and Figure 4.2 to see how to recognize the source of each migrated document. Clearly, this is the most challenging step in the migration. Figure 4.10 gives you an impression of the migrated tables in a small demo system.

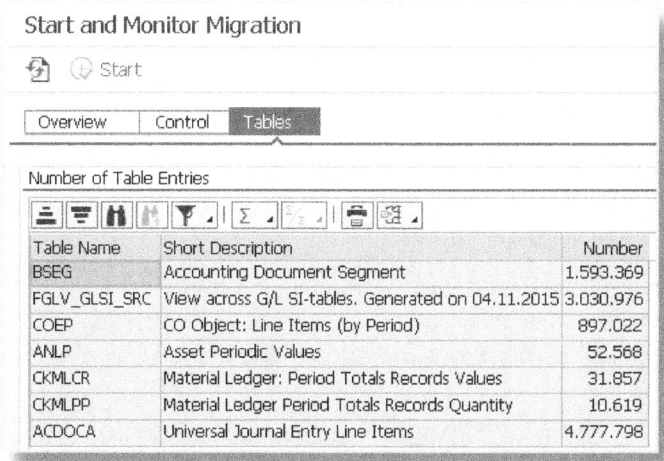

Figure 4.10: Table entries handled during a migration

4.5.4 Migrating balances

Executing the MIGRATION OF BALANCES step in the IMG ensures that where line items had been archived such that the sum of the line items does not match the associated entry in the totals table, a *correction posting* is created. These entries will only contain a handful of reporting dimensions because the totals tables do not contain many fields and the system cannot invent information when the supporting line item has been removed. Again, refer back to Figure 4.2 to understand how to later recognize such migrated totals. This step is necessary to ensure that the financial documents can be audited. It also ensures that processes such as results analysis and settlement, which consider the life time of an individual order or project rather than a specific accounting period, will find all the data that they need for further processing.

Another shift in the new data model is that the balance carryforward values can no longer be stored in the totals tables. The migration creates a new document to represent the balance carryforward.

4.5.5 Migrating depreciation values

In terms of project planning, you do not have to wait until SAP S/4HANA to activate new Asset Accounting; you can switch it on earlier if you are already using SAP ERP General Ledger Accounting with the ledger solution.

4.5.6 Migrating the Material Ledger

As of SAP S/4HANA 1511, you have to perform this step even if you did not use the Material Ledger or Actual Costing in the past. For further information, refer to the following SAP notes:

- ▶ SAP Note 2332591—"S4TWL – Technical Changes in Material Ledger", which can be found at: *https://launchpad.support.sap.com/#/notes/0002332591*. This walks you through the steps in the process in edition 1511.

- ▶ SAP Note 2352383—"S4TWL – Conversion to S/4HANA 1610 Material Ledger and Actual Costing", available at: *https://launchpad.support.sap.com/#/notes/0002352383*. This note walks you through the steps in the process in edition 1610.

4.5.7 Partitioning the universal journal table

Partitioning is a key element of the HANA story in that data is divided into *hot data* that is readily accessible and *cold data* that is not kept in memory. This means that during migration, the system sorts the data into the correct category and sets the flag for data aging, as shown in Figure 4.1. For more advice about partitioning and performance, refer to SAP Note 2289491[17].

4.5.8 SAP Core Data Service (CDS) views

CDS views with the same name as the old tables are created during the migration for the index tables and totals tables that we discussed in Chapter 1. The data that is no longer required is moved to back-up tables—if you refer back to Figure 1.2, you will see that the field names for Table GLT0 now end in _BCK. Similar views are created for all the totals tables and index tables that we discussed in Chapter 1, Section 1.3.1.

CDS views are also created for all the transactional tables made redundant by the move to the universal journal. To understand this, let us think about what happens to the controlling line item table COEP. During migration, the system creates an equivalent view V_COEP for table COEP and redirects all select statements to V_COEP instead of COEP. When a program calls the old table COEP, V_COEP is used to aggregate the data in the relevant journal entries from the universal journal.

4.6 Activities after migration

If you refer back to the steps shown in Figure 4.8, you will see that there are a number of steps to be performed once the migration has completed.

These include the following:

- Moving deleted index tables into cold store partitions
- Filling out due dates in FI documents

---

[17] SAP Note 2289491: "Best Practices for Partitioning of Finance Tables" (*https://launchpad.support.sap.com/#/notes/2289491*)

- Filling clearing accounts
- Deactivating the reconciliation ledger because it is no longer needed

While many SAP ERP customers have already successfully migrated to SAP S/4HANA, others have chosen not to migrate. Instead, they have set up a separate SAP S/4HANA system that collects accounting data from multiple systems in a new structure; this option is Central Finance. We will explore this next, before we look at how to perform group reporting (or consolidation) in SAP S/4HANA.

5 Deploying Central Finance

If you have a system landscape that comprises multiple ERP systems, Central Finance can provide an alternative to migrating each of the separate systems to SAP S/4HANA Finance. Any SAP S/4HANA Finance system can be deployed as a Central Finance system provided you set up the appropriate connections between the central system and the sending systems. The advantage of this approach is that you can experiment with the new finance structures without making significant changes to your existing system landscape.

The idea behind Central Finance is that it provides a *central reporting layer* which collects accounting information from each of the sending systems. It can therefore provide the base layer for your consolidation, planning, and much of your management reporting. You can also implement the cash and treasury functions to work on the same system instance. Of course, the use of Central Finance and a data warehouse are not mutually exclusive: you can extract data from the universal journal to SAP BW using the SAP S/4HANA Finance extractor (DataSource: 0FI_ACDOCA_10) which includes all relevant fields for reporting from the universal journal.

Central Finance is available as of SAP S/4HANA Finance 1503. You can access the documentation via *http://help.sap.com/saphelp_sfin200/helpdata/en /48/57c0540cf5ef05e10000000a4450e5/frameset.htm* and frequently asked questions can be found in SAP Note 2184567[18].

5.1 Replication approach for documents

As you post each accounting document in the local system, this triggers the creation of a **new** financial document in the central system that links back to the original document in the sending system. The document in the Central Finance system is effectively a **shadow** of the original financial document.

This might sound like the sort of thing that has been going on in data warehouses for years, but the difference is that this approach is **document-based**. Every document runs through the same master data checks and

---

[18] SAP Note 2184567: "Central Finance: Frequently Asked Questions" (*https://launchpad.support.sap.com/#/notes/0002184567*)

validations as a normal journal entry that is processed by the accounting interface and carries with it a link back to the sending system.

In order to allow these checks and validations, you have to create master data in the Central Finance system for all the organizational units (controlling areas, companies, company codes, plants, and so on) and all the master data (cost centers, profit centers, materials, customers, vendors, and so on) for which you will be transferring transactional data.

The easiest way to understand this is to look at an example. Figure 5.1 shows a sample journal entry for DOCUMENT NUMBER 100000000 in COMPANY CODE 3000 and FISCAL YEAR 2016. The document looks like a normal journal entry except that if you navigate to the DOCUMENT HEADER, you can see that it was originally created as DOCUMENT NUMBER 100037384 in COMPANY CODE 3000 and FISCAL YEAR 2016 in the sender system (ECN_00_000). The document has not been cloned but **reposted** in the central system, while keeping that all-important audit link back to the local system.

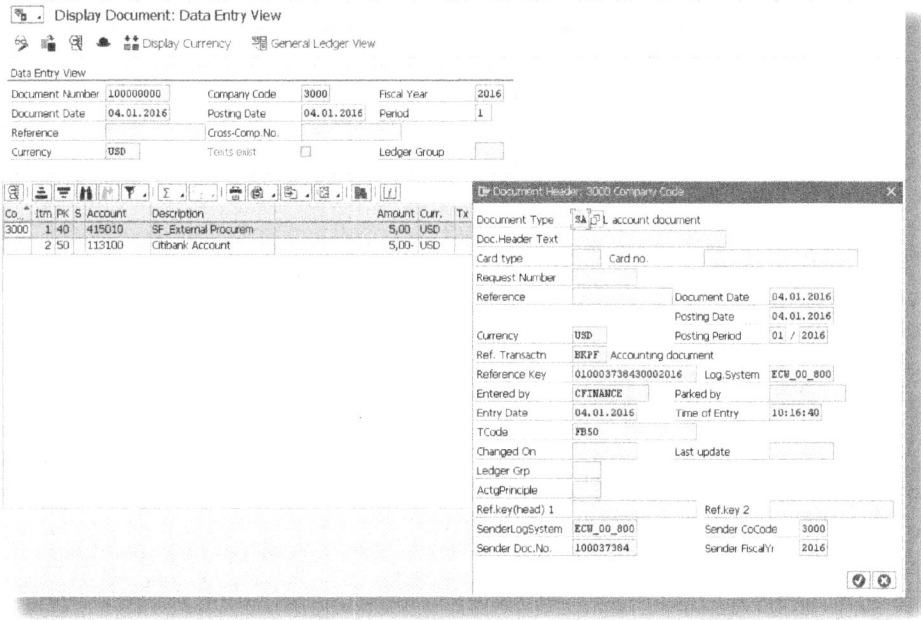

Figure 5.1: Journal entry in Central Finance

The idea that the document is reposted might make you fear that system reconciliation could become a major headache, but if you call up the Do-

CUMENT RELATIONSHIP BROWSER as shown in Figure 5.2, you will see a different example of a journal entry in which the ACCOUNTING DOCUMENT in the central system is 1400000058 in FISCAL YEAR 2016 and the original ACCOUNTING DOCUMENT in the local system is 4900000057 in FISCAL YEAR 2016. The system uses the links we saw in Figure 5.1 not just to link the source document and its shadow document in the central system but also to display the material document, delivery document, sales order, and so on associated with the original document. This involves making a *remote function call* to the local system to call up all pertinent documents that explain the accounting document in the central system. Auditors and managers reporting from the central system have access to exactly the same information as users looking at the accounting document in the local system. SAP delivers standard RFCs to make such calls to SAP ERP systems. If the sending system is a non-SAP system, then a *user exit* can be implemented to pass parameters and call the document details in the sending systems.

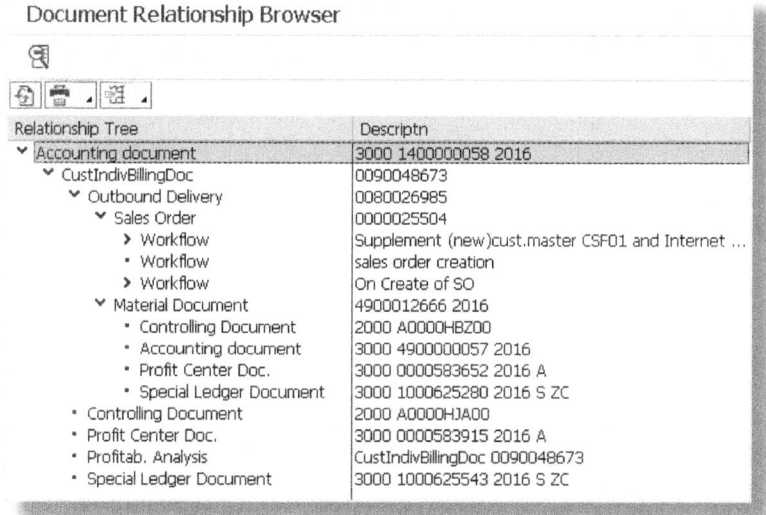

Figure 5.2: Document Relationship Browser showing the audit trail to original documents in the sender system

5.1.1 Master data

In these examples, the shadow accounting document in the central system was more or less a **copy** of the original accounting document. However, one of the advantages of this approach is that you can transform the reporting entities in the accounting document—for example, you might map your local accounts to a new set of group accounts in the central system or harmonize your cost centers via *mapping tables* as you post the document. This transformation can take place as each of the accounting documents is posted rather being a major data cleansing exercise at period close, bringing you closer to the idea of a real-time close. This master data can also form the basis for consolidation, so be sure to understand the entities for which you currently perform eliminations as you design your Central Finance approach.

As you build up your document design, you need to distinguish between entities that are being **passed on** within the accounting document and potentially transformed via mapping tables (organizational units, accounts, cost centers, customers, and so on) and entities that can be **derived** afresh in the central system if required (such as profit centers or CO-PA characteristics). It is also possible to transfer orders and projects and it is important to decide whether you want a 1:1 relationship between the local and central orders or whether you want to post multiple local production orders to a single internal order or product cost collector in the central system. But before we look at the business details, let us first look at the high-level system landscape.

5.2 System landscape

Figure 5.3 shows a high-level architecture of the Central Finance approach. In Figure 5.1 and Figure 5.2, we looked at a journal entry that was created in the Central Finance instance as a **shadow** of an accounting document created in a local instance of SAP ERP. The sending system can be on any version of SAP ERP, and therefore, many customers are actually leaving these systems on fairly old versions of the software. The sending system can also be the latest version of SAP S/4HANA, however. The sender systems do not even need to be SAP systems at all, and plenty of projects are underway to bring accounting data from non-SAP ERP systems into the Central Finance instance. Stay abreast of changes by following SAP Note 2148893[19].

---

[19] SAP Note 2148893: "Central Finance: Implementation and Configuration" (*https://launchpad.support.sap.com/#/notes/0002148893*)

Deploying Central Finance

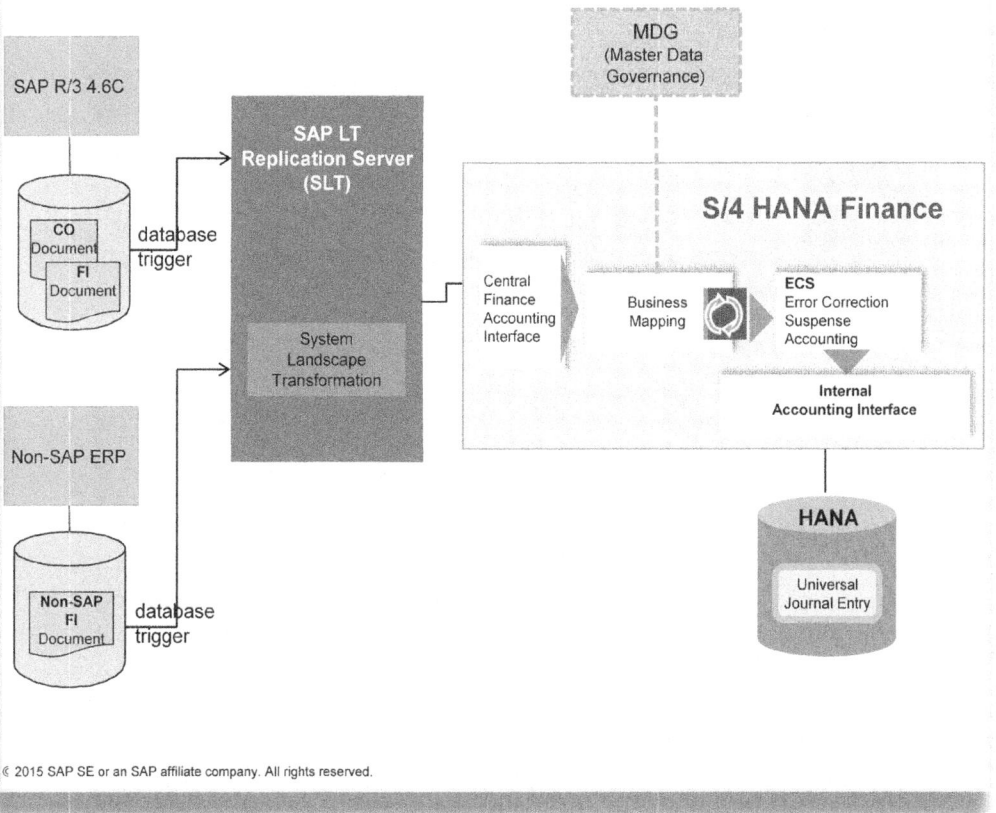

Figure 5.3 Central Finance architecture

5.2.1 SAP Landscape Transformation

As we can see in Figure 5.3., the system connections are made via SAP Landscape Transformation (SAP LT)—the middle box in the diagram. SLT works at the database level, so while you can connect and read tables from SAP systems, it is relatively easy to connect non-SAP systems to your Central Finance instance because only the database of the non-SAP system needs to be accessed, rather than the application. This means that you do not need to make modifications to the application server of the sender system. You can install the SLT software as a separate system on top of any of the source systems or the Central Finance system. To make the connections you have to make sure that the add-on DMIS 2011_1_700 or higher is installed on both the source and the target systems (Support Package [SP]

141

08 is recommended) and that you have implemented SAP Note 2124481[20] on these systems.

> **Administration Guide**
>
>  For more details on the system landscape and setting up the necessary connections, you can refer to the Administration Guide for Central Finance available on the SAP Service Marketplace, provided that you have a log-on for the SAP Service Marketplace:
>
> *https://service.sap.com/~sapidb/012002523100007722892015E/SFIN_ CF_INST_GUIDE.PDF*

5.2.2 Master data governance

Because clean master data is a key element of the Central Finance approach, it is also a good idea to consider *master data governance* as part of the project. This does not mean that all the associated systems have to have consistent master data (this is very rarely the case). However, note the Central Finance Accounting Interface in Figure 5.3, which enables you to harmonize master data between systems by setting up mapping tables or, if you use SAP Master Data Governance for distributing master data, then you can reuse the entries in the SAP Master Data Governance tool. What happens then is that as the document is prepared and checked for posting in the central system, the local reporting dimensions can be switched in accordance with the mapping tables. You can also run additional derivation steps (for example, if you want to fill the profit center) and make substitutions before the document is passed to the accounting interface.

As well as mapping master data, you also have to consider what happens when the master data is not available in the central system. This might happen if you are sending a cost center that does not yet exist in the central system. If this is the case, the documents containing that cost center are parked in a *message list* for subsequent correction.

---

[20] SAP Note 2124481: "SLT SP 08, Correction 3" (*https://launchpad.support.sap.com/#/ notes/0002124481*)

To get an idea of all the implementation steps associated with Central Finance, take a look at Figure 5.4, which shows the Implementation Guide for Central Finance which is available in all SAP S/4HANA Finance systems. This means that you can also run Central Finance in a hybrid mode, where the SAP S/4HANA Finance system is the system of record for some of the journal entries but not for others, allowing you to bring data from newly acquired companies into the SAP instance quickly and efficiently.

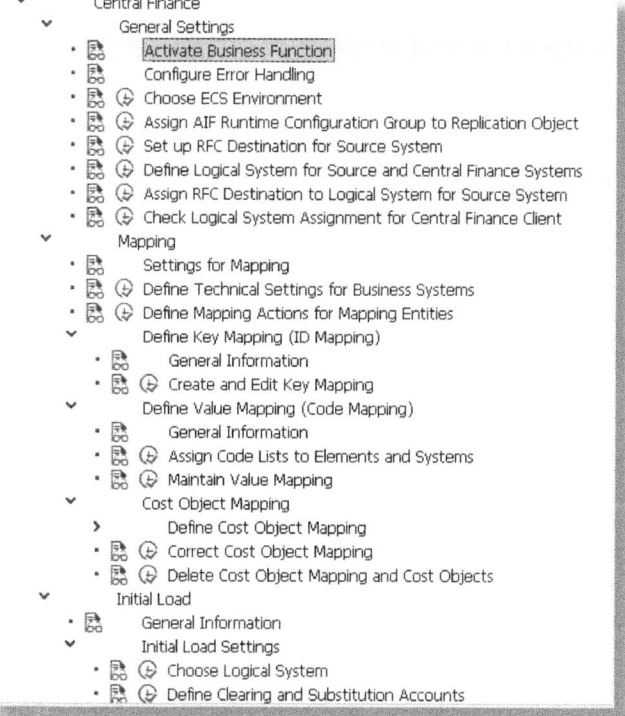

Figure 5.4: Implementation Guide for Central Finance

Start in the GENERAL SETTINGS section by having your administrator activate the business function FINS_CFIN (Central Finance). The use of this business function has license implications so make sure that the appropriate licensing arrangements are in place.

In SAP S/4 HANA Finance 1503, Error Correction and Suspense Accounting was used to handle any journal entries arriving with master data for which no equivalent was available in Central Finance. In subsequent editions, SAP Application Interface Framework is used to handle errors.

143

You also need to work with your system administrators to set up your system landscape. You need:

- RFC destinations for each sender system:
  We used an RFC (remote function call) to recreate the audit trail for the accounting documents shown in Figure 5.2. You also use RFCs during the initial data load and to create the mappings between the master data (including projects) in each of the linked systems.
- Logical systems:
  The *logical system* acts as a unique identifier for each system in your landscape. You can see the name of the field in the SENDER-LOGSYSTEM field in Figure 5.1.

We will look at the initial data load in Section 5.2.9, but before we do that, we will explain the accounting interface and how to set up the master data you need before you can post an accounting document.

5.2.3 Accounting interface for Central Finance

The key difference between Central Finance and a data warehouse is that the Central Finance approach is **document-based** and all documents are posted via the accounting interface. If the connected system is an SAP system, then you effectively read table ACCIT where the raw data for a document is stored before the accounting document is created via the accounting interface in the local system. The reason you do this rather than transferring the complete accounting document **after** posting is that all the **detail** is still available in the interface. As we discussed earlier, if the invoice contains so many items that it hits the 999 line item limit in BSEG, the local system is set up to **summarize** the material column to reduce the number of line items in order to allow posting. If you pick up the entry in ACCIT, then you can transfer all the posting line items from the invoice to the central system. The invoice contains sales conditions that are used in costing-based CO-PA but these do not appear in the accounting document because posting line items are only created for those conditions that are mapped to G/L accounts and the other line items are rejected. If you use SAP ERP General Ledger Accounting, you effectively send the entry view and document splitting is performed in the central system.

Figure 5.5 shows the new transfer structure for the accounting documents. We have called up the new development package FIN_CFIN_INTEGRATION and the header table CFIN_ACCHD that will act as the trigger for the transfer of the relevant accounting documents. Note that the tables listed on the left do not just include the accounting document itself but also the profitability segments that will be needed for a posting to CO-PA, a cost component split if you are valuing your cost of goods sold with the standard costs from a cost estimate, withholding tax, clearing information, and so on. Assuming that your local systems are not yet on SAP S/4HANA, you also need to set up a database trigger to read the CO documents from table COBK (if the local system is already on SAP S/4HANA Finance, then secondary costs will be part of the universal journal). If you plan to do order controlling or cost object controlling, you need to set up a database trigger to read new order master records from table AUFK. Note that these tables contain the **transactional data**. All related master data has to be in place **before** you start to trigger postings for the transactional data because the postings are validated against this master data.

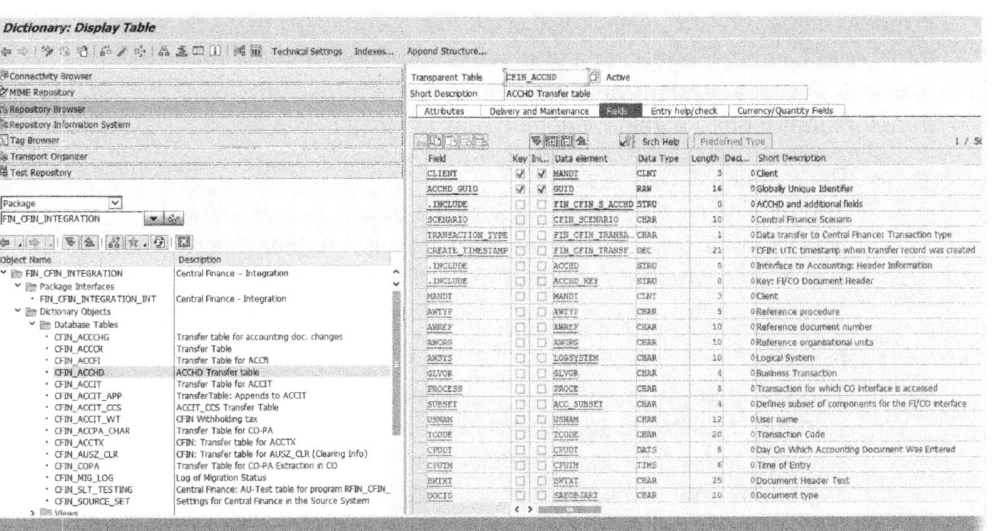

Figure 5.5: Transfer structure for accounting documents

SAP Landscape Transformation uses the database trigger to identify the existence of a record to be transferred to Central Finance. This is a largely technical step. The business logic takes place in the interface, where the accounting document is subjected to exactly the same checks as if it were being posted directly as a result of a business transaction in the central system. This means that checks are performed to check that all the organizational data exists (controlling area, company code, and so on) along with the accounts, the account assignment (cost center, order, project, and so on) and any other data needed for the posting (such as the tax settings or an activity type). Setting up this master data can require significant data cleansing but it means that the quality of the data in your Central Finance instance is likely to be better than the quality in a typical data warehouse.

Now that we have explained the basic idea of the Central Finance interface, we will look at the mapping options for the master data, assuming that you do not want a 1:1 relationship between each item of master data.

5.2.4 Value mapping for organizational data

If you refer back to the transfer structure shown in Figure 5.5, then the easiest way to create a document is simply to post a copy of that document in the central system as we did in Figure 5.1. Doing this means that you miss a huge opportunity to **harmonize** a heterogeneous finance landscape. It makes sense to start with a list of all the parameters that you want to transfer to Central Finance and to use this to understand the relationships between the local system and the central system. In terms of global parameters that require a value mapping, this list might include:

- Participating Countries:
  You have to create master data for the countries and make sure that you prepare a list of any country-specific reporting requirements and decide whether in future these will be met in the local or in the central system.

- Participating Companies:
  The companies are the basis for consolidation so instead of considering the companies in isolation, think about the relationships between these trading partners and specifically, how you are going to perform intercompany reconciliation centrally and how you will handle the sequence of implementation for any intercompany relationships.

- Participating Company Codes:
  As you define the settings for the company code, it becomes clear that you are dealing not simply with a reporting layer but rather you are defining key settings for the chart of accounts and the fiscal year variant. You do this using the same IMG steps as you would for a company code for which the Central Finance instance is the system of record.

- Number of Ledgers:
  You need a ledger for each accounting principle and must make sure that you take account of the new currency options that we discussed in Chapter 2.

▶ Controlling Area:
This setting controls the fiscal year variant, the chart of accounts (do not forget the secondary cost elements), and the group currency. It also controls which components are active and thus which account assignments are updated (cost center, order, project, and so on).

▶ Operating Concern:
This setting controls the CO-PA dimensions that you use centrally. This may be a subset of all the dimensions you have in the local systems and should be harmonized so that the reporting dimensions are consistent across the world.

These global parameters are usually handled using *value mapping* in Central Finance. This approach is also used for Customizing settings that are usually set up at the start of a project and then remain stable, such as the dunning areas and payment terms for a customer. You can define these in the IMG (see Figure 5.4) under MAPPING • SETTINGS FOR MAPPING. Figure 5.6 gives you an idea of the number of entities that can be covered in Central Finance.

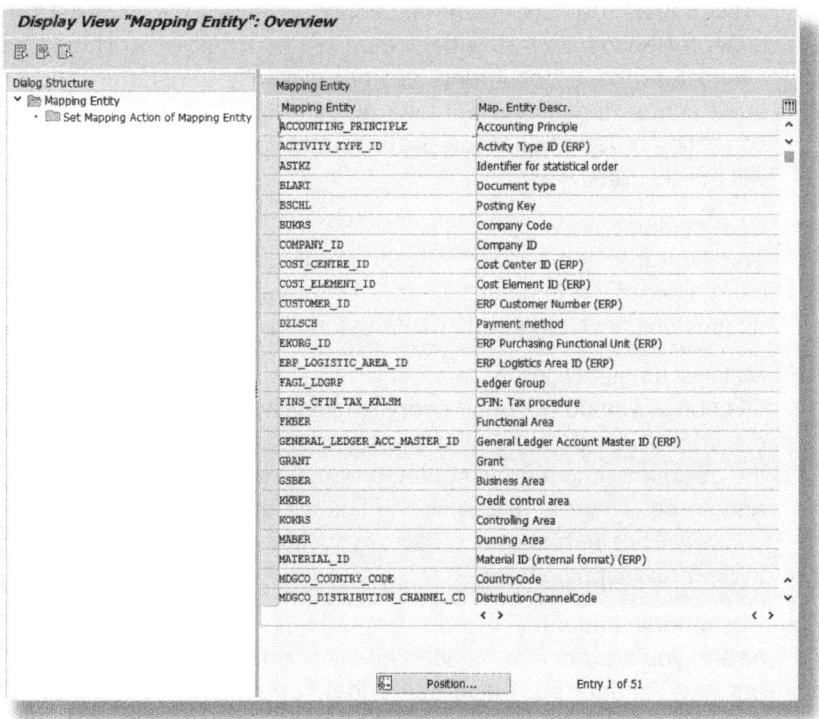

Figure 5.6: Mapping entities for global parameters and master data in Central Finance

147

5.2.5 Key mapping for master data

By contrast, the master data is usually handled via *key mapping*. The case for Central Finance often goes hand in hand with a case for better master data governance, so this topic needs to be handled properly. Again, you will probably want to draw up a list that includes:

- ▶ G/L accounts:
  Start with the trial balance for each relevant country and then include the secondary cost elements (unless the sending system is an SAP S/4HANA Finance system). Then decide if you want a 1:1 transfer or if you need to set up mapping tables to bring your entries into a single chart of accounts.

- ▶ Profit centers and segments:
  You do not have to run Profit Center Accounting in the local systems—you can also derive the profit centers afresh in the central system provided you set up the relevant master data (cost centers, materials, orders, and so on) needed for the derivation. Note that the profit center is only transferred in the document if the sending system uses SAP ERP General Ledger Accounting. If you run Profit Center Accounting as a dedicated ledger locally, you should be aware that these documents are not currently transferred and all profit center derivations will take place in the central system. Any correction or reclassification postings that you perform in ledger 8A will not be transferred.

- ▶ Cost centers:
  This is probably the most critical item of master data after the account because it is used to derive so many of the other reporting dimensions, including profit centers, functional areas, and so on.

- ▶ Material master records:
  Of course, you do not need every single view in the material master record, but you do need all the assignments for reporting, including the assignment to a profit center, product hierarchy, material group, and so on. There is also a strong chance that the material master codes will not be harmonized across systems and that you will need to perform mapping here.

- ▶ Customers/vendors:
  Again, you are not interested in all the master data for the customers and vendors but those items that you need for intercompany reconciliation and to derive CO-PA characteristics for reporting.

Once you have your list of master data, you need to decide where you can define a 1:1 transfer from the sending system and where you need to perform key mapping as shown in Figure 5.7. Here, you see a simple mapping of the customers from the local system (ECW_800) to the central system (ECNCLNT800). You should create key mappings for all those entities that are added on a regular basis, such as vendors, customers, materials, and G/L accounts. The most common mapping type is a *pair mapping*, in which account A in the local system maps to account B in Central Finance. To prepare this pair mapping, use the Web Dynpro application MDG_BS_WD_ID_MATCH_SERVICE. Where you need a more complicated mapping, consider using the BAdI BADI_FINS_CFIN_MAPPING_RULE to implement the required logic.

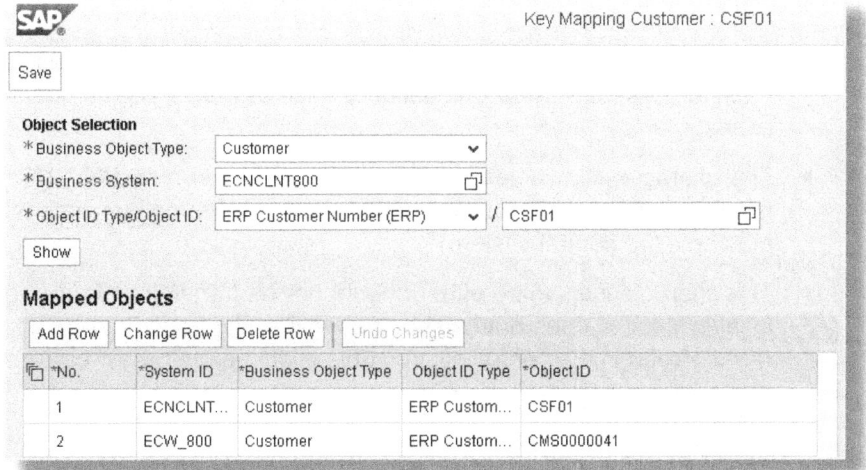

Figure 5.7: Key mapping for customers in a Central Finance instance

Because Central Finance uses the universal journal, make sure that you consider the CO-PA characteristics in your master data lists and understand how the derivations work and where you want to perform a validation to ensure that the relevant master data exists. In your local system, the CO-PA characteristics for the various dimensions are stored in table CE4 and are always read in combination with the transactional table (CE1 for costing-based Profitability Analysis and COEP for account-based Profitability Analysis). In Chapter 2, we saw that the universal journal includes a column for each characteristic in your operating concern. The decision as to which characteristics to use for reporting becomes more critical in Central Finance because many organizations have built operating concerns that are specific to individual countries or lines of business and struggle to consolidate the different reporting entities. The challenge is to understand how the standard fields have been used in terms of naming conventions and so on and to understand how company-specific characteristics are derived. Do not forget that the limit of 60 characteristics for an operating concern still applies because table CE4 continues to be updated.

As you think about transferring the characteristics, refer back to Figure 5.5 and note the transfer structure CFIN_ACCPA_CHAR, which is used to transfer CO-PA characteristics between systems. Although you can potentially transfer all the relevant characteristics from the local system, the technical name for the combination of characteristics, field PAOBJNR, will be different in each system because you are creating a new document by reposting. There are three ways of transferring characteristics from the local system:

- The characteristic values are the **same** in both systems (this is often the case for organizational units such as plants and company codes)
- The characteristic values require **mapping** between systems (this might be the case if you are harmonizing codes for the material master in the central system)
- The characteristic value either should not be transferred from the local system or does not exist in the local system and is to be **derived afresh** in the central system (this might be the case if you are assigning products to new product hierarchies in the central system)

5.2.6 Mapping cost objects for transactional objects

Before you can post costs by order, you have to make sure that the master data for these cost objects is available in the central system. This need not be a problem for long-living internal orders that behave much like cost centers, but many orders are extremely dynamic and we often find production orders, process orders, and maintenance orders that are created and closed on the same day. Clearly, creating the master data for such orders before you start is not practical because it would involve the creation of new orders on a daily basis. Instead, Central Finance enables you to set up product cost collectors to collect the costs of the many production orders or keep a 1:1 relationship between cost objects if you prefer. The various options are delivered as *scenarios*. The key point here is that the master data for the orders and product cost collectors is considered **transactional**

data in terms of Central Finance and transfer is triggered by a new entry in table AUFK.

Figure 5.8 gives an overview of the scenarios delivered for mapping cost objects between the local and the central systems. Note the CARDINALITY column, which determines whether there is an N:1 relationship between the orders in the local system, as we see for Scenario SAP001, where N production orders map to one product cost collector, or Scenario SAP004, where N maintenance orders map to one central maintenance order, or a 1:1 relationship as we see for Scenario SAP002, where product cost collectors already exist locally and are transferred 1:1, or in Scenario SAP003, where internal orders are transferred 1:1. There is also an additional scenario that maps maintenance or production orders to internal orders in the central system.

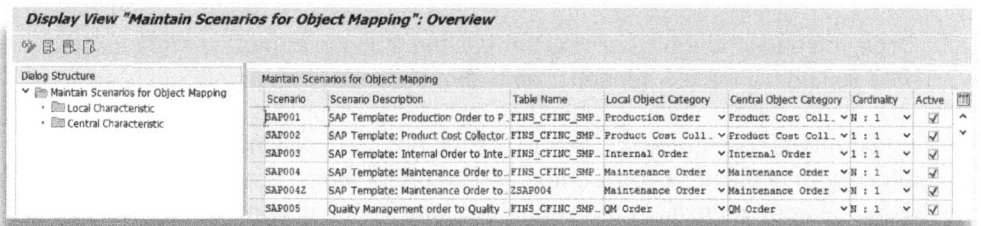

Figure 5.8: Scenarios for object mapping in Central Finance (edition 1503)

If you want to check the link between the local cost objects and the cost objects in the central system, refer to the entries in table FINS_CFINT_ASGNT. This will show you the relationships between the many local production orders (object category PROD_ORD) and the single product cost collector (object category PCC).

5.2.7 Central project reporting

From a Central Finance point of view, projects are somewhere between the stable master data, such as profit centers and cost centers, and the short-lived production orders and maintenance orders. Large engineering and investment projects can exist for several years, but project management typically takes place locally. The projects and assigned WBS elements are created in the local systems, such as production orders, but the transfer mechanism relies on ALE (Application Link Enabling) to bring the projects from the local systems into the central system. To ensure consistency, all maintenance of the projects and assigned WBS elements takes place in the local systems and you are not allowed to make master data changes in the central system.

Because the same project ID can exist in more than one assigned system, a new project ID is generated in the Central Finance system with the initial load of a new project. Before you can transfer projects, you will need to set up the ALE connection and the selection filters in the source systems and enable the appropriate mappings in the central system. Once a connection is established between the local project and its counterpart in the central system, you will not be able to delete the local project.

5.2.8 Error handling using the SAP Application Interface Framework

Once you have thought your way through the global parameters and master data settings, it makes sense to think about how the system should react if key master data is missing when you transfer a document. The SAP Application Interface Framework (AIF) handles any transactional records arriving with an account, a cost center, and so on for which appropriate master data does not yet exist in the central system. These documents will not be posted as accounting documents but stored for post-processing.

Figure 5.9 shows an overview of the three types of interface that are monitored for Central Finance:

- ▶ Accounting Documents
- ▶ Controlling Documents
- ▶ Cost Objects
- ▶ Projects (available as of edition 1709)

Figure 5.10 shows a list of errors in the accounting documents. You can navigate to details of the error by selecting an item and then reprocess the item once the underlying problem (such as missing master data) has been fixed.

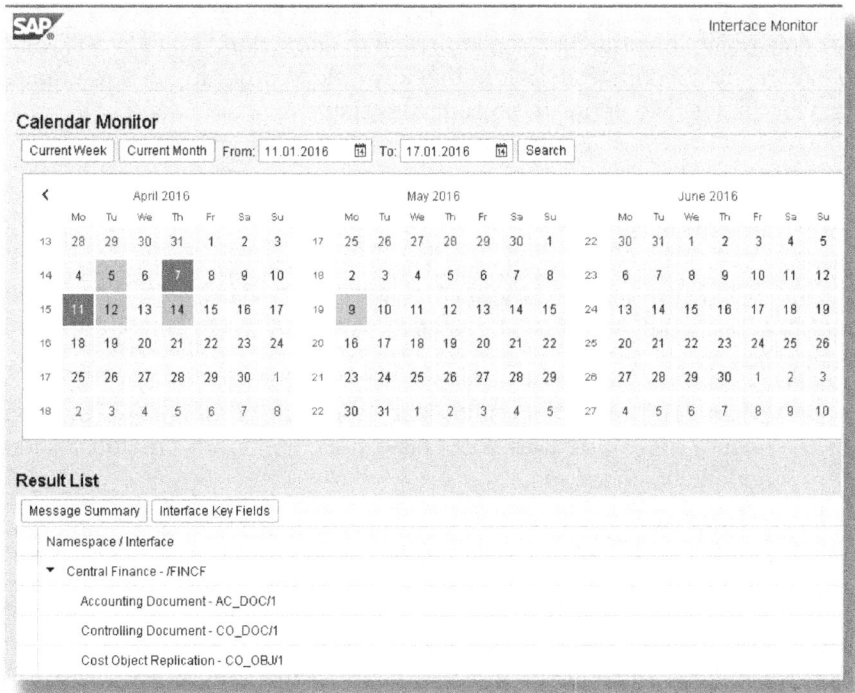

Figure 5.9: Interface monitor

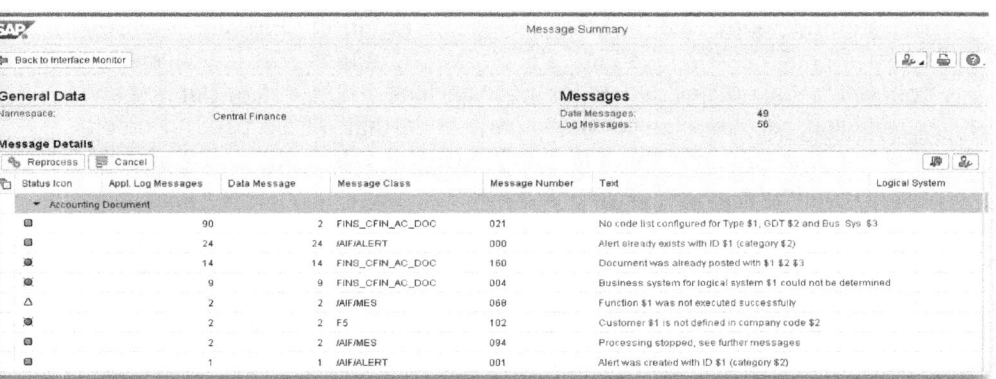

Figure 5.10: Summary of error messages in SAP AIF

While this gives you an idea about how to load transactional data from a key date going forward, it is also important to understand that you will want to load historical data from before that key date in order to have reference data for the last two years in the central system.

5.2.9 Initial data load

In Figure 5.4, we can see the main steps for the initial data load in the central system, but there are of course key precautions to take in the local system first.

- ▶ While you are loading data, lock users out of the local system to ensure that no further accounting documents are created for the periods being loaded.
- ▶ Ensure that period close is complete in Asset Accounting and prepare the balance carryforwards for all currencies and subledgers.
- ▶ Before you start, there are a series of check reports to ensure that the data being transferred is clean, so make sure that you reconcile Financial Accounting with Materials Management and with Accounts Payable and Accounts Receivable and check that the index entries are clean.

You are now ready to define the settings shown in the INITIAL LOAD SETTINGS area of the IMG (see Figure 5.4). Start by entering the logical system from which you will select data for the initial load. Then, define clearing and substitution accounts for each company code that will be used to create offsetting entries during the data load. Once the data load is complete, the balance on these accounts should be zero.

You can execute the initial data load steps from the IMG. In many cases, you will find a simulation step before each load step so that you can check that the mappings are correct before you start to load data in bulk. In the case of the Financial Accounting documents, it makes sense to simulate and load data company code by company code. You should also distinguish between the time periods for which you need full line item details (usually two years) and the prior periods where balance information is sufficient. You maintain this information in table VCFIN_SOURCE_SET.

With the initial data load complete, you are now ready to create your first journal entries to Central Finance. At this point, you should set the initial data load status to complete because the procedure for loading real-time data is different.

5.3 Group reporting

If we think of real-time Finance as the ultimate aim for SAP S/4HANA, the group close (or consolidation) process is often the furthest from this goal. Headquarters often has to wait several days for each subsidiary to submit its financial data. Various cleansing and validation steps are then performed before work finally begins on the elimination of intercompany profits, and adjustments are made to reflect the ownership structure of the affiliated companies. Only then can headquarters finally deliver consolidated figures for the group as a whole. The introduction of Group Reporting with SAP S/4HANA 1809 changes all this. If the data is available from the subsidiaries in near real-time, and does not arrive several days after closing, and has already been transformed and cleansed according to the corporate guidelines, then the only step that remains to complete the group close is the elimination of the intercompany profits and capital consolidation to reflect the ownership structure within the group. Group Reporting does not have to sit on top of a Central Finance system, but can be used in combination with the universal journal in the local system if you run a single instance of SAP S/4HANA.

Figure 5.11 provides a high-level view of how Group Reporting works in combination with the underlying local accounting system(s). Remember also the contents of Figure 1.8. The idea is that the Accounting and Controlling data in the universal journal should provide the starting point for Group Reporting, without transformation or cleansing. What is happening is that you are working with shared master data—the same accounts, cost centers, profit centers, etc., as exist in the accounting system—but you are organizing it by the reporting entities for group reporting: the consolidation units and consolidation groups, and by financial statement items. This shared master data enables a drill-back to Accounting and Controlling from the group reports, again keeping the idea of a single source of truth for financial reporting.

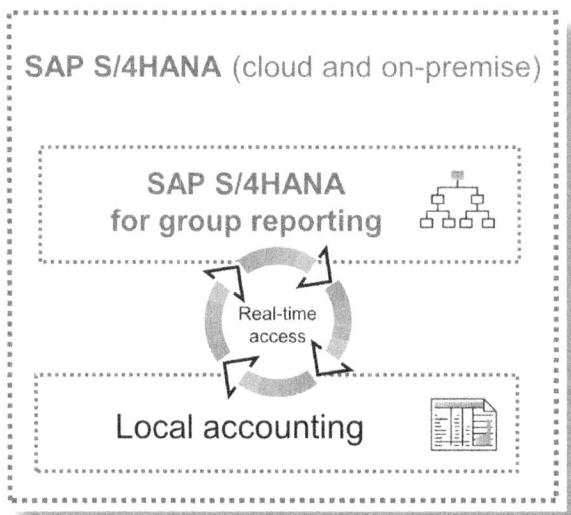

Figure 5.11: Group Reporting and Local Accounting

Figure 5.12 gives a sense of how the reporting architecture is simplified by having the underlying accounting table provide the base layer for group reporting. It shows the ACDOCU consolidation table and those fields that are accessed directly from the universal journal, including fields from the general ledger, controlling and profitability analysis. This shared data model means that there is significantly less data modelling and transformation than in a classic consolidation approach. The accounts, profit centers, and so on are the same as in the underlying ACDOCA table. This shared data model makes it easy to jump from the consolidated financial statements back to the underlying journal entries in the operational system.

For consolidation purposes, you can organize your accounts differently by assigning them to the appropriate financial statement items. In this context, SAP Group Reporting enables you to define different financial statement items, profit center hierarchies, and so on, from those used for local accounting. However, the tool to create these groupings is the same as in Accounting. Group Reporting uses the Global Accounting Hierarchy app that we will explore in Chapter 6.

Group Reporting is designed to handle financial data from an SAP S/4HANA system, but it can also use financial data from an external system using the classic data collection approach. In this case, the base data is stored in the ACDOCU table alongside the data aggregated from the underlying ACDOCA table.

DEPLOYING CENTRAL FINANCE

Transparent Table:	ACDOCU		Active				
Short Description:	SAP Universal Consolidation Journal Entries						
Attributes	Delivery and Maintenance	Fields	Input Help/Check	Currency/Quantity Fields	Indexes		

Field	Key	Initi...	Data element	Data Type	Length	Decim...	Coordinate	Short Description
.INCLUDE			ACDOC_SI_GL_ACCAS	STRU	0	0	0	Universal Journal Entry: G/L additional account assignments
RCNTR			KOSTL	CHAR	10	0	0	Cost Center
PRCTR			PRCTR	CHAR	10	0	0	Profit Center
RFAREA			FKBER	CHAR	16	0	0	Functional Area
RBUSA			GSBER	CHAR	4	0	0	Business Area
KOKRS			KOKRS	CHAR	4	0	0	Controlling Area
SEGMENT			FB_SEGMENT	CHAR	10	0	0	Segment for Segmental Reporting
SCNTR			SKOST	CHAR	10	0	0	Sender cost center
PPRCTR			PPRCTR	CHAR	10	0	0	Partner Profit Center

Figure 5.12: Journal Entries Table for Consolidation

To give a sense of how Accounting and Controlling merge with Group Reporting, refer to Figure 5.13, which displays the Consolidated P&L by Nature app. The DIMENSIONS list shows that the report includes entities from Group Reporting, such as the consolidation group (CONS. GROUP) and consolidation unit (CONS. UNIT). It also includes operational reporting entities, such as the ACCOUNT NUMBER, BILL-TO PARTY, BILLING TYPE, and BUSINESS AREA. There are even more if we scroll further down the DIMENSIONS list.

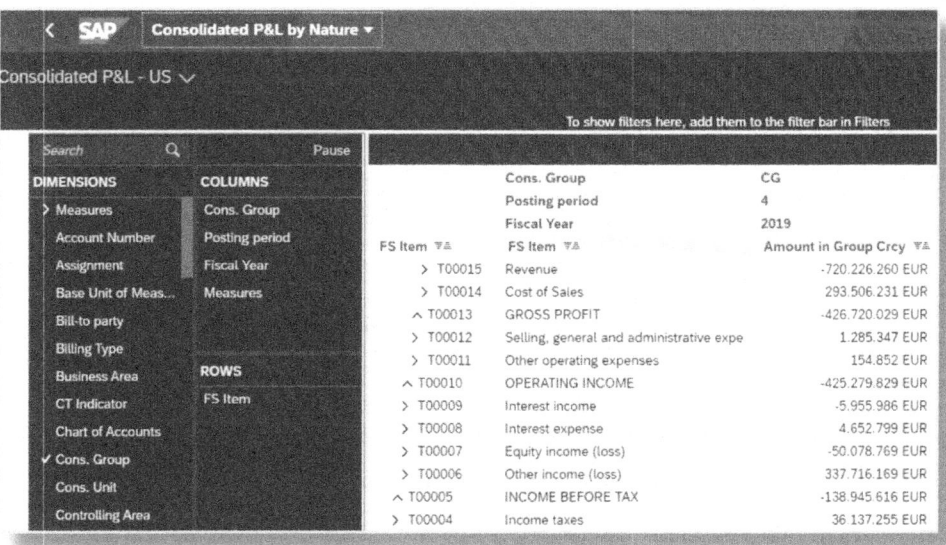

Figure 5.13: Consolidated P&L by Nature app

157

Note that in Group Reporting we are working with a consolidation chart of accounts (the FS ITEM in the report). The consolidation chart of accounts is a key element for running the consolidation process and reporting in S/4HANA Group Reporting. It not only controls how the accounts are displayed in the reports, but also how each item is processed during the group close. These are not only used for accounting purposes in the P&L statement (shown here), the balance sheet, and statement of retained earnings, but can also be used for maintaining metrics and key figures. For this purpose, statistical accounts can be assigned to Financial Statement Items alongside the operational accounts.

Figure 5.14 shows the Define Financial Statement Items app which can be used to display or update financial statement items and their properties. The properties include the consolidation chart of accounts, which can be different from the local account structure, item type and breakdown category. The new approach includes an elimination attribute, a currency translation attribute, and a role attribute, and these determine how the figures assigned to that account group will be handled during the group reporting process.

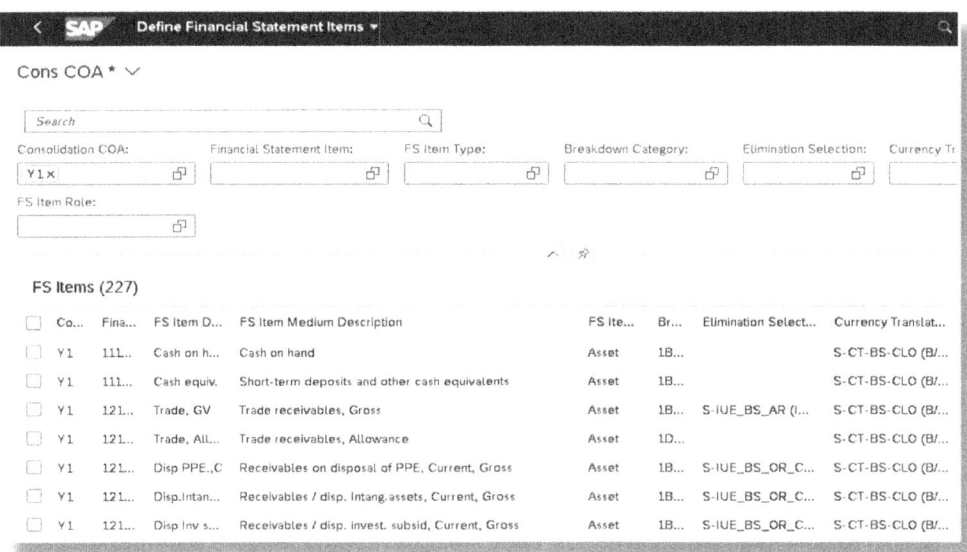

Figure 5.14: Define Financial Statement Items app

Figure 5.15 shows the detailed settings for FS Item 121100. Here we see the rules for currency translation and for elimination of intercompany profit for this item.

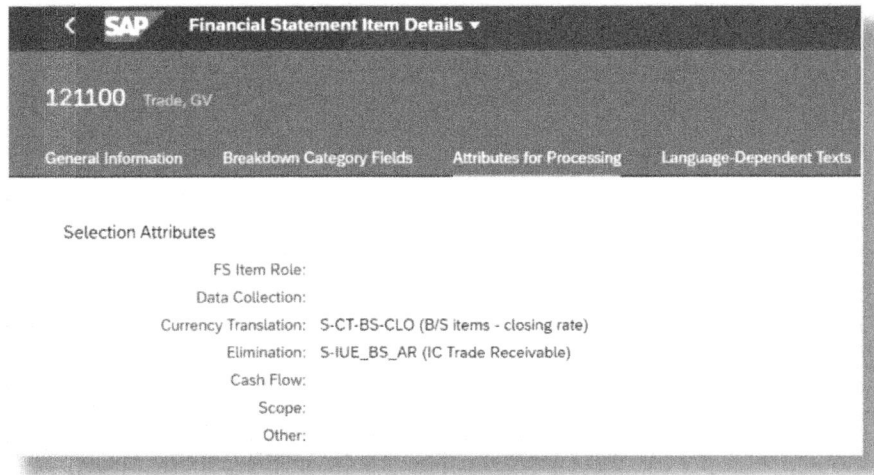

Figure 5.15: Financial Statement Item Details, showing rules for Currency Translation and Elimination

One of the key strengths that has been retained in Group Reporting from SAP EC-CS (Enterprise Controlling–Consolidation System) and SAP SEM-BCS (Strategic Enterprise Management–Business Consolidation System) is the principle of the accounting document. The idea is that the base layer of documents to be consolidated should provide a link back to the underlying accounting system, and each consolidation task should result in an auditable consolidation document. Therefore, we have documents that record the initial data load, the postings for interunit eliminations, the investment eliminations, and any manual postings for corrections. All these documents can be viewed in the Display Group Journal Entries app, as shown in Figure 5.16. Documents are filtered by choosing the appropriate DOCUMENT TYPE, VERSION and POSTING LEVEL.

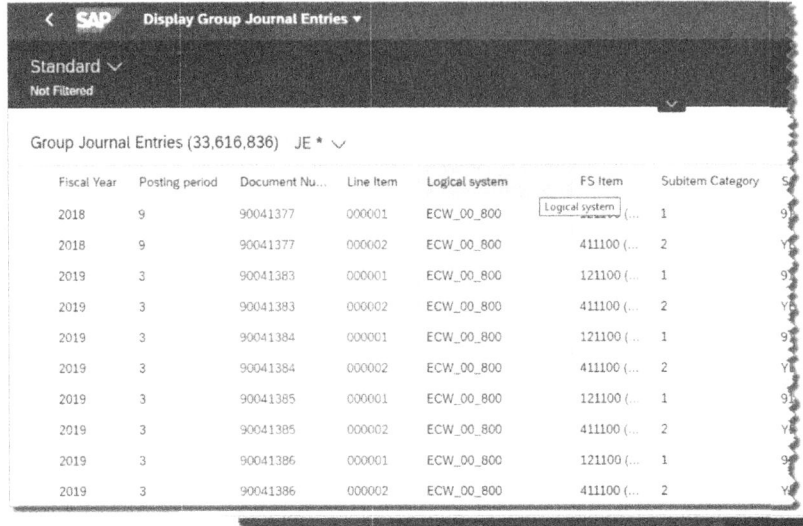

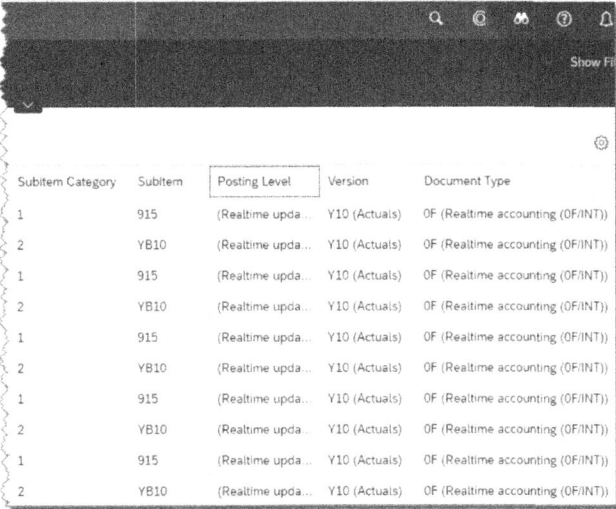

Figure 5.16: Display Group Journal Entries app

In this example, we are looking at the documents from the initial data load (POSTING LEVEL: REALTIME UPDATE). By clicking on the DOCUMENT NUMBER, it is possible to drill back directly to the underlying document(s) in the local accounting system, as we see in the Manage Journal Entries app for the selected document in Figure 5.17. Note the common look of the user interfaces for group reporting and accounting. This drill-back illustrates very powerfully the advantages of the common data model, where every consolidation specialist can explore the source data in the underlying accounting system.

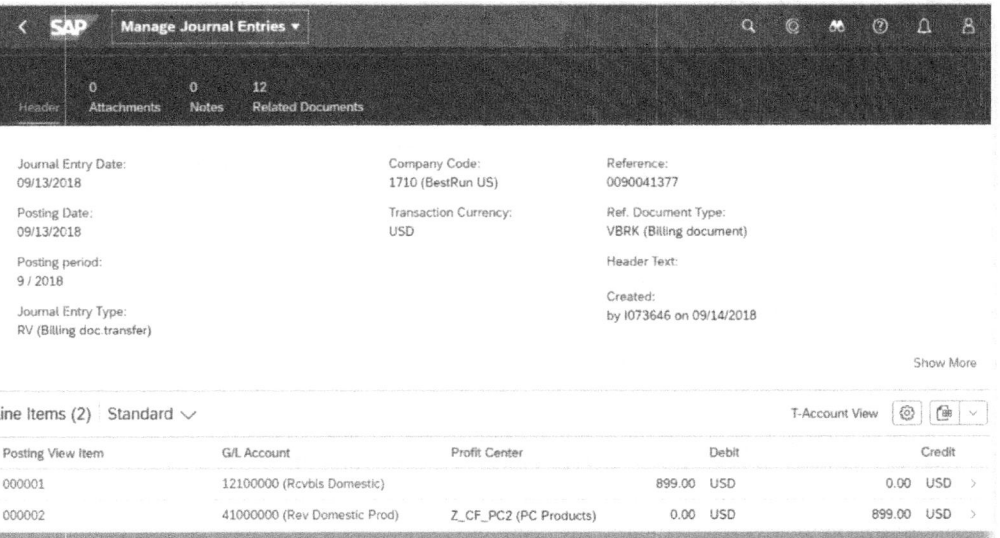

Figure 5.17: Manage Journal Entries app

This tight integration is also illustrated in the Data Monitor app shown in Figure 5.18. This tracks the data collection process (documents must first be released from the underlying accounting system) and includes steps such as validation and currency translation that run prior to consolidation proper.

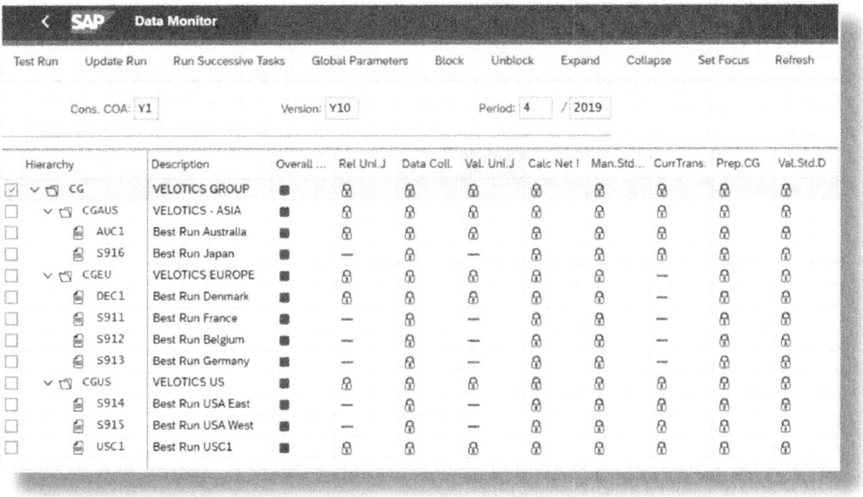

Figure 5.18: Data Monitor app

By contrast, the Consolidation Monitor app (see Figure 5.19) monitors all the tasks that form part of the group reporting process proper.

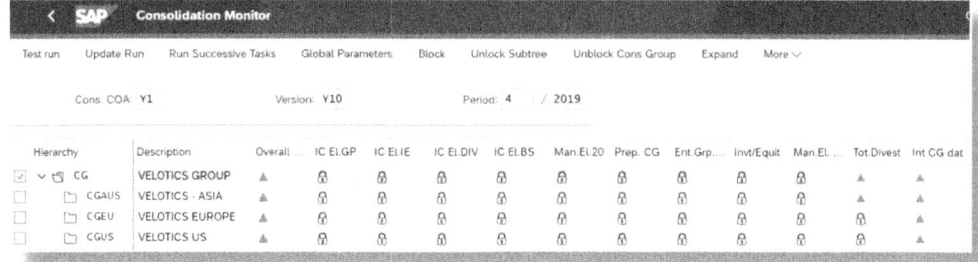

Figure 5.19: Consolidation Monitor app

Having looked at the flow of accounting and controlling into group reporting, we will end by focusing on SAP Fiori and will examine its role in delivering a consistent user experience in Finance.

6 SAP Fiori

In Chapter 1, we introduced the SAP Fiori applications as the new face of Finance for the end user. In this chapter, we explain how to set up the roles and business catalogs to provide your users with access to the Fiori applications. Because SAP Fiori is actually a design approach rather than a UI technology, we also explain how to understand the various types of Fiori applications.

SAP Fiori is SAP's new approach to user interface design and aims to ensure that all applications are:

- *Role-based*—designed with a specific user in mind
- *Responsive*—the application **responds** to the screen size of the device on which it is being run, regardless of whether this is the desktop, a tablet, or a mobile device
- *Simple*—the design paradigm here is 1-1-3 (1 user, 1 use case, 3 screens)
- *Coherent*—the applications all speak the same language
- *Instant value*—there is a low barrier to adoption

To check whether your devices are compatible with SAP Fiori and which Internet browsers are supported, refer to SAP Note 1935915[21]. Within the SAP Fiori umbrella there are several types of applications:

- *Analytical applications*, such as Overdue Receivables (see Chapter 1) and Trial Balance (see Chapter 2)
- *Transactional applications*, such as Manage Journal Entries, My Spend, and the Master Data Applications

One source of confusion in this area is the idea that SAP Fiori is a UI technology. The technology behind the SAP Fiori apps is often SAPUI5 but you will still find differences between the early apps, such as My Spend, which were largely custom built, and later apps, such as Predicted Revenue (see Chapter 2) and Commitments by Cost Center (see Chapter 3), that were built using smart templates to give a more consistent look. Then there are

---

[21] SAP Note 1935915: "Fiori for Business Suite: Browser / Devices / OS Information" (*https://launchpad.support.sap.com/#/notes/0001935915*)

accessible WebDynpro applications and various reporting technologies, including SAP Smart Business and SAP Design Studio.

To access the complete catalog of Fiori apps, see: *https://fioriappslibrary.hana.ondemand.com/sap/fix/externalViewer/*.

6.1 Roles and business catalogs

To access any of the Fiori applications, the user has to be assigned to a *role*. The roles structure the Fiori applications from a business perspective and user research is conducted to understand the typical tasks of each role and the context in which they work (shared service center, corporate headquarters, and so on). This is known in Fiori as the *persona description*. Examples of base roles (BR) in Finance include:

- Accounts Receivable Accountant (SAP_BR_AR_ACCOUNTANT)
- Accounts Receivable Manager (SAP_BR_AR_MANAGER)
- Accounts Payable Accountant (SAP_BR_AP_ACCOUNTANT)
- Accounts Payable Manager (SAP_BR_AP_MANAGER)
- General Ledger Accountant (SAP_BR_GL_ACCOUNTANT)
- Controller (SAP_BR_CONTROLLER)
- Consolidation Specialist (SAP_BR_CONSLDTN_SPECIALIST)

You can also find specializations of these roles, such as country-specific applications for Accounts Receivable or Accounts Payable, and refinements of the Controller role, such as:

- Overhead Accountant (SAP_BR_OVERHEAD_ACCOUNTANT)
- Inventory Accountant (SAP_BR_INVENTORY_ACCOUNTANT)
- Production Accountant (SAP_BR_PRODN_ACCOUNTANT)
- Sales Accountant (SAP_BR_SALES_ACCOUNTANT).

These roles are associated with *business catalogs* (BC) which contain the tiles that are used to access the Fiori applications that we saw in previous chapters. One role might be assigned to several business catalogs, as we see in the following examples:

- Accounts Receivable Accountant (SAP_SFIN_BC_AR_OPERATIONS, SAP_SFIN_BC_AR_DISPUTE_RES, SAP_SFIN_BC_REC_CLERK)
- Accounts Receivable Manager (SAP_SFIN_BC_AR_ANALYTICS)
- Accounts Payable Accountant (SAP_SFIN_BC_AP_OPERATIONS, SAP_SFIN_BC_APAR_OPER. SAP_SFIN_BC_AP_CHECK_PROC)
- Accounts Payable Manager (SAP_SFIN_BC_AP_ANALYTICS)
- General Ledger Accountant (SAP_SFIN_BC_GL_MASTER_DATA, SAP_SFIN_BC_GL_DOC_PROC. SAP_SFIN_BC_GL_GEN_REPORTING)

Figure 6.1 shows a sample tile catalog for ACCOUNTS RECEIVABLE – OPERATIONAL PROCESSING which is part of the Accounts Receivable Accountant role. Note the difference between these apps and those in the Accounts Receivable Manager role in that they show an icon rather than a color-coded KPI. This is the first difference between an *analytical app*, which calculates the trend for the KPI and shows the result so that you do not even need to go into the application if the trend is green, and a *transactional app*, which assumes that you are going to take action, by for example, processing receivables or collections.

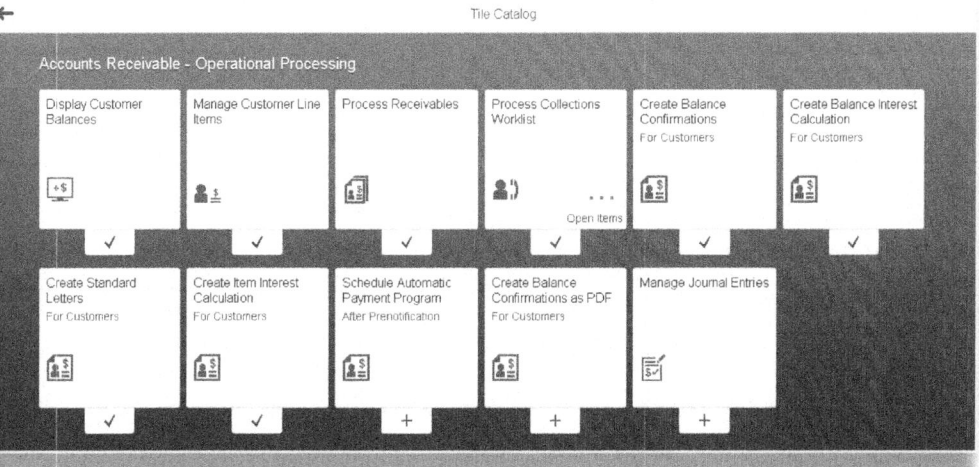

Figure 6.1: Tile catalog for operational processing in Accounts Receivable

A user can only execute the applications in these catalogs if they also have authorization for the individual applications in SAP S/4HANA. So, let's think for a moment about the technology stack involved in bringing the data from SAP S/4HANA to the business user:

- ▶ The user interface runs in a browser on your phone, tablet or PC, and the front end is usually built using SAPUI5.

- ▶ The application uses an *ODataService* in SAP Gateway as the connection between the user interface in SAP Fiori and the data in SAP S/4HANA.

- ▶ The ODataService uses one or more *CDS views* to select the relevant data from SAP S/4HANA. The CDS view combines the transactional data that provides the basis for the figures—the master data—including texts, and hierarchical information (if needed for the app).

Figure 6.2 shows the role for the OVERDUE PAYABLES application in SAP S/4HANA. The role for the OVERDUE RECEIVABLES application that we looked at in Chapter 1 has to be created manually and this role controls the authorizations that determine which user is allowed to see what data.

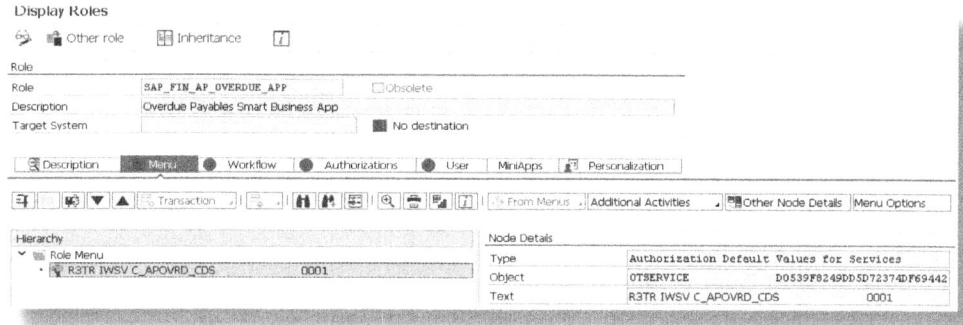

Figure 6.2: Role for the Overdue Payables application

The best way to find out about the link between the role, the business catalog, and the ODataServices is to use the Fiori library that we referenced at the beginning of the chapter. Figure 6.3 shows the configuration details for the OVERDUE RECEIVABLES application with the PFCG role, the business catalog, and the oDataService. From here, you can access more details on how to implement the application.

SAP Fiori

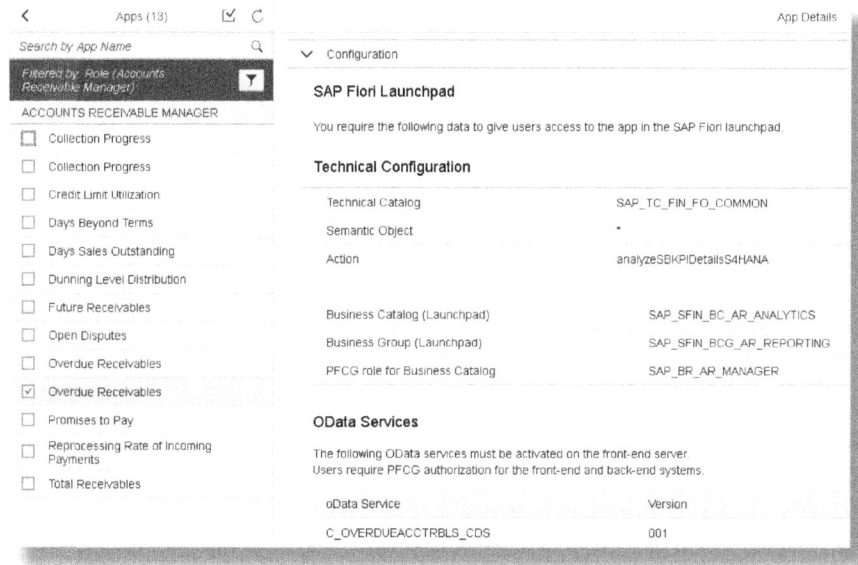

Figure 6.3: Role, business catalog and OData service for Overdue Receivables

6.2 Fiori apps for My Spend

The first wave of SAP Fiori development focused on casual users, who might not usually work with SAP data directly, and the mobile use case. MY SPEND was the first app of this kind in Finance and was designed specifically for the casual user—the manager on the go, who needs a quick update on their budget situation. Figure 6.4 shows the MY SPEND tile in the Fiori launchpad. Note that, like the SAP Smart Business KPIs that we looked at in Chapter 1, you can immediately see the total spend for a manager's cost centers.

167

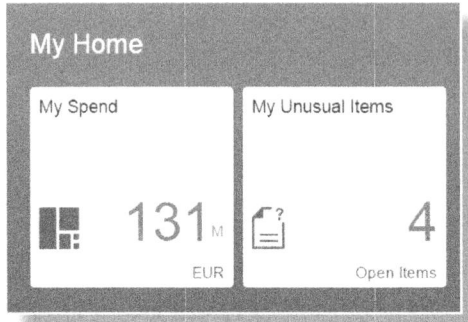

Figure 6.4: My Spend tile in Fiori launchpad

As we drill down, we can see the relative spending for each of the departments for which the manager is responsible. Each department is compared against the plan for that cost center to determine whether the area should be red, yellow, or green (see Figure 6.5).

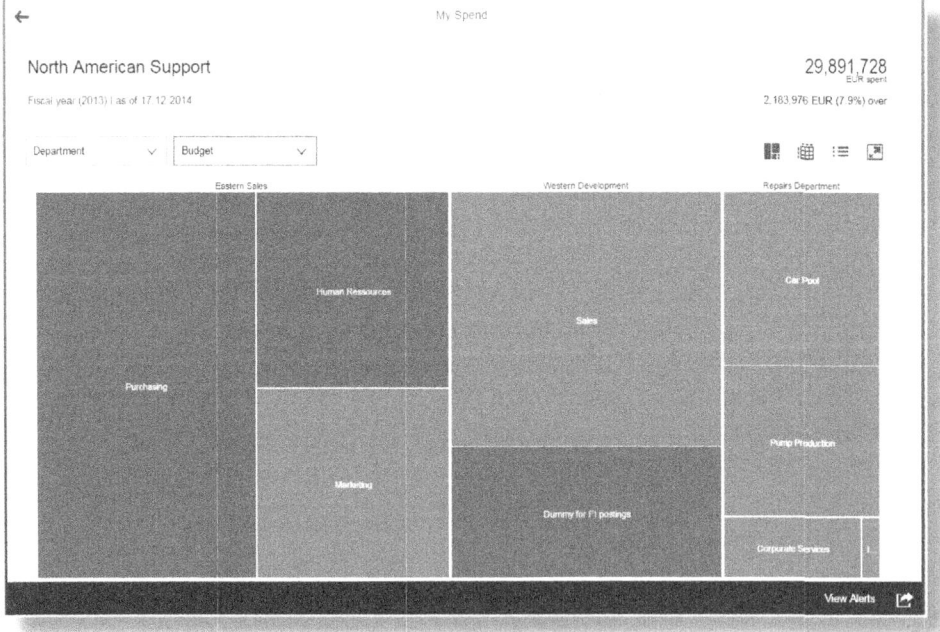

Figure 6.5: Relative spending in each department

By clicking on one of the blocks, users arrives at the view shown in Figure 6.6, which displays the individual spend categories and ultimately the line items for each item. Note that the app also shows the sum of actual and committed spending.

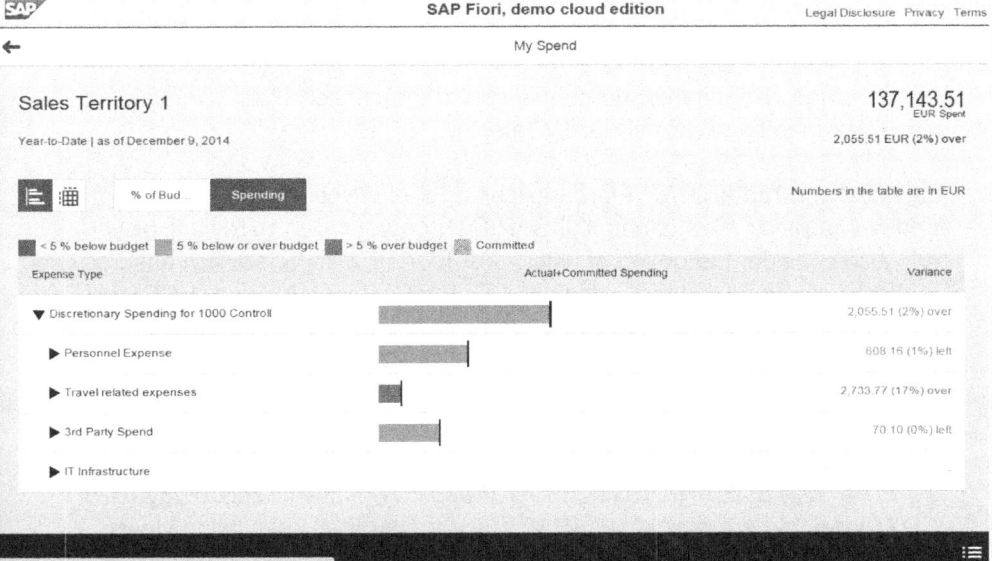

Figure 6.6: Details of spending

While this app might be too simple for the expert controller, it can be a perfect way of getting managers to take ownership of their budgets and monitor spending regularly, and ensure buy-in to the SAP S/4HANA project. It is also an excellent way of gradually weaning managers away from their spreadsheets and the static reporting we talked about in Chapter 1, and into the real-time world of SAP S/4HANA Finance.

6.3 SAP Smart Business apps

Moving away now from the manager who might never have consumed SAP data directly before SAP S/4HANA, the SAP Smart Business apps represent a way of presenting financial data simply to Finance users.

In Chapter 1, we looked at the SAP Smart Business application for Overdue Receivables. The best way to find out how to implement these apps is also in the Fiori library. Figure 6.7 shows the front-end and back-end components for the OVERDUE RECEIVABLES app.

- ► The back-end components are essentially the latest versions of the S/4HANA software layers with the coding for the existing transactions and the all-important access to the data in the SAP S/4HANA tables.
- ► The front-end components are where the user interface itself resides. They make the connection to the backend that contains the data to be shown via SAP Gateway.

Obviously, to run an SAP Fiori application, it is critical to have both components in place. You can install SAP Fiori on your own hardware or you can also consider the option of using SAP Fiori as a service which ensures that the new Fiori UI layer is deployed on the SAP HANA cloud (HCP) and is connected to your on-premise systems. While the decision about where your SAP Fiori will be deployed is best left to IT, it is critical to understand the difference between the various front-end and back-end layers. In the context of SAP Smart Business, this knowledge is important because the SAP S/4HANA Finance 1503 and 1605 apps use a different view technology to the SAP S/4HANA 1511 and 1610 apps. The newer technology uses CDS views that are part of the ABAP stack, rather than calculation views.

App Details

The app consists of front-end components (such as the user interfaces) and back-end components (such as the OData service). The back-end and front-end components are delivered with separate products and have to be installed in a system landscape that is enabled for SAP Fiori.

Front-End Components

Product Version	SAP FIORI FOR SAP S/4HANA 1909
	SAP Fiori for SAP S/4HANA 1909
Support Package Stack	02 (05/2020) FP
Software Component Version	UIAPFI70 700 - SP 0002
Prerequisite for installation	SAP FIORI FOR SAP S/4HANA 1909 - SPS 02 (05/2020) FP is an Add On to
	SAP FIORI FRONT-END SERVER 6.0 - SPS SP01 (02/2020)

Back-End Components (ABAP)

Product Version	SAP S/4HANA 1909
	SAP S/4HANA 1909
Support Package Stack	02 (05/2020) FP
Software Component Version	S4CORE 104 - SP 0002

Figure 6.7: Front-end and back-end components for the Overdue Receivables app

Figure 6.7 shows the entries in the SAP Fiori library for the 1909 back-end edition and the SAP Fiori for SAP S/4HANA 1909 front-end.

Whichever back-end environment you work with, you need to distinguish in the front end between the SAP Smart Business *runtime*, which controls what you see in the overview tile and the configuration drill-downs, and the SAP Smart Business *design time*, which is used to define the KPI, the filters, and thresholds (the evaluation) and the visualization in the app. One of the advantages of using SAP Smart Business is that every KPI has a coherent look, making it easy for a user in a shared service center to move from Accounts Receivable to Accounts Payable and from there to the Cash KPIs.

6.4 Fiori apps for professional users

Mobile apps and smart KPIs might satisfy one group of users, but the lion's share of Financial users are professionals who spend a significant amount of their day working in SAP S/4HANA. In SAP S/4HANA Cloud, all users access their tasks using the apps in a Fiori launchpad. In the on-premise environment, organizations can choose between continuing to use the classic transactions or implementing SAP Fiori. In some cases only SAP Fiori applications are available, so you will only see the predictive journal entries that we showed in Chapters 2 and 3 in apps such as Incoming Sales Orders or Commitments by Cost Center, and you will only see the production costs assigned to work centers and operations in apps such as Production Cost Analysis and Costs by Work Center and Operation.

To get a feel for how to work with the new apps we will begin by looking at the FINANCIAL STATEMENT app shown in Figure 6.8. If you compare this app with classic reporting transactions, you will notice immediately that the selection parameters are part of the application. You no longer have to return to the selection screen to change reporting periods or company codes, making the application immediately more intuitive. You can, of course, navigate through the various nodes of the chart of accounts but you can also enter an account name or part of one in the SEARCH field and have the application search for the relevant account names. This immediately makes it easier to bring new users who are not familiar with your chart of accounts up to speed in their daily work.

SAP Fiori

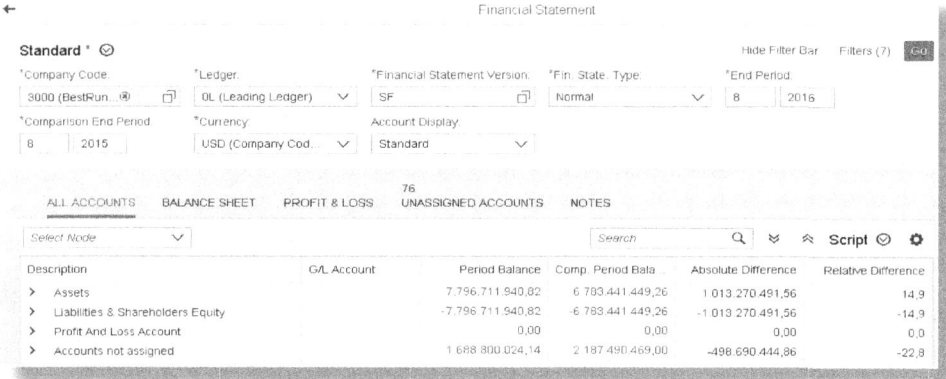

Figure 6.8: Financial Statement app

Figure 6.9 shows a different example—the Manage Customer Line Items app.

If you compare Figure 6.8 and Figure 6.9, you will immediately see similarities in the way the search works and the look of the results list.

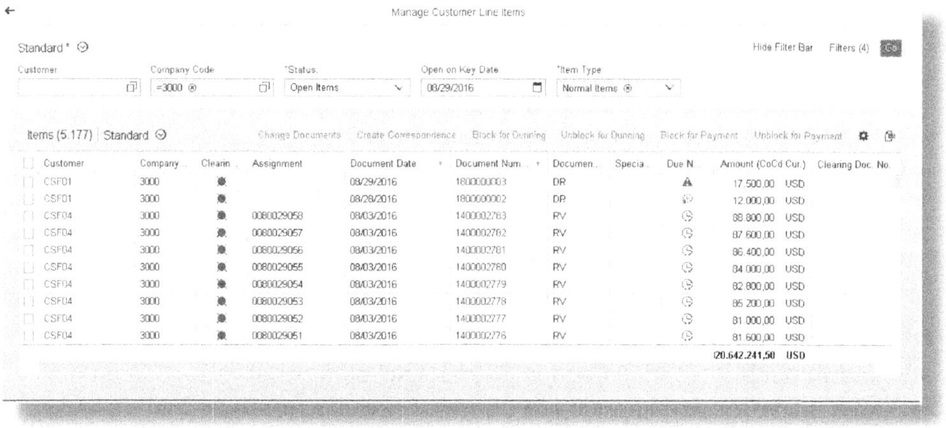

Figure 6.9: Manage Customer Line Items app

Another key aspect of such applications is the ability to navigate to other applications. Figure 6.10 shows a list of the other applications that you can navigate to from the MANAGE CUSTOMER LINE ITEMS app.

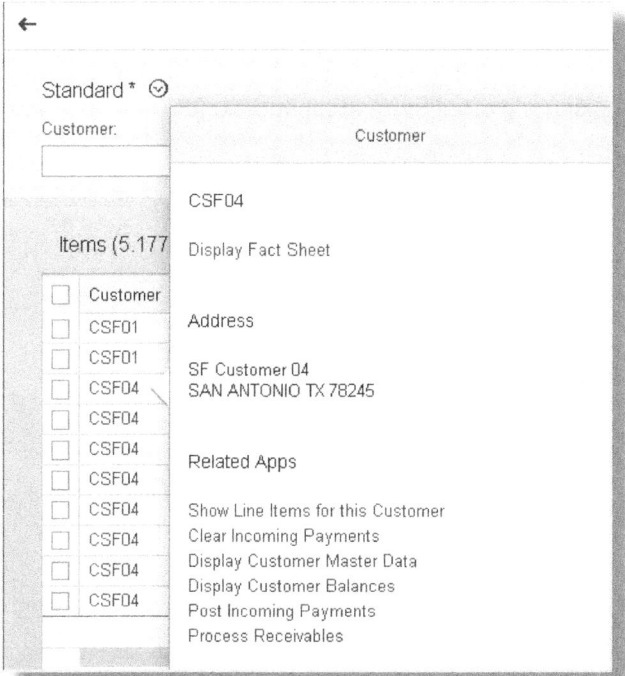

Figure 6.10: Navigation targets associated with customer CSF04

Of course, there are posting apps as well as reporting apps. The MANAGE JOURNAL ENTRIES app (see Figure 6.11) displays a list of the journal entries that meet your selected criteria.

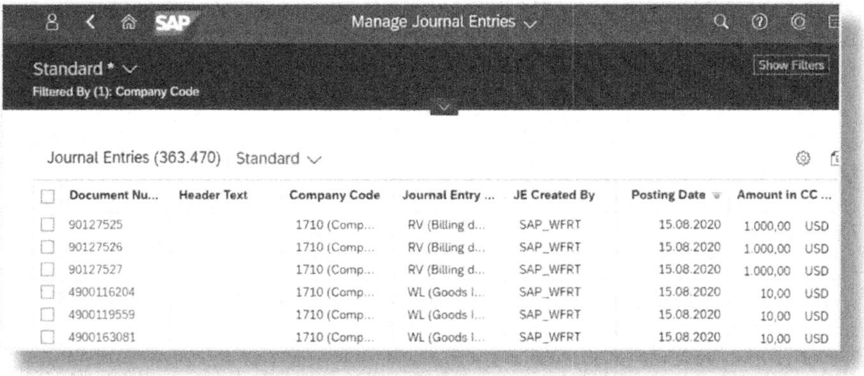

Figure 6.11: Manage Journal Entries app

From here you can navigate to the POST GENERAL JOURNAL ENTRIES app, as shown in Figure 6.12. This is first and foremost a posting app to capture general journal entries and also enables you to upload attachments to document why you are making a journal entry at all and what the rationale for the posting is.

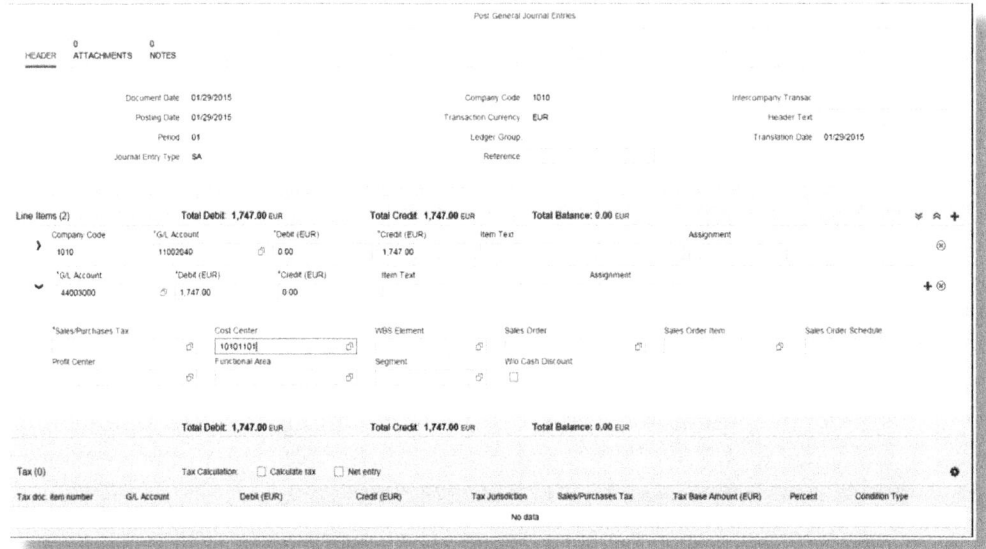

Figure 6.12: Post General Journal Entry app

Many of these early apps were built using custom UI5. Over time, various smart templates were introduced to make it easier for users to work within the same pattern and for developers to deliver SAP Fiori applications with less effort. We have already seen various examples of these applications including: Gross Margin – Predictive Accounting in Chapter 2, and Cost Center Budget and Commitments by Cost Center in Chapter 3. These applications are all analytical apps, but the same technology can be used to build transactional apps, such as the Monitor Predictive Accounting app (see Figure 6.13), that is used to show errors that prevented the posting of the predictive journal entries and to perform the associated corrections.

Instead of displaying the G/L account that we looked at in Figure 2.5 using a classic user interface, we can use the MANAGE G/L ACCOUNT MASTER DATA app to access the same data that we see in Figure 6.14.

SAP Fiori

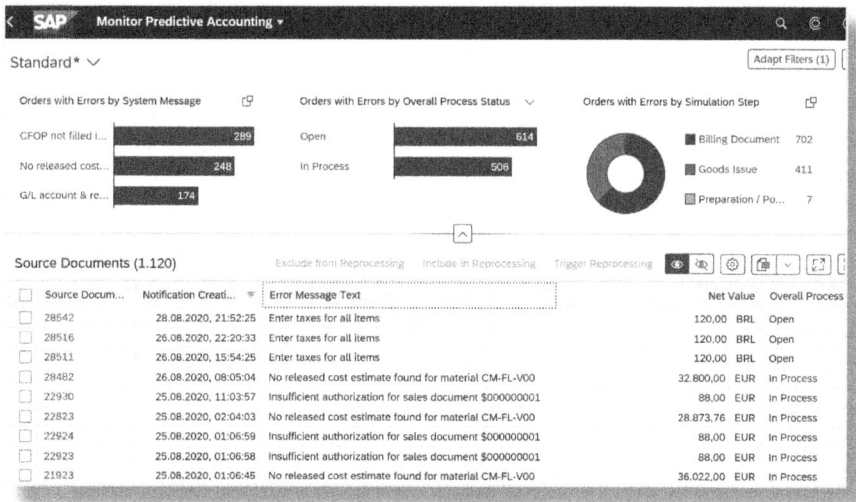

Figure 6.13: Monitor Predictive Accounting app

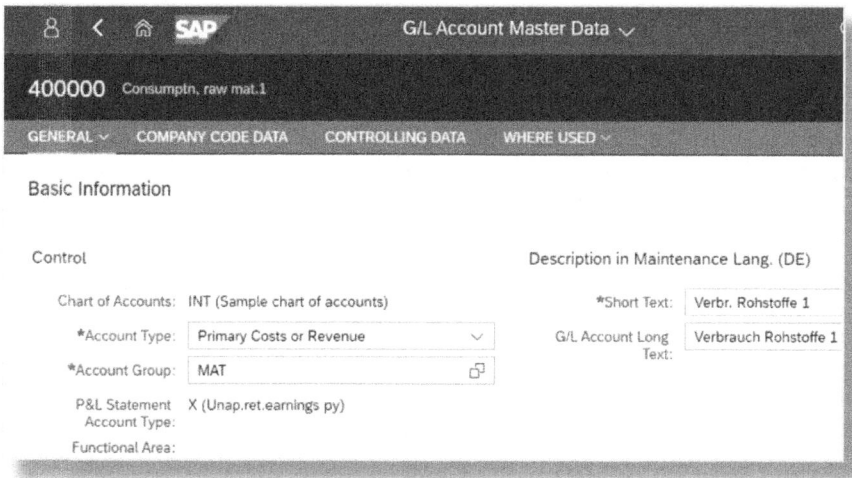

Figure 6.14: G/L Account Master Data app

Similar apps are available to manage profit centers, cost centers, internal orders, activity types, and statistical key figures. Figure 6.15 shows the MANAGE COST CENTERS app. We looked at the details of this app when we explained how to activate budget availability control in Chapter 3 (see Figure 3.22).

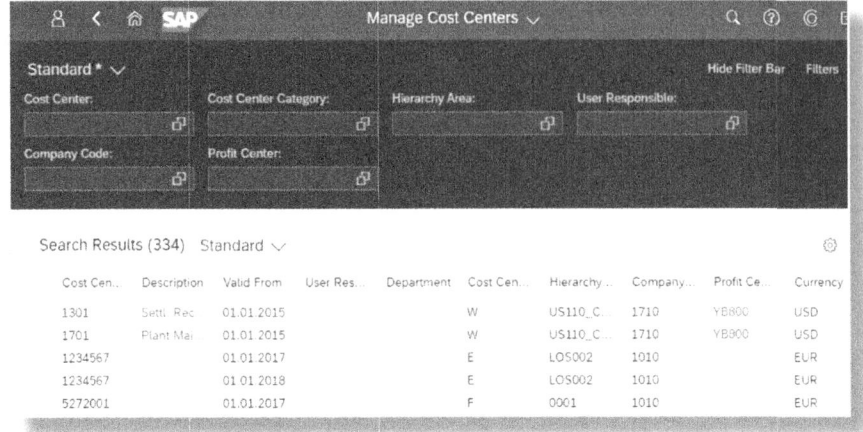

Figure 6.15: Manage Cost Centers app

One key aspect of the master data that has been retained from SAP ERP is the idea of a *where-used list*, as shown in Figure 6.16. Here, we can see the ACTIVITY TYPES, COMPANY CODES, COST ALLOCATION CYCLES, COST ALLOCATION SEGMENTS, FIXED ASSETS, GROUPS AND HIERARCHY, PROFIT CENTERS and SPLITTING STRUCTURES associated with the selected cost center.

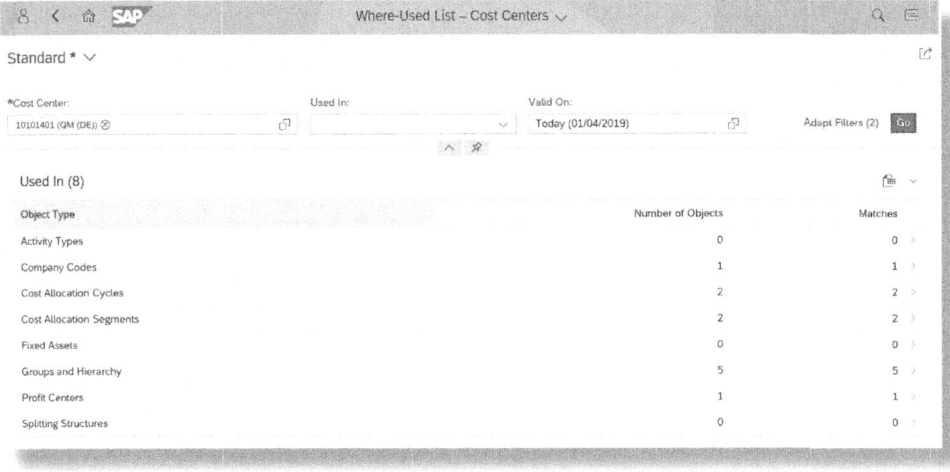

Figure 6.16: Where-Used List in the Cost Centers app

6.5 Hierarchies in Finance

Having looked at the financial master data, it is also important to understand how to create hierarchies in SAP S/4HANA. This is because the financial statement versions, profit center hierarchies, cost center hierarchies, etc., are key to structuring financial data for analysis and to aid selection during allocations. While the classic set tables continue to exist in SAP S/4HANA, a new table has been introduced to accelerate reporting and you will want to make a choice in your reporting approach as to whether to remain in the old world or to move your hierarchies to the new world. The first difference is that financial statement versions and account groups are now stored in the same table structure as cost center groups, profit center groups, and so on. These are all maintained using the Manage Global Accounting Hierarchy app that we will look at next.

6.5.1 Global Accounting hierarchies

The Manage Global Accounting Hierarchy app, shown in Figure 6.17, can be used to manage the following hierarchy types for Accounting and Controlling:

- Financial statement versions
- Account hierarchies/groups
- Profit center hierarchies/groups
- Cost center hierarchies/groups
- Company code groups
- Custom hierarchies

The same app is used to create hierarchies for group reporting. This hierarchy offers new features, such as status management and time dependency, and stores the tree structures in a new table—the HRRP table (hierarchy runtime replication).

We will start by looking at how to set up *financial statement versions* in the global accounting hierarchy. SAP delivers financial statement versions for both general reporting purposes and to handle country-specific reporting requirements. A financial statement version is a hierarchical grouping of accounts, together with a classification (assets, liabilities, etc.) and debit/credit indicators. Financial statement versions maintained using the new app can be time dependent and provide the option of status management (draft, released, etc.) features which are not available for financial statement versions maintained using transactions OB58, FSE2 and FSE3.

For performance reasons, you must first replicate your existing financial statement versions to the new HRRP table before you can use them in the new reports. When you change a financial statement version using the classic transactions, you will be asked whether you wish to activate the financial statement version. This will transfer the structure to the new data store for reporting. You can copy classic financial statement versions into the Manage Global Accounting Hierarchies app as a draft and process them further using the app. Note, however, that changes made using the app will not be reflected in the old financial statement versions.

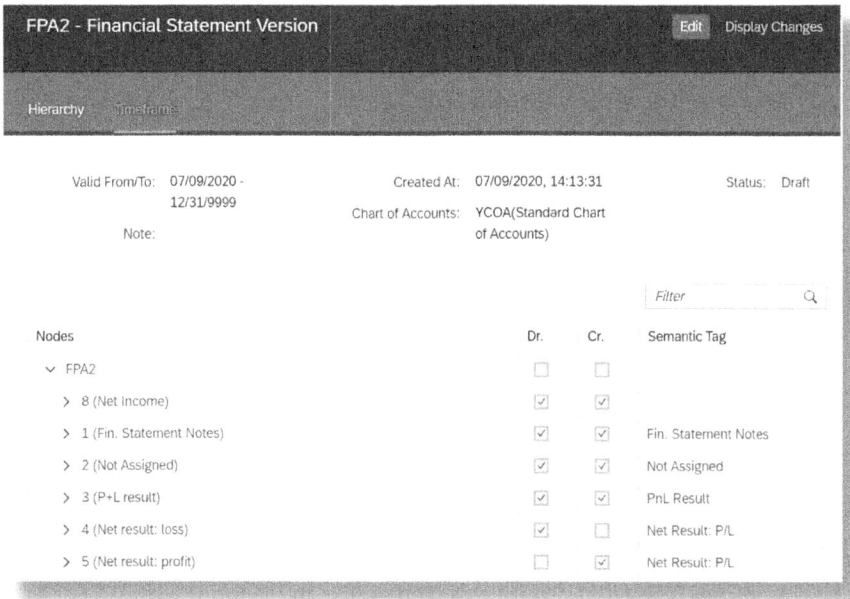

Figure 6.17: Manage Global Accounting Hierarchies app, showing Financial Statement Version

You can then use these hierarchies in all SAP Fiori reporting apps and in SAP Analysis for Office Microsoft, as shown in Figure 6.18.

Trial Balance				
System: HE4 / User GLMGR				
Company Code: 1710 Ledger: 0L				
Posting Date From: 01.01.2019				
Posting Date To: 31.12.2019				
				Starting Balance in Company Code Crcy
Company Code		G/L Account		
1710	BestRun US	[-] Z900/0Z900	FINANCIAL STATEMENTS	0.00
		[-] Z900/00ASSETS	ASSETS	135,848,821,923.83
		[+] Z900/076	Current Assets	135,820,586,025.43
		[+] Z900/012	Long Term Assets	28,235,898.40
		[-] Z900/00LIABILITS	LIABILITIES and STOC	-135,998,156,622.17
		[+] Z900/037	Current Liabilities	-8,821,282,283.95
		[+] Z900/038	Long Term Liabilitie	18,610,245.70
		[+] Z900/039	Shareholders Equity	-127,195,484,583.92
		[-] Z900/057	PROFIT & LOSS STATEM	0.00
		[-] Z900/050	Net Profit After Tax	0.00
		[+] Z900/051	Income Before Taxes	0.00
		[+] Z900/082	Taxes	0.00
		[+] Z900/00NOTASSGND	ACCOUNTS NOT ASSIGNE	149,334,698.34
Overall Result				0.00

Figure 6.18: Financial Statement Version displayed in the Trial Balance app

Account groups maintained using the new app are also status-dependent and time-dependent—features which are not available for cost element groups maintained using transactions KAH1, KAH2 and KAH3, or for account groups maintained using transactions KDH1, KDH2 and KDH3. You can make these classic groups available for reporting by replicating them to the HRRP tables using the Replicate Runtime Hierarchy app. You may have defined many account groups over the years, so before you replicate, use the Set Reporting Relevancy app to flag set class 0102 (cost element groups) and set class 0109 (account groups) as relevant, before you plan the transfer in the app. If you continue to maintain your account and cost element groups using the classic transactions, you will need to replicate them to the HRRP tables after each change, or set up a regular job to do so. This same basic pattern also applies to cost center groups, profit center groups, and so on.

6.5.2 Flexible hierarchies

While the Manage Global Accounting Hierarchies app enables you to build up the tree structures for reporting manually, a new option was introduced with SAP S/4HANA 1709 to generate hierarchies using the underlying master data. Figure 6.19 shows a sample hierarchy that was created using the Manage Flexible Hierarchies app and generating the tree using the entries in the cost center category field (Administration, Development, Logistics, and so on). This idea is not new. The same approach was used to summarize orders and WBS elements in SAP ERP, but the approach is new for cost centers and profit centers. The challenge with cost centers and profit centers is that their master data does not typically include as many attribute fields as we find in orders and WBS elements.

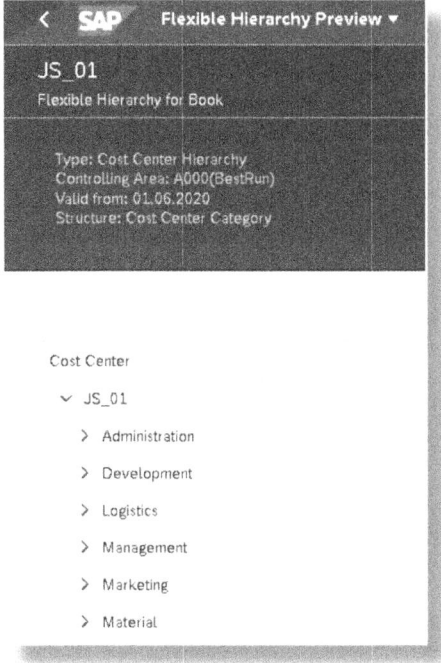

Figure 6.19: Flexible Hierarchy using cost center categories

In Figure 6.20 we have started to build up a profit center hierarchy using the attributes NAME 1, NAME 2, etc., but none of these fields are delivered within the profit center master data. To take this approach, we must extend the master data and we will look at this in the next section.

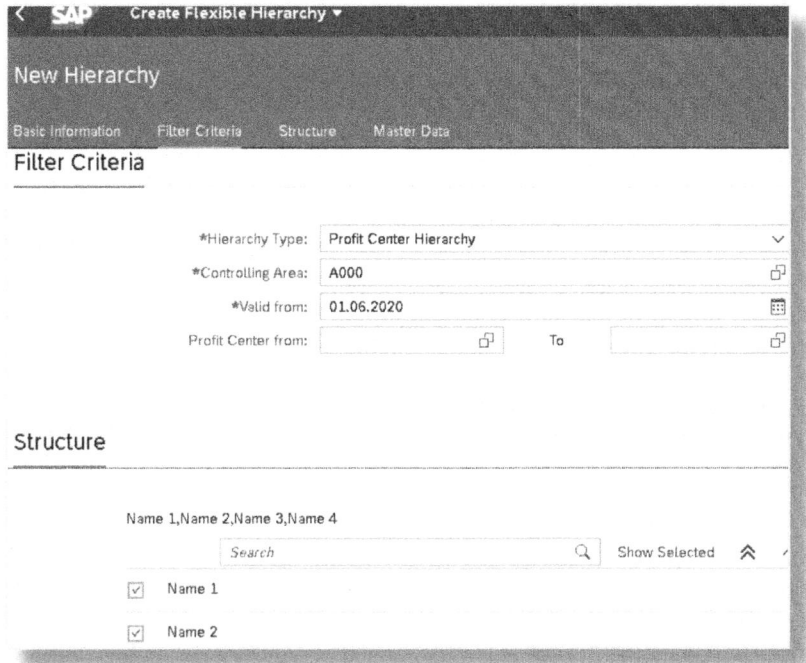

Figure 6.20: Flexible Hierarchy using profit center attributes

6.6 Extensibility in SAP Fiori

As organizations choose between continuing to use the classic transactions and moving to SAP Fiori, one of the arguments in favor of SAP Fiori is the ability to add reporting dimensions based on their unique requirements. In SAP ERP, tools such as Report Writer and Report Painter offer little opportunity for extensibility and if you have worked with some of the industry solutions in SAP ERP, you will know that separate reports delivered for public sector accounting overlap with the existing financial reports to include fields specific to the public sector. With SAP Fiori, you can create custom fields and add them to the universal journal, or use them to extend the master data (see Figure 2.9) and extend the associated apps to show these new fields.

6.6.1 Additional fields in the universal journal

In Chapter 2, we showed the place holders to extend the universal journal. We will now explain how to use these in the context of reporting. Keep in mind, however, that SAP has also been performing its own extensions to the universal journal, so production controllers will be interested to learn that the work center and operation are now part of the universal journal. This means that you can now report on your production orders by looking at the costs for the work centers where each operation was performed, as shown in Figure 6.21. Similar enhancements have been made to include fields relevant for maintenance controlling in the universal journal.

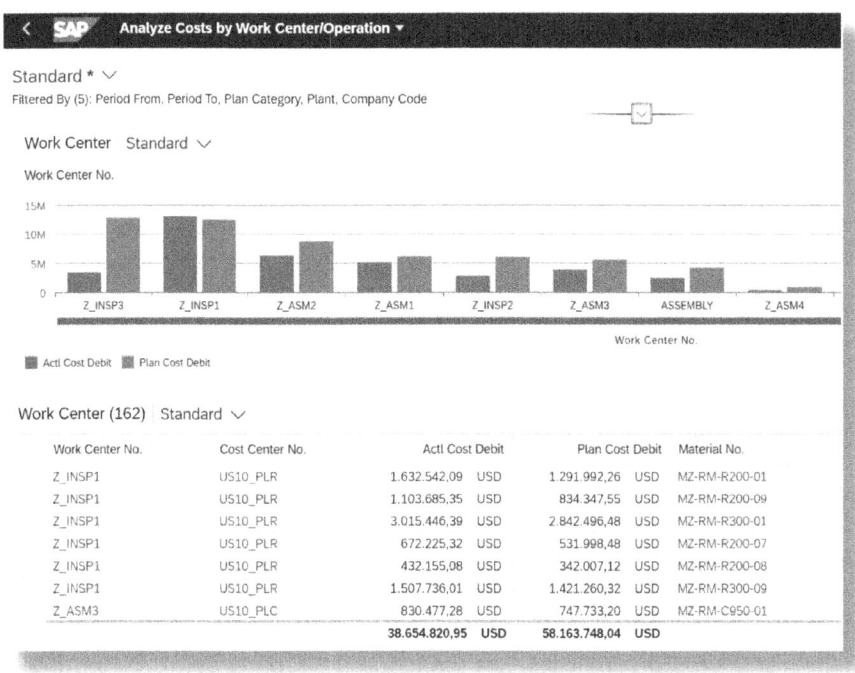

Figure 6.21: Analyze Costs by Work Center/Operation app

6.6.2 Adding fields to the coding block

Many organizations will be familiar with the ability to add new fields to the coding block from SAP ERP, and any fields you added previously will be taken over to the universal journal during migration.

In the new approach, you use the Custom Fields and Logic app to add fields to your coding block. The link is made using a business context—

ACCOUNTING: CODING BLOCK. This link ensures that the new field becomes part of the coding block section of the universal journal. Figure 6.22 shows how to create a new field (LOB) to be included in the coding block.

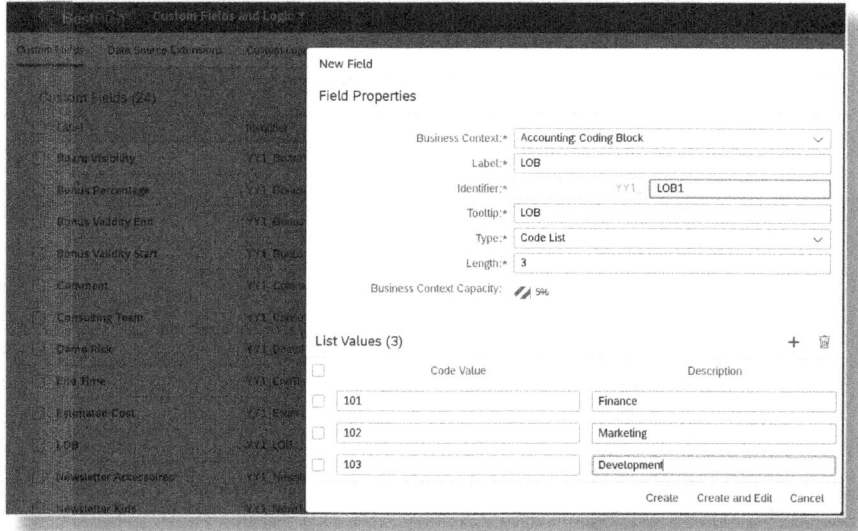

Figure 6.22: Custom Fields and Logic app—New Field for coding block

The next step is to choose the UIs that currently display fields from the coding block, as shown in Figure 6.23. You continue this process to publish the new field and the associated structures.

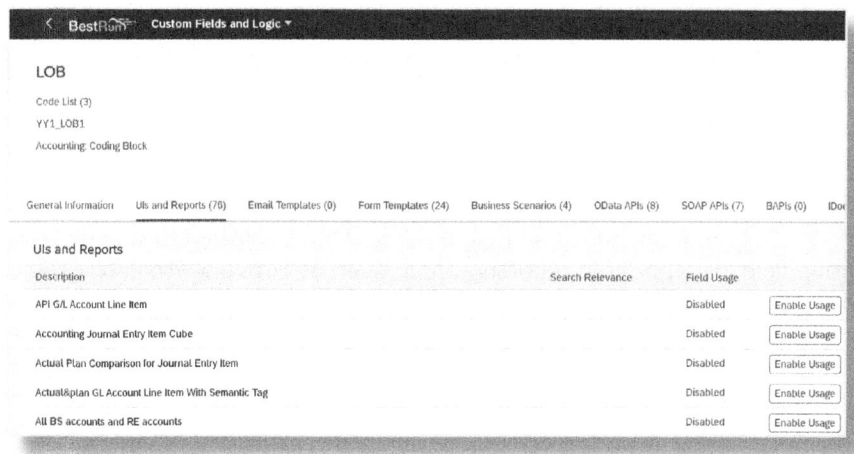

Figure 6.23: Custom Fields and Logic app—UIs for new coding block field

183

6.6.3 Adding fields to the market segment

The market segments in your operating concern will also be transferred to the universal journal during migration, and will be available both for reporting and in apps, such as assessment and top-down distribution.

The new approach to add fields to Margin Analysis is again to use the Custom Fields and Logic app, but this time to use the ACCOUNTING: MARKET SEGMENT business context, as shown in Figure 6.24.

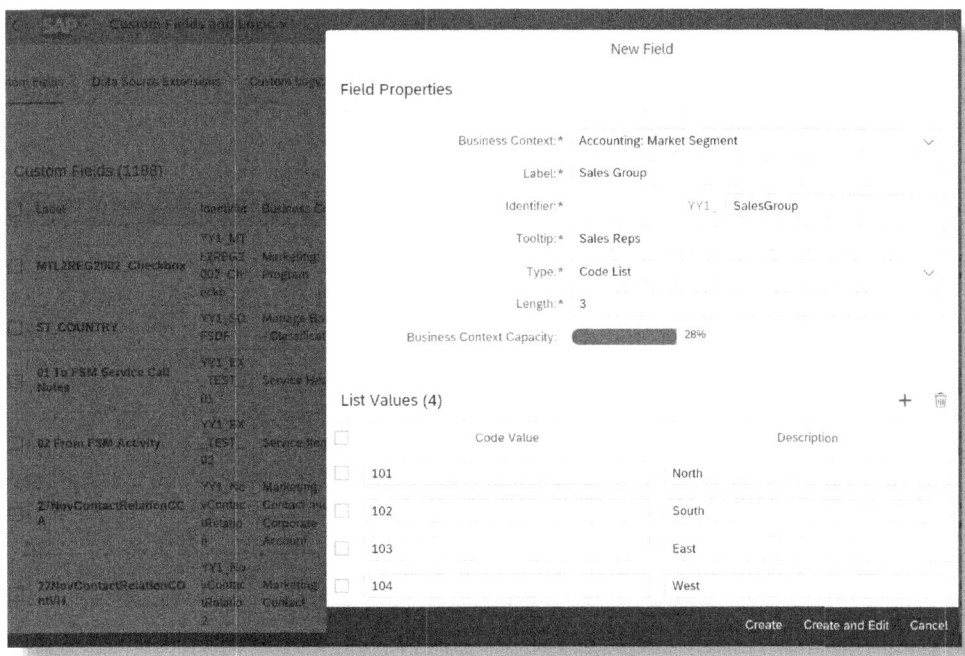

Figure 6.24: Custom Fields and Logic—New Field for market segment

The next step is to choose the UIs that currently display fields from the market segment, as shown in Figure 6.25. Once published, the new sales group field will appear in reporting apps, such as Product Profitability, and the allocation apps that we looked at in Chapter 2.

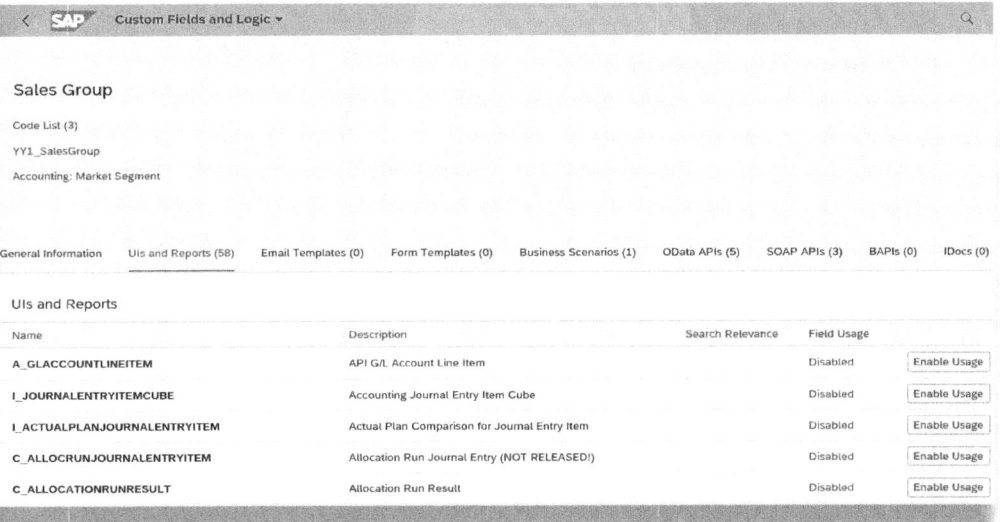

Figure 6.25: Custom Fields and Logic—UIs for market segment

6.7 Semantic tags in Accounting

In Chapter 2, we looked at the Product Profitability app (see Figure 2.4) and the Project Profitability app (see Figure 2.36). We will now look at a key aspect of their design—how to build the measures that form the rows of the Product Profitability app and the columns of the Project Profitability app. These measures, or key figures, are defined using *semantic tags*. Semantic tags enable SAP to deliver stable report structures. There is no equivalent structure in SAP ERP, but the idea is that SAP can deliver measures such as billed revenue or realized revenue. In order to use the key figures in these apps, customers only need to assign their own accounts to the relevant semantic tags by selecting the appropriate financial statement items.

To check the delivered semantic tags, follow the IMG menu path: ACCOUNTING • GENERAL LEDGER ACCOUNTING • MASTER DATA • G/L ACCOUNTS • DEFINE SEMANTIC TAGS FOR BALANCE SHEET AND PROFIT AND LOSS STRUCTURES. Sample semantic tags from a test system are shown in Figure 6.26. You can create your own semantic tags and link them with the relevant queries. For further details, refer to SAP Note 2538634[22].

---

[22] SAP Note 2538634: "Semantic Tagging for FSV and CDS Query Extension" (*https://launchpad.support.sap.com/#/notes/2538634*)

List of Semantic Tags

Sem. Tag	Semantic Tag Long Name
ACCPAY	Increase (Decrease) in Accounts Payable
ACCPAY_OTH	Increase (Decrease) in Other Payables
ACCREC	Increase (Decrease) in Accounts Receivable (Net)
ACCREC_OTH	Increase (Decrease) in Accounts Other Receivable
ACR_COST	Accrued Cost
ACR_REV	Accrued Revenue
ACT_COST	Actual Cost
ADJ_COS	COS Adjustments
ADJ_REV	Revenue Adjustments
AMORINASST	Amortization of Intangible Assets
ASSET	Assets
BILL_REV	Billed Revenue
CHGFARET	Gain/Loss from Retirement of Fixed Assets

Figure 6.26: List of semantic tags delivered in SAP

Semantic tags cannot be used in isolation, but must be linked with a financial statement version and the relevant accounts (and functional area) in order to select the data stored in your system. To select data for the "billed revenue" tag, you will need to enter the accounts used to capture the relevant revenues. Figure 6.27 shows the link between the semantic tags we saw in Figure 6.26 and the financial statement items that have been built up to group these accounts. If you work with different financial statement versions in the various countries that you operate in, work with one semantic tag to enable you to use the same report in every country, and assign the country-specific accounts using the relevant financial statement versions. To assign accounts and, if necessary, functional areas to the delivered semantic tags, follow the IMG menu path: ACCOUNTING • GENERAL LEDGER ACCOUNTING • MASTER DATA • G/L ACCOUNTS • ASSIGN SEMANTIC TAGS FOR BALANCE SHEET AND PROFIT AND LOSS STRUCTURES.

An additional assignment is used for the project cost reports that are delivered as part of the Project Financial Controller role. These tags are also used to determine the accounts that are considered relevant for the active availability control checks.

Mapping of Financial Statement Version to Semantic Tag

	FS Vers	FS Item	Sem. Tag	Account From	Account To	Func. Area From	Functl. Area To
☐	11C0	1000210	DPRTASSET				
☐	11C0	1000220	AMORINASST				
☐	11C0	1000230	CHGFARET				
☐	11C0	1000310	PROVISIONS				
☐	11C0	1000320	INVENTORY				
☐	11C0	1000330	ACCREC				
☐	11C0	1000340	ACCREC_OTH				
☐	11C0	1000350	ACCPAY				
☐	11C0	1000360	ACCPAY_OTH				
☐	11C0	2000100	TANGASSETS				
☐	11C0	2000200	ITANGASSET				
☐	11C0	2000300	CHGFARET				
☐	11C0	2000400	GLTINV				
☐	11C0	3000100	COMNSTOCK				
☐	11C0	3000200	NOTERECEIV				
☐	11C0	4000000	CSH_CSHEQV				

Figure 6.27: Assignment of financial statement items to semantic tags

6.8 Digitizing the finance function

As you work through the list of Fiori apps, you need a strategy for which apps to approach and in what sequence. You could try to tempt new users online by offering apps such as MY SPEND or some of the key figure apps in SAP Smart Business. Alternatively, you might focus on a particular role where there is high coverage, such as those in Accounts Receivable, Accounts Payable, or Cash Management. It is not generally a good idea to go directly from a transaction to a Fiori app. The POST GENERAL JOURNAL ENTRIES app that we looked at in Figure 6.12 is the natural follow-up to transaction FB50 and there is a link between the old master data transactions and the new apps. You need to consider the work performed in the various finance departments and determine how you can help users in these departments to work more efficiently. A transaction list alone does not tell you the whole story and it can be just as interesting to look at the spreadsheets documenting who has done what and why to understand how a key business process is carried out. Digitizing the finance function can be a simple matter of bringing these spreadsheets online. You might, for example, transform a list of closing tasks, and the individuals responsible for them, into entries in the SAP Financial Closing Cockpit, or consider implementing Dispute Management in Accounts Receivable.

6.8.1 Intercompany reconciliation

The process of intercompany reconciliation is another good example in this context. Everybody documents open items between affiliated companies before they go into the consolidation process, and many organizations already worked with INTERCOMPANY RECONCILIATION in SAP ERP. This enabled the system to match whichever intercompany open items it could, and then offer a list of those that it was unable to match, which therefore required clarification.

In edition 1909, a new process was introduced —SAP Intercompany Matching and Reconciliation—that was completely rearchitected based on the universal journal, and which further automates the reconciliation process. As discussed in Chapter 5, data transfer takes place more frequently than before and we can now drill-down directly from Group Reporting to the underlying data in Accounting. Again, matching rules are used to match payables against receivables, as far as possible, for the affiliated companies. If this fails, the consolidation specialist can drill down to the line items from both companies to determine what data might be missing.

Figure 6.28 shows the Manage Assignments app and the items for COMPANY 1010 that need to be matched against the items in the partner unit. In Figure 6.29, we have scrolled left to see the items in the affiliated company and the steps that can be performed to clear these items.

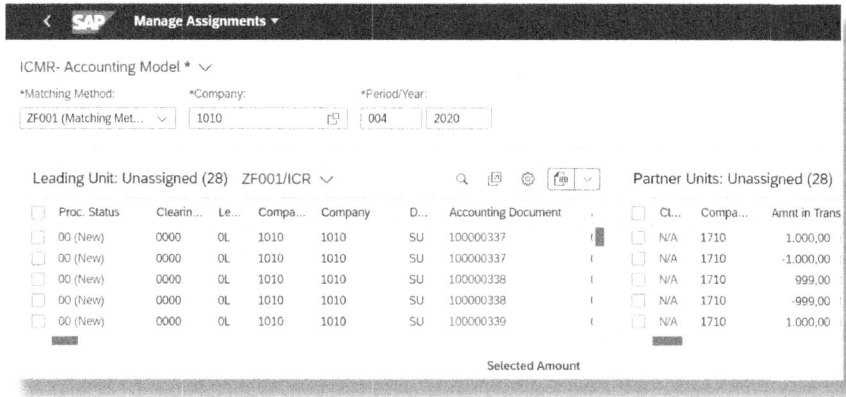

Figure 6.28: Manage Assignments app, showing the units to be matched

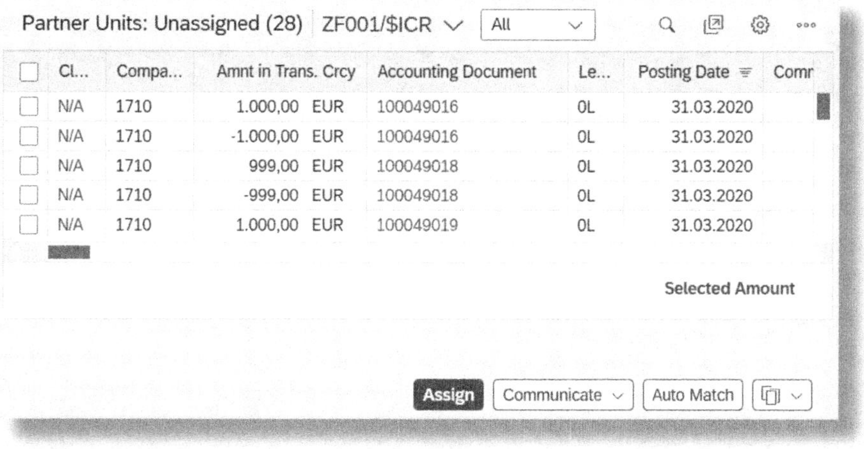

Cl...	Compa...	Amnt in Trans. Crcy		Accounting Document	Le...	Posting Date ⇅	Comr
N/A	1710	1.000,00	EUR	100049016	0L	31.03.2020	
N/A	1710	-1.000,00	EUR	100049016	0L	31.03.2020	
N/A	1710	999,00	EUR	100049018	0L	31.03.2020	
N/A	1710	-999,00	EUR	100049018	0L	31.03.2020	
N/A	1710	1.000,00	EUR	100049019	0L	31.03.2020	

Partner Units: Unassigned (28)   ZF001/$ICR   All

Selected Amount

[Assign] [Communicate ∨] [Auto Match] [📋 ∨]

Figure 6.29: Manage Assignments app, showing the steps to assign the selected items

6.8.2 GR/IR monitor

If you have worked in finance, you will be familiar with the business problem that the invoice receipt does not always match the goods receipt. Sometimes, this is because we are simply waiting for one of the documents, and sometimes it is because the values in the two documents are different. In either case, the classic approach is to open a spreadsheet and start documenting why the two do not match before ultimately writing off the difference if the issues cannot be clarified satisfactorily.

Figure 6.30 shows an application built to handle exactly this problem. The system reads the relevant data in procurement and makes a proposal for the differences (invoice values that are higher than the goods receipt values, goods receipt values that are higher than the invoice receipt values, etc.). In the past, every shared service center had its own version of a spreadsheet to handle these differences, but now the application matches what it can and a rules framework makes proposals. Finally, a worker in the shared service center can document the situation to explain why there is a difference and whether there is an expectation that the missing invoice receipt will follow at some point. Research conducted with users in the shared service centers was used to identify the typical causes of variances. The documents are now shown sorted by these variances for easier analysis. The process can be extended by machine learning to have the system propose what the next step should be.

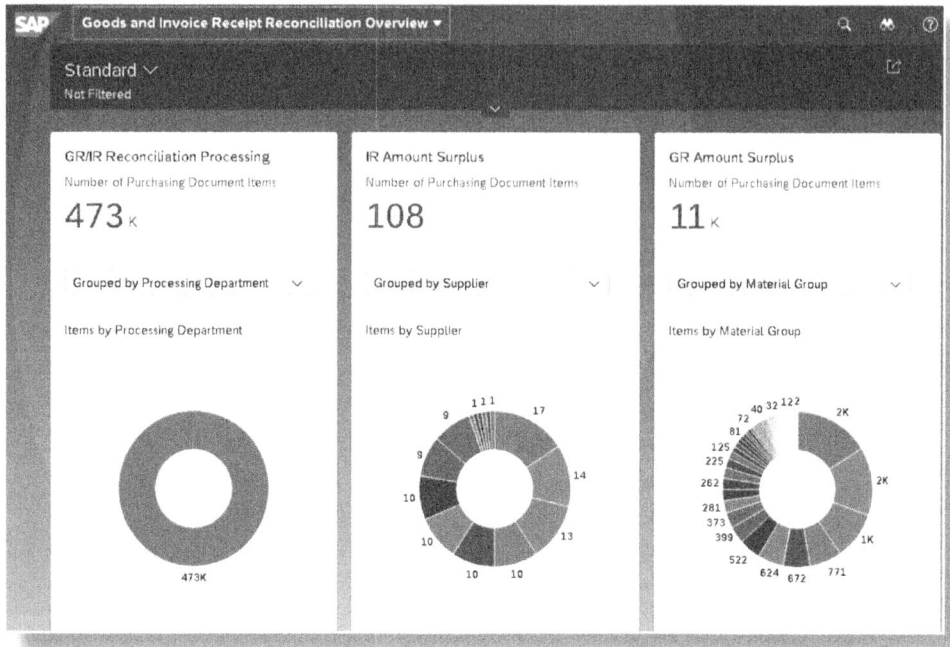

Figure 6.30: Goods and Invoice Receipt Reconciliation Overview app

7 Outlook

Probably the most common question during presentations on SAP S/4HANA is about what comes next. As the business world evolves and changes, so do the requirements of a financial system. Finance departments are being asked to do more with less and this is changing the type of software systems that they use. Most organizations now use cloud software in some form or other and this brings about its own changes.

7.1 On-premise and cloud editions

Most of the screenshots in this book were captured from a demo system running not *on premise* (the deployment option with which most of us are currently familiar) but in the *cloud*, in this case, the SAP HANA Enterprise Cloud. It is becoming increasingly common for organizations to run their migration testing for S/4HANA Finance on a cloned version of their operational system or to implement Central Finance on an SAP HANA Enterprise Cloud rather than installing a new system for the purpose. What this means is that the systems run in a secure data center, such as the one in St Leon Rot in Germany, rather than on site at the customer's premises.

This changes the dynamics of a software investment for a CIO—instead of a significant **capital investment** in hardware, software, and consulting services to make the system available to the users, the investment is in **operational expenses** where an organization pays a monthly fee for the use of the software services in the cloud. This shift in approach has been compared to the early industrial age where organizations ran their own power plants as long as there was no reliable power grid and gradually shifted to using power companies to supply the power. The new power companies in turn benefited from economies of scale that enabled them to offer power more cheaply and efficiently. Essentially, the cloud gives organizations the option to be more flexible because they are not constrained by their own IT resources. It also enables them to scale where their own growth outstrips the performance of their IT systems.

Running SAP S/4HANA Finance in a data center that is not your own is one option, referred to as the *managed cloud*, but SAP has also begun to offer versions of the software designed specifically for the *private cloud*. This shift in approach is reflected in the product names, so you will notice that all software editions have a new notation that denotes the year of release (1503 released in March 2015, 1511 in November 2015, and so on) and either OP for on premise or CE for the cloud edition, the idea being that all cloud customers have the latest version of the software rather than waiting months or even years to implement the next wave of enhancements.

Innovations are being shipped first in the cloud edition and then made available on premise. One example of this is the SAP S/4HANA Professional Services Cloud. The package uses S/4HANA Finance as its core, so it contains the universal journal, new Asset Accounting, new Cash Management, and so on, but it offers features that are designed for a specific industry, namely professional services. The focus is on creating a customer project, recording consulting time, procurement, and travel expenses against that project, billing for the services rendered, and checking the profitability of the project. While there are already consulting houses running SAP ERP, what is interesting is the specific features that have been added to make the package attractive to the industry in question.

> **S/4HANA cloud edition**
>
>
> To access the Feature Scope Description for the SAP S/4HANA cloud edition, refer to the following document:
>
> *https://cp.hana.ondemand.com/dps/d/preview/pdf5eb7d4d30 467d917131b698a509e3/1503%20000/en-US/FSD_PC1506. pdf*

7.2 SAP S/4HANA professional services cloud

The first industry for which dedicated cloud software was offered was the professional service industry. While many of the finance and logistics features described in the document above could be used in any industry, a few are specific to the professional service industry. Service providers are typically concerned about the effectiveness of every consultant, which has led to plenty of workarounds in the past because the employee was not generally recorded in the financial applications. For the cloud edition, the universal journal has been extended to include the field PERSONNEL NUMBER and the HANA views and reports extended to include this field using the same techniques we described in Chapter 5. The financial transactions associated with that employee (time recording, procurement, travel, billing, and so on) now update the universal journal with the personnel number of the employee recording his/her work.

Professional service companies do not typically calculate an activity price by dividing the cost center expenses by the number of hours delivered; instead, they set rates dependent on the seniority of the consultant, the country out of which he/she is operating, and so on. The manual activity rates that we are all used to maintaining using transaction KP26 have been replaced by sales conditions which enable organizations to define their activity rates depending on a number of factors.

Service companies also typically have plenty of work in process, in the form of work that has been performed but not yet billed to the customer. Now, event-based revenue recognition immediately creates a revenue journal entry as the time recording is posted. New functions are also available for intercompany projects.

These functions were originally offered in the S/4HANA cloud edition but are not offered as part of the on-premise edition from 1610 for use not just by pure professional service companies but also by manufacturers who have an additional service business or by engineer-to-order companies who have contractors working to put the final machine together at the customer's site.

7.3 SAP S/4HANA Cloud for other industries

SAP has taken the cloud approach further and now offers cloud solutions for chemical companies, the upstream oil and gas industry, and the public sector. The solutions provide dedicated business content in the form of configuration settings (or best practices) that are described in the following link: *https://rapid.sap.com/bp/#/BP_CLD_ENTPR*.

The settings are packaged as scope items, together with business descriptions and test scripts. The following scope items describe the scenarios in this book:

- ▶ Accounting and Financial Close (J58)
- ▶ Accounting for Incoming Sales Orders (2FD)
- ▶ Actual Costing (33Q)
- ▶ Asset Accounting (J62)

- Asset Under Construction (BFH)
- Commitment Management (2I3)
- Event-Based Production Cost Posting (3FO)
- Financial Planning and Analysis (2FM)
- Group Reporting (1SG)
- Intercompany Reconciliation Process (40Y)
- Margin Analysis (J55)
- Monitoring of Goods and Invoice Receipts (2V7)
- Overhead Cost Accounting (J54)
- Project Financial Control (1NT)
- Statistical Sales Conditions (34B)
- Universal Allocation (2QL)

7.4 SAP S/4HANA as the digital core

It is not just SAP S/4HANA Finance in the cloud that concerns us, but also the connectivity between other cloud products and SAP S/4HANA. Gradually, SAP S/4HANA is evolving to become the *digital core* to which many cloud systems connect, including Success Factors, Ariba, Concur, Fieldglass, and so on. Figure 7.1 shows the vision of how the various *business networks* will connect to SAP S/4HANA. Similarly, the *Internet of Things* completely changes the amount of data being collected about a business process: instead of a single backflush and confirmation at the end of the production line, we have sensors all along the line. In theory, this will enable much more accurate views of work in process than were previously possible, but such data volumes change our understanding of a financial document and what must be stored and audited dramatically. Most financial users barely consider *social networks* in their professional lives but in future, applications such as sentiment analysis will start to enter their working sphere and we will see many controllers becoming data scientists as they look for patterns in the data. Some of these innovations are possible today. Others will evolve over the next several years.

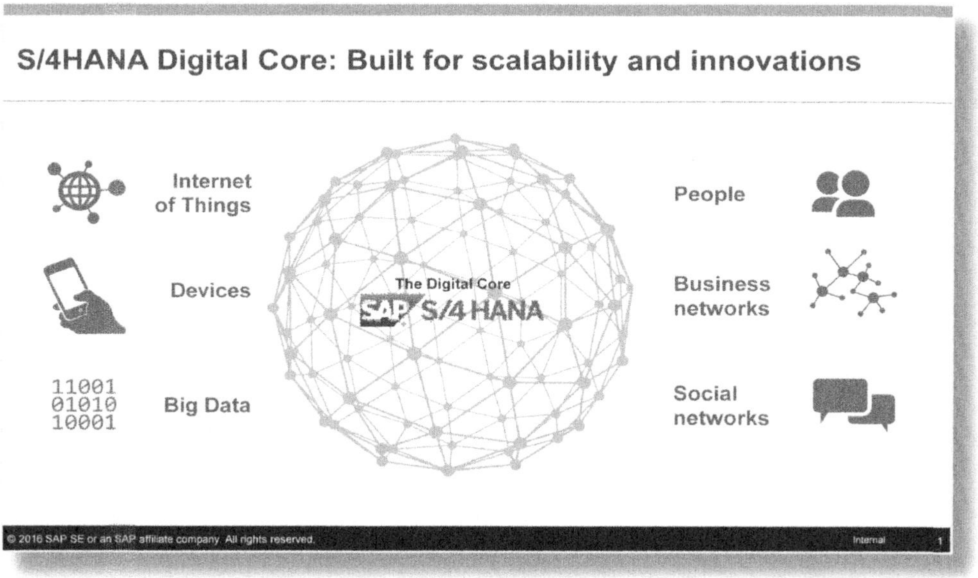

Figure 7.1: SAP S/4HANA as the digital core

You have finished the book.

Sign up for our newsletter!

Stay up to date!

Sign up for our newsletter for updates on new SAP book releases and exclusive discounts.

http://newsletter.espresso-tutorials.com.

A The Author

Janet Salmon is currently the Chief Product Owner for Management Accounting at SAP SE in Walldorf and has accompanied many developments in the Controlling components of SAP ERP and SAP S/4HANA.

Janet joined SAP AG as a translator in 1992, having gained a degree in Modern and Medieval Languages from Downing College, Cambridge and a post-graduate qualification in Interpreting and Translating from the University of Bath.

Janet became a technical writer for the Product Costing area in 1993 and a product manager in 1996. In 1998, she received an award from the Society of Technical Communication for her paper "Functions in Detail: Product Cost Controlling". She is an advisor and regular contributor to SAP Financials Expert (*http://www.financialsexpertonline.com*) and regularly presents at Financials conferences.

B Index

A

Account assignments 42, 56
Account-based Profitability Analysis 63, 128
Account groups 179
Accounting interface 138, 144
Accounting principles 32, 47, 130
Accounts 44, 186
Accounts Receivable Accountant 165
Accounts Receivable Manager 20
Accruals 130
ACDOCA 18, 19, 27
ACDOCP 88, 90
ACDOCU 156
Actual Costing 37, 78
Affiliated companies 188
Aggregations 29
Asset Accounting 32, 33, 51, 129
Asset acquisition 55
Assets under construction 47
Auxiliary cost component split 68
Availability control 92, 108

B

Back-end components 170
Backup tables 117
Balance carryforward 134
Batch processes 9
BSEG 19, 31
Budget 108
Budget availability control 92
Budget Availability Control 108
Business catalogs 164
Business partner 26
Business transactions 27

C

Central Finance 137
Central reporting layer 137
Charts of depreciation 129
CI_COBL 44
Classic General Ledger Accounting 30
Client/server architecture 9
Cloud, 191
Coding block 183
COEP 43
COFIT 30
Column store 12
Commitments 109
Commitments by Cost Center 110
Compatibility views 17
Consolidated P&L by Nature 157
Consolidation Monitor 162
Consolidation table 156
Contract Accounts Receivable and Payable 38
CO-PA accelerator 15
Correction entry 118
Cost and activity planning 97
Cost breakdown 65
Cost Center Budget Report 108
Cost Element Category 45, 58
Cost elements 44
Costing-based Profitability Analysis 77
Cost object mapping 150
Cost of goods sold 63
Currencies 50

D

Data cleansing 140
Data Monitor 161

199

Index

DataSource 0FI_ACDOCA_10 137
Data warehouses 10
Define Financial Statement Items 158
Delivery quantity 69
Deprecated transactions 122
Depreciation 53
Depreciation areas 54
Derivation rules 63
Digital core 12, 194
Direct activity allocation 57
Display Costs by Work Center or Operation 112
Display Group Journal Entries 159
Document splitting 127, 144

E

Employee Self-Service 10
Enriching actual data 132
Entry view 54
Extensibility 181
Extension ledgers 49

F

FAGLFLEXA 31
FAGLFLEXP 87
Financial Planning and Analysis 94
Financial Statement 171
Financial statement version 177
Financial statement versions 177
Fixed Asset 52
Flexible Hierarchies 179
Front-end components 170

G

General Ledger Accounting 30, 42
General ledger data 125
General ledger view 54
G/L account 174
G/L accounts 44

Global Accounting Hierarchy 156, 177
Granularity 29
Graphical user interface 10
GR/IR Monitor 189
Gross Margin 72
Group Reporting 155
Group valuation 48

I

Import Financial Plan Data 92
Incoming Sales Orders 71
Index tables 16
Initial data load 154
In-Memory Data Management 11
Innovation without disruption 13
Insert 14
Integrated Financial Planning 95
Intercompany Matching and Reconciliation 188
Intercompany reconciliation 188
Internal order 140
Inventory Accounting 79

K

Key mapping 148

L

Ledger 32, 47
Ledgers 127
Locks 14

M

Main cost component split 68
Mainframes 9
Manage Allocations 60
Manage Cost Centers 108, 175
Manage Customer Line Items 172
Managed cloud 191
Manage Flexible Hierarchies 179

Manage G/L Account Master Data 174
Manage Global Accounting Hierarchy 177
Manage Journal Entries 160, 173
Manage Material Valuation 37
Management information systems 10
Manager Self-Service 10
Mapping tables 140
Margin Analysis 35, 63
Market segments 184
Master data governance 142
MATDOC 26, 80, 81
Material Ledger 37, 78
Material number 26
Material Price Analysis 82
Migration of balances 134
Migration of the line items 133
Migration source 116
MLDOC 26
MLDOCCCS 26
Monitor Predictive Accounting 174
Moving average price 81
Multidimensional reporting 10
My Spend 167

N

New Asset Accounting 32, 129
New Asset Accounting 51
New data structures 120
New General Ledger Accounting 31
Non-operating accounts 45
Not assigned costs 42

O

Object number 56
Online analytical processing 10
On premise 191
Open item management 38
Operating concern 35, 63
Overdue Receivables 21, 166, 169

P

Pair mapping 149
Parallel cost of goods manufactured 62
Partner dimension 42
Partner object 56
Partner object number 56
Periodic Valuation 68
Plan categories 91
Plan Cost Center Expenses 97
Planning model 88
Planning transactions 87
Post General Journal Entry 174
Predictive accounting 49, 71
Price Determination 80
Primary cost elements 131
Primary cost posting 33
Primary Costs 45
Primary database 15
Private cloud 191
Product cost collector 140
Product cost simulation 103
Production Cost Analysis 112, 113
Production variances 112
Product Profitability 36
Profitability Analysis 13, 35
Profit center valuation 48
Project Budget Report 110
Project planning 105
Project Profitability 76

R

Real-time derivation 74
Receiver 57
Reconciliation account 34
Reconciliation ledger 18, 30
Reconciliation objects 78
Remote function call 139
Reorganization 65
Reporting characteristics 13
Roles 164
Row store 12

Rules framework 189
Run Allocations 61

S

Sales and profitability planning 102
SAP Accounting 24
SAP Analytics Cloud 94
SAP BPC for SAP S/4HANA 94
SAP Business Suite powered by HANA 25
SAP Digital Boardroom 11
SAP ERP General Ledger Accounting 31
SAP Fiori 12, 163
SAP Gateway 166
SAP HANA 12
SAP HANA Enterprise Cloud 191
SAP Landscape Transformation 141
SAP S/4HANA 25
SAP S/4HANA Finance 11, 25
SAP Simple Finance Add-On for SAP Business Suite powered by HANA 25
Scenarios 31
Scope items 193
Secondary cost element 57
Secondary cost elements 58, 131
Secondary cost posting 34
Secondary database 15
Select statement 13
Semantic tags 185
Sender 57
Sender-receiver relationship 57
Sender-receiver relationships 58
Service providers 192
Side-car approach 15
Simplification items 121
Simplification list 122
Single source of truth 29
Single valuation ledgers 49
Soft close 59

Sparsely filled matrix 41
Special Ledger 42
Splitting scheme 66
Spreadsheet 11
Star schema 10
Statistical postings 43
Statistical sales conditions 73
Statistical sales conditions 74
Substitutions 43
Summarization 29
Summarization in BSEG 19
Summarization levels 14

T

T-Accounts 22
Target costs 112
Three-tier architecture 10
Timeliness 10
Totals records 87
Totals tables 16, 80
Transfer structure 144
Trial balance 39, 52

U

Unified data structure 27
Universal allocation 60
Universal journal 18, 27, 115
Update 14
User interface 20

V

Validations 43
Value fields 35
Value mapping 146
Version 62
View technology 170

W

Web services 10
Weighted average cost 78
Work in process 47, 59

C Disclaimer

This publication contains references to the products of SAP SE.

SAP, R/3, SAP NetWeaver, Duet, PartnerEdge, ByDesign, SAP BusinessObjects Explorer, StreamWork, and other SAP products and services mentioned herein as well as their respective logos are trademarks or registered trademarks of SAP SE in Germany and other countries.

Business Objects and the Business Objects logo, BusinessObjects, Crystal Reports, Crystal Decisions, Web Intelligence, Xcelsius, and other Business Objects products and services mentioned herein as well as their respective logos are trademarks or registered trademarks of Business Objects Software Ltd. Business Objects is an SAP company.

Sybase and Adaptive Server, iAnywhere, Sybase 365, SQL Anywhere, and other Sybase products and services mentioned herein as well as their respective logos are trademarks or registered trademarks of Sybase, Inc. Sybase is an SAP company.

SAP SE is neither the author nor the publisher of this publication and is not responsible for its content. SAP Group shall not be liable for errors or omissions with respect to the materials. The only warranties for SAP Group products and services are those that are set forth in the express warranty statements accompanying such products and services, if any. Nothing herein should be construed as constituting an additional warranty.

More Espresso Tutorials Books

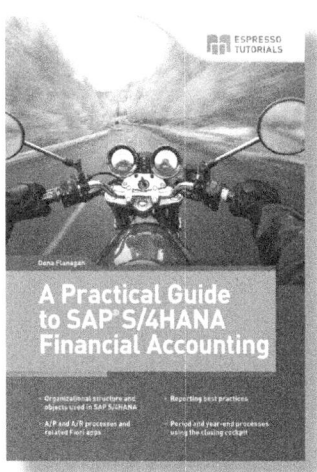

Oona Flanagan:

A Practical Guide to SAP® S/4HANA Financial Accounting

- Financial accounting processes in SAP S/4HANA
- Finance organizational structure, key financial master data
- Daily transactions using SAP Fiori apps
- SAP Fiori apps for displaying and reporting financial data

http://5320.espresso-tutorials.com

Oona Flanagan:

Delta from SAP ERP Financials to SAP® S/4HANA Finance

- Key changes to financial accounting and structure in SAP S/4HANA Finance
- New general ledger structure in the universal journal
- Master data changes in G/L accounts and the business partner
- SAP S/4HANA preparation and migration tools

http://5321.espresso-tutorials.com

Kees van Westerop:

New Fixed Asset Accounting in SAP® S/4HANA

- ▶ Describes SAP Fixed Asset Accounting functionality in SAP S/4HANA with SAP Fiori examples
- ▶ Explores the complete lifecycle of an asset in SAP
- ▶ Identifies differences between classic Fixed Asset Accounting and the new SAP S/4HANA Fixed Asset Accounting
- ▶ Examines how Fixed Asset Accounting is integrated with other SAP modules

http://5409.espresso-tutorials.com

Ann Cacciottolli:

First Steps in SAP® Financial Accounting (FI)

- ▶ Overview of key SAP Financials functionality and SAP ERP integration
- ▶ Step-by-step guide to entering transactions
- ▶ SAP Financials reporting capabilities
- ▶ Hands-on instruction based on examples and screenshots

http://5095.espresso-tutorials.com

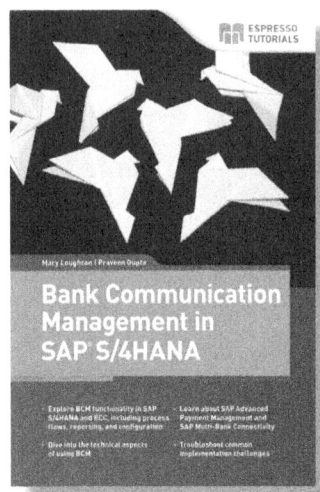

Mary Loughran, Praveen Gupta:

Bank Communication Management in SAP® S/4HANA

- ▶ Explore BCM functionality in SAP S/4HANA and ECC, including process flows, reporting, and configuration
- ▶ Dive into the technical aspects of using BCM
- ▶ Learn about SAP Advanced Payment Management and SAP Multi-Bank Connectivity
- ▶ Troubleshoot common implementation challenges

http://5469.espresso-tutorials.com

Robin Schneider:

Practical Guide to SAP® Business Partner Functions and Integration with SAP S/4HANA

- ▶ The SAP Business Partner concept
- ▶ SAP Business Partner integration in SAP ERP and SAP S/4HANA
- ▶ SAP Business Partner synchronization and Customer-Vendor Integration (CVI)
- ▶ Overview of customization settings and master data maintenance

http://5494.espresso-tutorials.com

Oona Flanagan:

A Practical Guide to Accounts Payable in SAP® S/4HANA Fiori

- ▶ SAP Business Partner integration in SAP ERP and SAP S/4HANA
- ▶ SAP Business Partner synchronization and Customer-Vendor Integration (CVI)
- ▶ Overview of customization settings and master data maintenance

https://www.espresso-tutorials.de/produkt/a-practical-guide-to-accounts-payable-in-sap-s-4hana/

Oona Flanagan:

Introduction to New Asset Accounting in SAP® S/4HANA (FI-AA)

- ▶ Explore new asset accounting (FI-AA) functionality in SAP S/4HANA
- ▶ Unlock key fixed asset transactions for capitalization, retirement, and more
- ▶ Plan your migration

http://5567.espresso-tutorials.com

Made in the USA
Coppell, TX
23 July 2023